THE LIFE OF GAUTAMA BUDDHA

THE LIFE
OF
GAUTAMA BUDDHA

(Original Pāli Text with English Translation)

Edited with furnishing
Original Pāli Text, Revised Translation,
Index and Glossary
By

DR. N. C. PANDA
Panjab University,
Hoshiyarpur,
Punjab

BHARATIYA KALA PRAKASHAN
DELHI (INDIA)

Revised and Enlarge Edition : 2010

Published by **C.P. Gautam**
BHARATIYA KALA PRAKASHAN
3421-A, IInd Floor Narang Colony, Tri Nagar,
Delhi-110035. Phone : 27393083, 32967505 (O)
E-Mail : bkp3421@yahoo.co.in
Website : www.bkpbooks.com

ISBN : 978-81-8090-262-8

Printed By :
BDH Printer at Salasar Imaging Systems,
Delhi

DEDICATION

Dedicated with Profound Respects

to

My Revered Teacher

PROF. DR. SURYAPRAKASH VYAS

An Ideal Teacher, an Eminent Scholar

of

Sanskrit, Kashmir Saivism,

Pali & Buddhism

And

Professor & Former Head

Dept.of Jaina-Bauddha Darshana

SANSKRIT LEARNING & THEOLOGY

BANARAS HINDU UNIVERSITY

VARANASI

CONTENTS

PREFACE

Buddhism is undoubtedly one of the oldest systems of Indian Philosophy. The life of Gautama Buddha, the founder of the Buddhist School of Thought, is fairly well known. He was born some two thousand and six hundred years ago on the full-moon day of Vaisakha, in the city of Kapilavastu. He intently retired to the forest and deeply pursued various existing systems of Indian religious and philosophical disciplines, until he returned to find out for himself his own code of life. Following that and after a stupendous struggle of six strenuous years, in his 35th year Gautama became 'a Buddha'. The term *'Buddha'* means the 'Enlightened One' or the 'Awakened One' and signifies that the person to whom it is applied has solved the riddle of existence, and discovered the doctrine for the cessation of misery. After obtaining the great knowledge of truth, he went about preaching his newly acquired doctrine in Sarnath, Magadha, Kośala and elsewhere until his death, *i.e.* Mahāparinirvāṇa in Kusinagara.

In the Jataka texts, twenty-four mythical Buddhas are mentioned to have appeared before Gautama in preceding cycles of time. Many particulars about them are given, including their birthplaces, the length of their lives and their statures. Gautama himself is said to have met some of them during his transmigrations. Even the sacred trees under which they obtained Supreme Wisdom are enumerated. Their names are: Dīpankara, Kauṇḍinya, Maṅgala, Sumana, Raivata, Sobhita, Anomadarsin, Padma, Nārada, Padmottara, Sumedha, Sujāta, Priyardarśin, Arthadarśin, Dharmadarśin, Siddhārtha, Tiṣya,

Puṣya, Vipaśyin, Śikhin, Viśvabhū, Kakusandha, Koṇāgamana, and Kāśyapa. The Buddhavaṁśa adds three more names with this list, viz. Taṇhaṅkara, Meghankara, Śaraṇaṅkara. Thus, the number goes up to twenty-seven. The Lalitavistara gives a list of fifty five Buddhas, viz. (1) Padmottara, (2) Dharmaketu, (3) Dīpaṅkara, (4) Guṇaketu, (5) Mahākara, (6) Ṛṣideva, (7) Śrītajā, (8) Satyaketu, (9) Vajrasamhata, (10) Sarvābhimū, (11) Hemavarṇa, (12) Atyuccagāmī, (13) Pravālasāgara, (14) Puṣyaketu, (15) Vararūpa, (16) Sui ocana, (17) Ṛṣigupta, (18) Jinacakra, (19) Dnnata, (20) Puṣpita, (21) Ūrṇateja, (22) Puṣ kara, (23) Suraśmi, (24) Maṅgala, (25) Sudarśana, (26) Mahāsiṁhatejā, (27) Sthitabuddhidatta, (28) Vasantagandhi, (29) Satyadharmāvipulakīrti, (30) Tiṣya, (31) Puṣya, (32) Lokasundara, (33) Vistirṇatejā, (34) Ratnakīrti, (35) Ugratejā, (36) Brahmatejā, (37) Sughoṣa, (38) Supuṣya, (39) Sumanojñaghoṣa, (40) Suceṣṭarupa, (41) Prahasitanetra, (42) Guṇarāśi, (43) Meghasvara, (44) Sundaravarṇa, (45) Āyustejā, (46) Salīlagajagāmī, (47) Lokābhilāṣita, (48) Jitaśatru, (49) Saṅpūjita, (50) Vipaśyī, (51) Śikhī, (52) Viśvabhū, (53) Krakucchanda, and (54) Kanakamuni.

The earliest account of the life of Gautama Buddha is contained in Mahapadana Sutta of the Dīgha Nikāya and contains an autobiography of Buddha. In addition to the numerous legends about the life of Buddha, which sometimes are contradictory with each other, there are five ancient works giving us the glimpses of the life of Buddha, *viz.* (1) The Mahāvastu, (2) the Lalitavistara, (3) the Buddhacarita, (4) the Nidānakathā, (5) the Abhinishkramaṇa Sūtra. Besides these, there are stray pieces in Sanskrit and Pali, depicting certain periods or events in the life of Buddha. From these old records as well as from the traditions and legends that have easily come down to us, we are in a position to reconstruct, more or less accurately, the life of Gautama Buddha.

Lord Buddha recruited a large number of devotees who became monks, and framed a new monastic order having monasteries built for them by the lay devotees. He also framed the general rules for the Sangha or the assemblage of monks, and permitted relaxation of these rules in extraordinary circumstances. He was primarily interested in the cloistered life of a hermit. He emphasized the psycho-ethical training, which would enable a *bhikkhu* to know the reality or *tathatā* and attain eternal wisdom or Nirvāṇa. However, Lord Buddha was very positive for the mental and physical upliftment of the monks. He taught common people, how to exercise their will, and realize in themselves the highest possibilities that are open to human beings. He advised them not to waste their . time on splitting hairs about the formalities of religion. Ignorance is the main cause of all human sufferings. No one gets freedom unless he tries to remove these tJtrough the practice of religious austerity, sacrifices and other spiritual acts prescribed by the Holy Scriptures. Lıkewise, Gautama Buddha also tried to free human beings from the chain of sufferings through his teachings, which may be said to be threefold: Four Noble Truths, the Noble Eightfold Path and the Doctrine of Dependent Origination.

The Four Noble Truths *(catvtiri-tiryasatytini)* are: (1) *Dukkha* (suffering), (2) *dukkhasamudayo* (cause of suffering), (3) *dukkhanirodha* (cessation of suffering), (4) *dukkhanirodha-gtimini pratipada* (way for leading to the cessation of suffering).

The Noble Eightfold Path *(Ārya-aṣṭāṅgika-mārga)* consists of eight steps which are: (1) *samyag dṛṣṭi* (right views), (2) *samyag saṅkalpa* (right resolve), (3) *samyag vtik* (right speech), (4) *samyag karmtinta* (right action), (5) *samyag ājīva* (right living), (6) *samyag vyāyāma* (right effort or exertion), (7) *samyag smṛti* (right thought or recollection), (8) *samyag samādhi* (right meditation or concentration).

In the old scriptures, we also find mention of a triple path consisting of *śīla* (conduct), *samādhi* (concentration) and *prajñā* (wisdom). They roughly correspond to *darśana, jñāna* and *caritra* of Jainism. *Śīla* and *samādhi* lead to *prajñā, which* is the direct cause of liberation or Nirvāṇa. Buddha's ethical 'middle path' is like the 'golden mean' of Aristotle. In his very first sermon at Sarnath, he has stated: there are two extremes, from which he who leads a religious life must abstain. One is a life of pleasure, devoted to desire and enjoyment: that is base, ignoble, unspiritual and unreal. The other is a life of mortification: it is gloomy, unworthy and unreal. There is a 'middle path', discovered by the Buddha, a path which enlightens the eyes, enlightens the mind, and bestows understanding, which leads to peace, to insight, to the higherwisdom, to Nirvāṇa.

The doctrine of *'Pratīyasamutpāda'* or Dependent Origination is the foundation of all the teachings of Gautama Buddha. Due to the chain of phenomenal cause and effect the birth and rebirth occur. It tells us that in the empirical world dominated by the intellect everything is relative, conditional, dependent, subject to birth and death and therefore impennanent. The causal formula is: this being, that arises *(asmin sati idam bhavati), i.e.* depending on the cause, the effect arises. We get the twelve links *(dvādaśa nidāna)* of the causal wheel of dependent origination, *viz. avidyā* (ignorance), *saṁskāra* (impression of kārmic forces), *vijñāna* (consciousness), *nāma-rūpa* (psycho-physical organism), *ṣaḍāyatana* (six sense organs including mind), *sparśa* (sense object contact), *vedanā* (feeling), *tṛṣṇā* (craving), *upādāna* (clinging to this enjoyment), *bhava* (process of becoming),jāti (rebirth), *jarāmaraṇa* (old age & death). Out of these twelve links, the first two are related to past life, the last two to future life and the rest to present life. This is the cycle of birth and death. Besides, this is the twelve-spoked wheel of dependent origination. It is called the *bhava-cakra, samsāra-cakra, dharma-cakra, janma-maraṇa-cakra,* etc. It can be destroyed only when its root cause, ignorance, is destroyed. Ignorance *(avidyā)* can be destroyed only by sacred wisdom or knowledge. Hence, ignorance is bondage and knowledge is liberation (Nirvāṇa).

Therefore, the doctrine of dependent origination is the central teaching of the Buddha and his other teachings can easily be deduced from it as corollaries. The theory of *karma* is based on this, being an implication of the law of causation. Our present life is due to the impressions of the *karmas* of the past life and it will shape our future life. In the earlier system of

Buddhist thought, the doctrine of *karma* plays a very important part, in as much as, this law explains completely the process of evolution. In fact, in the Milinda Pañha, we find that Nāgasena says: "it is through a difference in their *karma* that men are not all like. But some long lived, some short lived, some healthy and some sickly, some handsome and some ugly, some powerful and some weak, some rich and some poor, some of high degree and some of low degree, some wise and some foolish.¿ The Lord Buddha himself has formulated in so many words the existence of this theory of *karma.* When a persecuted disciple came to Lord Buddha, the Lord consoled him with the words Ṣsuffer it be so, oh Bhikkhu, you are now feeling the results of your *karma,* that might have cost you centuries of suffering in purgatory."

Nirvāṇa consti.tutes the highest and ultimate goal of all Buddhist aspirations. The',word Nirvāṇa means 'blowing out'. It is the dissolution of the five *skandhas.* It is the cessation of all activities and of all becoming *(bhavanirodha).* It is said to be the Supreme and indestructible state, which gives happiness here and hereafter. So it is known as the 'highest bliss'. In the early Buddhism, however, there are passages, which indicated that Nírvāṇa means eternal and exalted beatitude.

Gautama Buddha denied the existence of a permanent substratum of Reality or the Self. This is known as the theory of not self or *anātma-vāda.* According to Buddhism, consciousness *(vijñāna),* which operates to project a new being or *'nāma-rūpa'* into existence, is not a transmigratory soul, but is merely a *salitsktira,* which is changeable and unsubstantial in character. In the Milinda Pañha, it is stated that, just as a body is a complex of many parts or elements, so also, what we call a *jīva* or an individual, is a similar complex of physical and psychical elements, and that, both were ultimately liable to dissolution into their component elements. Thus, the theory of non-existence of the soul *(antitmavtida)* amounts only to a denial of the estimative persistence of it. This theory of *anāmavāda* has been much misunderstood and has been responsible for a lot of confusion in later philosophy. However, if we clearly analyze the pristine teachings of Buddha, we find that he, as a practical teacher that he was, refused to define in terms of language, an experience, that transcends thought itself. He really wanted human beings to practice his teachings and experience for themselves, the 'great truth', and was not interested in verbal quarrels about its nature and principles.

Lord Buddha's life and teachings have a great importance today for the common people to live in peace and to maintain goodwill in the society. Besides, the basic principles of Buddhism are full of moral and ethical values, which may provide proper discipline, self-confidence, sacred thoughts, energetic livelihood and true concentration of mind to the seeker of truth and spiritual harmony. The book 'Buddhism in Translations' is really a great contribution of Henry Clarke Warren to the people of Buddhist world. In this work, the authorhas given the basic ideas of Buddhism found in original Pāli Texts *(i.e. Buddhavacana).In* fact, the Pāli texts contain the main concepts of Lord Buddha's moral teachings. Therefore, the author has collected and translated into English the essence of Buddhist ideas and conceptions found in Pali Canons. However, in this work, he has not given the Original Pāli texts with the selected translations. Hence, I have tried my best to furnish the Pali text with its English translation. Now, the learned readers will find both the text as well as its English translation at one place.

The work is divided into twelve Chapters. It embodies a detailed discussion on the Life of Gautama Buddha. The chapters are: the story of Sumedha, a list of former Buddhas, Characteristic of future Buddha, birth of the Buddha, the young Gotamid Prince, the Great Retirement, the Great Struggle,

the attainment of Buddhaship, first events after the attainment of Buddhaship, the conversion of Sāripttta and Moggallāna,the Buddha's daily Habits and his Death.

In presenting this work to the world of scholars, I have consulted a number of works extant either in Sanskrit or in Pali. Moreover, in this respect, I may assure to the learned readers that the text materials they will meet with in this work are culled from original and reliable sources and supported by the erudite scholars from both the East and the West. Although I have tried my best to add the exact texts, but sometimes the variant readings of the texts may differ from its translations. Therefore, the intelligent readers may bear with this.

A Geeral Index is added to this work and an addition of a Glossary of Buddhist technical terms is another notable feature of this worlr .

I hope the present edition would be immensely useful for the students and researchers of Pāli and Buddhism. Besides, it will also serve a much larger purpose of the general readers of Buddhist Philosophy and Religion.

I have mainly taken the help of the following editions, *viz.* Vipassana Research Institute, Igatpuri, Bauddha Bharati, Varanasi, Nava Nālandā Mahāvihāra, Bihar. I extend my sincere thanks to the publishers of these (Pāli text) editions. I have no words to express my gratitude to Prof. Surya Prakash Vyasa, Prof. Ramesh Chandra Panda, Prof. Ramesh Chandra Dwivedi, Prof. Gangadhar Panda, Prof. Gopabandhu Mishra, Prof. Surendra Mohan Mishra and Prof. Raghbir Singh and Prof. Ganesh Dutt Bhardwaj, for their scholarly guidance and constant encouragement. Apart from these pillars of knowledge, I must express my sincere thanks to Shri C.P. Gautam, Publisher of Bharatiya Kala Prakashan, Delhi, who happily undertood the work for publication.

27th April, 2010

—Narasingha Charan Panda

V.V.B.I.S. & I.S., Sadhu Ashram,
Panjab University, Hoshiarpur,
Punjab.

ABBREVIATIONS

A	Aṅguttara-Nikāya. Edited by Rev. Richard Morris. Pāli Text Society, London, 1885-8.
CV	Culla-Vagga. Edited by Hermann Oldenberg. Vinaya-Piṭaka, vol. ii., London, 1880.
D	Dīgha-Nikāya, vol. i. Edited by T.W.R. Davids and J.E. Carpenter. P. T. S., London, 1890.
Dhp	Dhammapada. Edited by V. Fausböll. Copenhagen. 1855. Grimblot. Sept Suttas Pālis. Edited by P. Grimblot. Paris, 1876.
J	Jātaka, together with its Commentary, 5 vols, Edited by V. Fausböll, 1877-91.
JPTS	Journal of the Pāli Text Society.
JRAS	Journal of the Royal Asiatic Society, London.
M	Majjhima-Nikāya. Edited by V. Trenckner. P. T. S., London, 1888.
Mil	Milindapañha. Edited by V. Trenckner. London, 1880.
MPS	Mahā-Parinibbāna-Sutta. Edited by R. C. Childers, London, 1878. JRAS, new series, vii; also separately.
MSS	Mahā-Satipaṭṭhāna-Sutta. Colombo, 1883.
MV	Mahā-Vagga. Edited by Hermann Oldenberg. Vinaya-Piṭaka, vol. i, London, 1879.

P's Aut	Mrs. Piozzi's Autobiography. Edited by Hayward. Boston, 1861.
S	Saṁyutta-Nikāya. Edited by Léon Feer. P. T. S. London, 1884-94.
Sum Vil	Sumaṅgala-Vilāsinī. Edited by T. W. R. Davids and J. E. Carpenter. P. T. S. London, 1886.
Ud	Udāna. Edited by Paul Steinthal. P. T. S. London, 1885.
Vis	Visuddhi-Magga.

The abbreviations and numbers at the upper inside corners of the pages of this book refer, as precisely as may be, to the chapter and other subdivisions or to the volume and page and line of the original work from which the beginning of the page concerned is translated.

अं /अ०नि०	=	अङ्गुत्तरनिकाय
अ / अट्ठ०	=	अट्ठकथा
अनुटी०	=	अनुटीका
अप० थेर०	=	अपदान
अप० थेरी०	=	अपदान
अभि० टी०	=	अभिनवटीका
इ / इतिवु०	=	इतिवुत्तक
उ / उदा०	=	उदान
कङ्खा० टी०	=	कङ्खवितरणी-टीका
कथा०	=	कथावत्थु
खु० नि०	=	खुद्दकनिकाय
खु० पा०	=	खुद्दकपाठ
चरिया०	=	चरियापिटक
चूळनि०/ चुनि	=	चूळनिद्देस
चुल्ल / चूळव०	=	चूळवग्ग
जा०	=	जातक संस्करण
जातक	=	जातकट्ठकथा

टी०	=	टीका
थेरगा०/ थेर	=	थेरगाथा
थेरीगा०	=	थेरीगाथा
दी / दी०नि०	=	दीघनिकाय
धा / धा०प०	=	धम्मपद
धम्म / धा०स०	=	धम्मसङ्गणि
धातु०	=	धातुकथा
नेत्ति०	=	नेत्तिप्पकरण
पटि/पटि० म०	=	पटिसम्भिदामग्ग
पट्ठा०	=	पट्ठान
पाचि०	=	पाचित्तिय
पारा०	=	पाराजिक
परि०	=	परिवार
पु०टी०	=	पुराणटीका
पु०प०	=	पुग्गलपञ्ञत्ति
पे०व० / पेत	=	पेतवत्थु
पेटको०	=	पेटकोपदेस
बु० वं०	=	बुद्धवंस
म/ म०नि०	=	मज्झिमनिकाय
महाटी०	=	महाटीका
महाव०	=	महावग्ग
महानि०/मनि	=	महानिद्देस
मि०प०	=	मिलिन्दपञ्ह
मूलटी०	=	मूलटीका
यम०	=	यमक
रो०	=	रोमन् (पालि टेक्स्ट सोसाइटी)
वजिर०टी०	=	वजिरबुद्धि-टीका
वि०व०/विमान	=	विमानवत्थु
वि०वि०टी०	=	विमति-विदोदनी-टीका
वि०सङ्ग०अट्ठ०	=	विनय-सङ्गह-अट्ठकथा
वि०वि०टी०	=	विनय-विनिच्छय-टीका

विभ०	=	विभङ्ग
विसुद्धि०	=	विसुद्धिमग्ग
सं०/ सं०नि०	=	संयुत्तनिकाय
सारत्थ० टी०	=	सारत्थदीपनी-टीका
सु/ सु०नि०	=	सुत्तनिपात

LIST OF TRANSLITERATIONS

अ	-	a	ए	-	e	ऋ	-	ṛ
आ	-	ā	ऐ	-	ai	ॠ	-	ṝ
इ	-	e	ओ	-	o	ऌ	-	lṛ
ई	-	ē	औ	-	au/ou	ॡ	-	lṝ
उ	-	u	अं	-	n			
ऊ	-	ū	अः	-	ḥ			

क्	-	k	च्	-	c	ट्	-	t	त्	-	t
ख्	-	kh	छ्	-	ch	ठ्	-	ṭ	थ्	-	th
ग्	-	g	ग्	-	j	ड्	-	d	द्	-	d
घ्	-	gh	झ्	-	jh	ढ्	-	ḍ	ध्	-	dh
ङ्	-	ṅ	ञ्	-	ñ	ण्	-	ṇ	न्	-	n
प्	-	p	य्	-	y	ष्	-	ṣ	क्ष्	-	kṣ
फ्	-	ph	र्	-	r	स्	-	s	त्र्	-	tr
ब्	-	b	ल्	-	l	ह्	-	h	ज्ञ्	-	jñ
भ्	-	bh	व्	-	v						
म्	-	m	श्	-	ś						

INTRODUCTION

In reading the Pāli Scriptures one is impressed with the strong personal influence exercised by The Buddha over the hearts of his followers. He was regarded, not as a mere formulator of dry metaphysical propositions, but as a very wise and compassionate friend of his fellow-men. He was full of tact, and all his ways were ways of peace. To allay discord he would tell a little story or fable with a moral, and his epithet for one of whom he disapproved was merely "vain man." Anger, in fact, had no place in his character, and the reader of this book will find that it had equally none in his religio-philosophic system.

The term "Buddha" means "Enlightened One," and signifies that the person to whom it is applied has solved the riddle of existence, and discovered the doctrine for the cessation of misery. It was by his attainment of this supreme "Enlightenment" or Wisdom that Gotama became a Buddha. During the thirty-five years of his life previous to that event, and during all previous existences from the time he set out towards the Buddhaship, he was a Bodhisatta, a term which I have freely translated "Future Buddha," but which is more literally rendered "He whose essence is Wisdom."

The Buddha's given name would appear to have been Siddhattha; but as the word means "Successful in his Objects," it looks as though it might be a simple epithet. The Buddha belonged to the Śākya clan. The word "Śākya" means

"Powerful;" and the families that bore the name had a reputation for pride and haughtiness. They were of the warrior caste, but cultivated the peaceful arts of agriculture. By his contemporaries The Buddha is usually called Gotama, or, as the word is sometimes Anglicized, the Gotamid. It is not quite clear why he and others of his clan should bear the name of Gotama in addition to that of Śākya. It may be they claimed descent from the ancient sage Gautama (Sanskrit "Gautama" becomes "Gotama" in Pāli), to whom are attributed some of the hymns of the Ṛgveda; or it may be, as Burnouf has suggested, "because Gautama was the sacerdotal family name of the military race of Śākyas, who, being of the warrior caste, had no ancestor or tutelar saint like the Brāhmaṇas, but might, as the Hindu law permits, have taken the name of the sage to whose family belonged their spiritual guide."

The Buddha was a Hindu, born not far from the Ganges, and during his long ministry wandered about from place to place in the section of country about Benares, very much as did Christ in Judea and Galilee. And just as Christ once left his native country and went to Egypt, so The Buddha is said by native authorities to have paid a couple of visits to Ceylon; but the statement is, I fear, somewhat mythical.

The date of Gotama Buddha is considered to be the sixth century before Christ. It would appear that he lived to his eightieth year, and the time of his death is given by scholars as about 480 B. C.

The first eight–sections of the present chapter are from the general introduction to the Jātaka ("Book of Birth-Stories"). These Birth-Stories, five hundred and fifty in number, are so called because they are tales of the anterior existences of Gotama Buddha, while he was as yet but a Future Buddha. The Jātaka is an extensive work; five volumes have already been edited by Professor V. Fausböll, of Copenhagen, and more is yet to come. It consists of the Birth-Stories themselves, with a commentary and a long introduction. Examples of these Birth-Stories will be given further on; here we have only to do with the

Introduction, the author of which and of the commentary is unknown.

After a few preliminary remarks concerning the inception and plan of his work, the author begins by quoting entire the Story of Sumedha as contained in the metrical work called the Buddha-Vaṁsa ("History of the Buddhas"). He does not quote it all consecutively, but a few stanzas at a time as authority for his prose statements. In this prose is also some matter of a commentary nature, apparently later glosses and not a part of the original text. In my first translation I give the Story of Sumedha as quoted in this Introduction to the Jātaka, but I give it consecutively and omit the prose, except that of some of the more interesting and explanatory passages, of the glosses especially, have made foot-notes.

After the Story of Sumedha our author gives formal descriptions of each of the twenty-four Buddhas that preceded Gotama. These descriptions, however, are tedious, and are not here translated. They mainly concern themselves with such details as the height of each Buddha, his length of life, how many conversions he made, the names of his father, mother, chief disciples, etc. But from the point where my second section begins to the end of the eighth I follow the native text without making any omissions, I have divided one continuous text into seven parts; and then given these divisions titles of my own devising.

The reader is thus brought up to the ministry of The Buddha. This ministry lasted some forty-five years, and an account of part of it is given by the author of the Introduction. It is, however, only a part that he gives, just enough to conduct his reader up to the time when The Buddha was presented with Jetavana monastery, the importance of which event to our author will be readily perceived when it is remembered that this was the monastery in which The Buddha is represented as having related the greater part of the Birth-Stories. As our author fails to give us a complete life of The Buddha, and as I know of none in Pāli literature, none is attempted in this book. But in order that the reader may have at an early stage an idea of what the matters were wherein The Buddha considered himself "enlightened," two passages are translated from the Mahā-Vagga. Then follows a description of the daily routine of The Buddha's ministry, and the last section of this chapter gives the Pāli account of how The Buddha died. It is not because the philosophical ideas expressed and the references to meditation and trance made in these four sections are supposed to be self-explanatory, that I make no comment on them in this chapter; but because the next three chapters, as I have already stated in my General Introduction, are devoted to the Doctrine, and constitute the philosophical and systematic part of this work. It appeared desirable to give the reader a general idea of what the Buddhists consider to be the salient features of their system of religion before beginning its detailed discussion.

'नमो तस्य भगवतो अरहतो समासम्बुद्धस्स।'

Chapter I

THE STORY OF SUMEDHA[1]

Translated from the Introduction to the Jātaka (i.31).

खुद्दक निकाये जातक अट्ठकथा, सुमेधकथा
"कप्पे च सतसहस्से, चतुरो च असङ्खिये।
अमरं नाम नगरं, दस्सनेय्यं मनोरमं।
दसहि सद्देहि अविवित्तं, अन्नपानसमायुत"न्ति।। 12।।

12. "A hundred thousand cycles vast
And four immensities ago,
There was a town named Amara,
A place of beauty and delights.
It had the noises ten complete[2]
And food and drink abundantly."

"हत्थिसद्दं अस्ससद्दं, भेरिसङ्खरथानि च।
खादथ पिवथ चेव, अन्नपानेन घोसित"न्ति।। 13।।

13. "The noise of elephant and horse,
Of conch-shell, drum, and chariot,
And invitations to partake—
"Eat ye, and drink!" — resounded loud."

नगरं सब्बङ्गसम्पन्नं, सब्बकम्ममुपागतं।।
सत्तरतनसम्पन्नं, नानाजनसमाकुलं।
समिद्धं देवनगरंव, आवासं पुञ्ञकम्मिनं।। 14।।

14. "A town complete in all its parts,
Where every industry was found,
And eke the seven precious gems,[3]
And foreigners from many lands.
A prosperous city of the gods,
Full of good works and holy men."

नगरे अमरवतिया, सुमेधो नाम ब्राह्मणो।
अनेककोटिसन्निचयो, पहूतधनधञ्ञवा।। 15।।

15. "Within this town of Amara
Sumedha lived, of Brāhmaṇa caste,
Who many tens of millions had,
And grain and treasure in full store."

अज्झायको मन्तधरो, तिण्णं वेदान पारगू।
लक्खणे इतिहासे च, सधम्मे पारमिं गतो"ति।। 16।।

16. "A student he, and wise in spells,
A master of the Vedas three.
He fortunes told, tradition knew,
And every duty of his caste."

रहोगतो निसीदित्वा, एवं चिन्तेसहं तदा।
दुक्खो पुनब्भवो नाम, सरीरस्स च भेदनं।। 17।।

17. "In secret then I sat me down,
And thus to ponder I began:
"What misery to be born again!
And have the flesh dissolve at death!"

जातिधम्मो जराधम्मो, ब्याधिधम्मो सहं तदा।
अजरं अमतं खेमं, परियेसिस्सामि निब्बुतिं।। 18।।

18. "Subject to birth, old age, disease,
Extinction will I seek to find,
Where no decay is ever known,
Nor death, but all security."

यंनूनिमं पूतिकायं, नानाकुणपपूरितं।
छड्डयित्वान गच्छेय्यं, अनपेक्खो अनत्थिको।। 19।।

19. "What if I now should rid me of
This body foul, this charnel-house,
And go my way without a care,
Or least regret for things behind!"

"अत्थि हेहिति सो मग्गो, न सो सक्का न हेतुये।
परियेसिस्सामि तं मग्गं, भवतो परिमुत्तिया"ति।। 20।।

20. "There is, there must be, an escape!
Impossible there should not be!
I'll make the search and find the way,
Which from existence shall release !"

यथापि दुक्खे विज्जन्ते, सुखं नामपि विज्ञति।
एवं भवे विज्जमाने, विभवोपि इच्छितब्बको।। 21।।

21. "Even as, although there misery is,
Yet happiness is also found;
So, though indeed existence is,
A non-existence should be sought."

यथापि उण्हे विज्जन्ते, अपरं विज्ञति सीतलं।
एवं तिविधग्गि विज्जन्ते, निब्बानं इच्छितब्बकं।। 22।।

22. "Even as, although there may be heat,
Yet grateful cold is also found;
So, though the threefold fire[4] exists,
Likewise Nirvāṇa should be sought."

"यथापि पापे विज्जन्ते, कल्याणमपि विज्ञति।
एवमेव जाति विज्जन्ते, अजातिपिच्छितब्बक"न्ति।। 23।।

23. "Even as, although there evil is,
That which is good is also found;
So, though't is true that birth exists,
That which is not birth should be sought."

यथा गूथगतो पुरिसो, तळाकं दिस्वान पूरितं।
न गवेसति तं तळाकं, न दोसो तळाकस्स सो।। 24।।

24. "Even as a man befouled with dung,
Seeing a brimming lake at hand,

And pathless bathing not therein,
Were senseless should he chide the lake;"

एवं किलेसमलधोवे, विज्जान्ते अमतन्तळे।
न गवेसति तं तळाकं, न दोसो अमतन्तळे।। 25।।

25. "So, when Nirvāṇa's lake exists
To wash away corruption's stain,
Should I not seek to bathe therein,
I might not then Nirvāṇa chide."

यथा अरीहि परिरुद्धो, विज्जन्ते गमनम्पथे।
न पलायति सो पुरिसो, न दोसो अज्जसस्स सो।। 26।।

26. "Even as a man hemmed in by foes,
Seeing a certain safe escape,
And nathless seeking not to flee,
Might not the blameless pathway chide;"

एवं किलेसपरिरुद्धो, विज्जमाने सिवे पथे।
न गवेसति तं मग्गं, न दोसो सिवमज्जसे।। 27।।

27. "So, when my passions hem me in,
And yet a way to bliss exists,
Should I not seek to follow it,
That way of bliss I might not chide."

यथापि ब्याधितो पुरिसो, विज्जमाने तिकिच्छके।
न तिकिच्छापेति तं ब्याधिं, न दोसो सो तिकिच्छके।। 28।।

28. "Even as a man who, sore diseased,
When a physician may be had,
Should fail to send to have him come,
Might the physician then not chide;"

"एवं किलेसब्याधीहि, दुक्खितो परिपीळितो।
न गवेसति तं आचरियं, न दोसो सो विनायके"ति।। 29।।

29. "So, when diseased with passion, sore
Oppressed, I seek the master not
Whose ghostly counsel me might cure,
The blame should not on him be laid."

यथापि कुणपं पुरिसो, कण्ठे बद्धं जिगुच्छिय।
मोचयित्वान गच्छेय्य, सुखी सेरी सयंवसी।। 30।।

30. "Even as a man might rid him of
A horrid corpse bound to his neck,
And then upon his way proceed,
Joyous, and free, and unconstrained;"

तथेविमं पूतिकायं, नानाकुणपसञ्चयं।
छड्डयित्वान गच्छेय्यं, अनपेक्खो अनत्थिको।। 31।।

31. "So must I likewise rid me of
This body foul, this charnel-house,
And go my way without a care,
Or least regret for things behind."

यथा उच्चारट्ठानम्हि, करीसं नरनारियो।
छड्डयित्वान गच्छन्ति, अनपेक्खा अनत्थिका।। 32।।

32. "As men and women rid them of
Their dung upon the refuse heap,
And go their ways without a care,
Or least regret for what they leave;"

एवमेवाहं इमं कायं, नानाकुणपपूरितं।
छड्डयित्वान गच्छिस्सं, वच्चं कत्वा यथा कुटिं।। 33।।

33. "So will I likewise rid me of
This body foul, this charnel-house,
And go my way as if I had
Cast out my filth into the draught."

यथापि जज्जरं नावं, पलुग्गं उदगाहिनिं।
सामी छड्डेत्वा गच्छन्ति, अनपेक्खा अनत्थिका।। 34।।

34. "Even as the owners leave and quit
A worn-out, shattered, leaky ship,
And go their ways without a care,
Or least regret for what they leave;"

एवमेवाहं इमं कायं, नवच्छिद्दं धुवस्सवं।
छड्डयित्वान गच्छिस्सं, जिण्णनावंव सामिका।। 35।।

35. "So will I likewise rid me of
This nine-holed,[5] ever-trickling frame,
And go my way, as owners do,
Who ship disrupted leave behind."

यथापि पुरिसो चोरेहि, गच्छन्तो भण्डमादिय।
भण्डच्छेदभयं दिस्वा, छड्डयित्वान गच्छति।। 36।।

36. "Even as a man who treasure bears,
And finds him in a robber-gang,
Will quickly flee and rid him of
The robbers, lest they steal his gold;"

"एवमेव अयं कायो, महाचोरसमो विय।
पहायिमं गमिस्सामि, कुसलच्छेदनाभया"ति।। 37।।

37. "So, to a mighty robber might
Be likened well this body's frame.
I 'll cast it off and go my way,
Lest of my welfare I be robbed."

एवाहं चिन्तयित्वान, नेककोटिसतं धनं।
नाथानाथानं दत्वान, हिमवन्तमुपागमिं।। 38।।

38. "Thus thinking, I on rich and poor
All that I had in alms bestowed;
Hundreds of millions spent I then,
And made to Himavant[6] my way."

हिमवन्तस्साविदूरे, धम्मिको नाम पब्बतो।
अस्समो सुकतो मय्हं, पण्णसाला सुमापिता।। 39।।

39. "Not far away from Himavant,
There was a hill named Dhammaka,
And here I made and patterned well
A hermitage and hut of leaves."

चङ्कमं तत्थ मापेसिं, पञ्चदोसविवज्जितं।
अट्ठगुणसमुपेतं, अभिञ्ञाबलमाहरिं।। 40।।

40. "A walking-place I then laid out,
Exempted from the five defects,[7]

And having all the virtues eight;[8]
And there I gained the Six High Powers."

साटकं पजहिं तत्थ, नवदोसमुपागतं।
वाकचीरं निवासेसिं, द्वादसगुणमुपागतं।। 41।।

41. "Then ceased I cloaks of cloth to wear,
For cloaks possess the nine defects,[9]
And girded on a barken dress,
Which is with virtues twelve endued."[10]

अट्ठदोससमाकिण्णं, पजहिं पण्णसालकं।
उपागमिं रुक्खमूलं, गुणे दसहुपागतं।। 42।।

42. "My hut of leaves I then forsook,
So crowded with the eight defects,[11]
And at the foot of trees I lived,
For such abodes have virtues ten."[12]

वापितं रोपितं धञ्ञ, पजहिं निरवसेसतो।
अनेकगुणसम्पन्नं, पवत्तफलमादियिं।। 43।।

43. "No sown and cultivated grain
Allowed I then to be my food;
But all the many benefits
Of wild-fruit fare I made my own."

"तत्थप्पधानं[4] पदहिं, निसज्जट्ठानचङ्कमे।
अब्भन्तरम्हि सत्ताहे, अभिञ्ञाबलपापुणि"न्ति।। 44।।

44. "And strenuous effort made I there,
The while I sat, or stood, or walked;
And ere seven days had passed away,
I had attained the Powers High."

एवं मे सिद्धिप्पत्तस्स, वसीभूतस्स सासने।
दीपङ्करो नाम जिनो, उप्पज्जि लोकनायको।। 45।।

45. "When I had thus success attained,
And made me master of the Law,
A Conqueror, Lord of All the World,
Was born, by name Dīpaṁkara."

"उप्पज्जन्ते च जायन्ते, बुज्झन्ते धम्मदेसने।
चतुरो निमित्ते नाद्दसं, झानरतिसमप्पितो"ति।। 46।।

46. "What time he was conceived, was born,
What time he Buddhaship attained,
When first he preached, the Signs[13] appeared.
I saw them not, deep sunk in trance."

पच्चन्तदेसविसये निमन्तेत्वा तथागतं।
तस्स आगमनं मग्गं, सोधेन्ति तुट्ठमानसा।। 47।।

47. "Then, in the distant border-land,
Invited they this Being Great,
And every one, with joyful heart,
The pathway for his coming cleared."

अहं तेन समयेन, निक्खमित्वा सकस्समा।
धुनन्तो वाकचीरानि, गच्छामि अम्बरे तदा।। 48।।

48. "Now so it happened at this time,
That I my hermitage had left,
And, barken garments rustling loud,
Was passing o'er them through the air."

वेदजातं जनं दिस्वा, तुट्ठहट्ठ पमोदितं।
ओरोहित्वान गगना, मनुस्से पुच्छि तावदे।। 49।।

49. "Then saw I every one alert,
Well-pleased, delighted, overjoyed;
And, coming downward from the sky,
The multitude I straightway asked:"

"तुट्ठहट्ठो पमुदितो, वेदजातो महाजनो।
कस्स सोधीयति मग्गो, अज्जसं वटुमायन"न्ति।। 50।।

50. "Well-pleased, delighted, overjoyed,
And all alert is every one;
For whom is being cleared the way,
The path, the track to travel on?"

"ते मे पुट्ठा वियाकंसु, 'बुद्धो लोके अनुत्तरो।

दीपङ्करो नाम जिनो, उप्पज्जि लोकनायको।
तस्स सोधीयति मग्गो, अज्जसं वटुमायनं"॥ 51॥

51. "When thus I asked, response was made:
A mighty Buddha has appeared,
A Conqueror, Lord of All the World,
Whose name is called Dīpaṁkara.
For him is being cleared the way,
The path, the track to travel on."

बुद्धोति मम सुत्वान, पीति उप्पज्जि तावदे।
बुद्धो बुद्धोति कथयन्तो, सोमनस्सं पवेदयिं॥ 52॥

52. "This word, "The Buddha," when I heard,
Joy sprang up straightway in my heart;
"A Buddha! Buddha!" cried I then,
And published my heart's content."

तत्थ ठत्वा विचिन्तेसिं, तुट्ठो संविग्गमानसो।
'इध बीजानि रोपिस्सं, खणो एव मा उपच्चगा॥ 53॥

53. "And standing there I pondered deep,
By joyous agitation seized :
"Here will I now some good seed sow,
Nor let this fitting season slip."

यदि बुद्धस्स सोधेथ, एकोकासं ददाथ मे।
अहम्पि सोधयिस्सामि, अज्जसं वटुमायनं॥ 54॥

54. "For a Buddha do ye clear the road?
Then, pray, grant also me a place!
I, too, will help to clear the way,
The path, the track to travel on."

अदंसु ते ममोकासं, सोधेतुं अज्जसं तदा।
बुद्धो बुद्धोति चिन्तेन्तो, मग्गं सोधेमहं तदा॥ 55

55. "And so they granted also me
A portion of the path to clear,
And I gan clear, while still my heart
Said "Buddha ! Buddha !" o'er and o'er."

अनिट्ठिते ममोकासे, दीपङ्करो महामुनि।

चतूहि सतसहस्सेहि, छळभिञ्ञेहि तादिहि।
खीणासवेहि विमलेहि, पटिपज्जि अञ्जसं जिनो।। 56।।

56. "But ere my part was yet complete,
Dīpaṁkara, the Mighty Sage,
The Conqueror, came that way along,
Thronged by four hundred thousand saints, "
Without depravity or spot,
And having each the Six High Powers."

पच्चुग्गमना वत्तन्ति, वज्जन्ति भेरियो बहू।
आमोदिता नरमरू, साधुकारं पवत्तयुं।। 57।।

57. "The people then their greetings gave,
And many kettle-drums were beat,
And men and gods, in joyous mood,
Loud shouted their applauding cries."

देवा मनुस्से पस्सन्ति, मनुस्सापि च देवता।
उभोपि ते पञ्जलिका, अनुयन्ति तथागतं।। 48।।

58. "Then men and gods together met,
And saw each other face to face;
And all with joined hands upraised
Followed The Buddha and his train."

देवा दिब्बेहि तुरियेहि, मनुस्सा मानुसेहि च।
उभोपि ते वज्जयन्ता, अनुयन्ति तथागतं।। 59।।

59. "The gods, with instruments divine,
The men, with those of human make,
Triumphant music played, the while
They followed in The Buddha's train."

दिब्बं मन्दारवं पुप्फं,पदुमं पारिछत्तकं।
दिसोदिसं ओकिरन्ति, आकासनभगता मरू।। 60।।

60. "Celestial beings from on high
Threw broadcast over all the earth
The Erythrina flowers of heaven,
The lotus and the coral-flower."

चम्पकं सललं नीपं, नागपुन्नागकेतकं।
दिसोदिसं उक्खिपन्ति, भूमितलगता नरा।। 61।।

61. "And men abiding on the ground
On every side flung up in air
Champakas, salaḷas, nīpas,
Nāgas, punnāgas, ketakas."

केसे मुञ्चित्वाहं तत्थ, वाकचीरञ्च चम्मकं।
कलले पत्थरित्वान, अवकुज्जो निपज्जहं।। 62।।

62. "Then loosened I my matted hair,
And, spreading out upon the mud
My dress of bark and cloak of skin,
I laid me down upon my face."

"अक्कमित्वान मं बुद्धो, सह सिस्सेहि गच्छतु।
मा नं कलले अक्कमित्थो, हिताय मे भविस्सती"ति।। 63।।

63. "Let now on me The Buddha tread,
With the disciples of his train;
Can I but keep him from the mire,
To me great merit shall accrue."

पथवियं निपन्नस्स, एवं मे आसि चेतसो।
इच्छमानो अहं अज्ज, किलेसे झापये मम। 64।।

64. "While thus I lay upon the ground,[14]
Arose within me many thoughts:
To-day, if such were my desire,
I my corruptions might consume."

किं मे अञ्ञातवेसेन, धम्मं सच्छिकतेनिध।
सब्बञ्ञुतं पापुणित्वा, बुद्धो हेस्सं सदेवके।। 65।।

65. "But why thus in an unknown guise
Should I the Doctrine's fruit secure?
Omniscience first will I achieve,
And be a Buddha in the world."

किं मे एकेन तिण्णेन, पुरिसेन थामदस्सिना।
सब्बञ्ञुतं पापुणित्वा, सन्तारेस्सं सदेवके।। 66

66. "Or why should I, a valorous man,
The ocean seek to cross alone?
"Omniscience first will I achieve,
And men and gods convey across."

इमिना मे अधिकारेन, कतेन पुरिसुत्तमे।
सब्बञ्ञुतं पापुणित्वा, तारेमि जनतं बहुं।। 67।।

67. "Since now I make this earnest wish,
In presence of this Best of Men,
Omniscience sometime I 'll achieve,
And multitudes convey across."

'संसारसोतं छिन्दित्वा, विद्धंसेत्वा तयो भवे।
धम्मनावं समारुय्ह, सन्तारेस्सं सदेवके'ति।। 68।।

68. "I'll rebirth's circling stream arrest,
Destroy existence's three modes;
I'll climb the sides of Doctrine's ship,
And men and gods convey across."

"मनुस्सत्तं लिङ्गसम्पत्ति, हेतु सत्थारदस्सनं।
पब्बज्जा गुणसम्पत्ति, अधिकारो व छन्दता।
अट्ठधम्मसमोधाना, अभिनीहारो समिज्झती"ति।। 69।।

69. "A human being,[15] male of sex,
Who saintship gains, a Teacher meets,
As hermit lives, and virtue loves,
Nor lacks resolve, nor fiery zeal,
Can by these eight conditions joined,
Make his most earnest wish succeed."

दीपङ्करो लोकविदू, आहुतीनं पटिग्गहो।
उस्सीसके मं ठत्वान, इदं वचनमब्रवि।। 70।।

70. "Dīpaṁkara, Who Knew All Worlds,
Recipient of Offerings,
Came to a halt my pillow near,
And thus addressed the multitudes:"

पस्सथ इमं तापसं, जटिलं उग्गतापनं।
अपरिमेय्ये इतो कप्पे, बुद्धो लोके भविस्सति।। 71।।

71. "Behold ye now this monk austere,
His matted locks, his penance fierce!
Lo! he, unnumbered cycles hence,
A Buddha in the world shall be."

अहु कपिलव्हया रम्मा, निक्खमित्वा तथागतो।
पधानं पदहित्वान, कत्वा दुक्करकारिकं।। 72।।

72. "From the fair town called Kapila
His Great Retirement shall be made.
Then, when his Struggle fierce is o'er,
His stern austerities performed,"

अजपालरुक्खमूले, निसीदित्वा तथागतो।
तत्थ पायासं पग्गय्ह, नेरञ्जरमुपेहिति।। 73।।

73. "He shall in quiet sit him down
Beneath the Ajapāla-tree;
There pottage made of rice receive,
And seek the stream Nerañjarā."

नेरञ्जराय तीरम्हि, पायासं अद सो जिनो।
पटियत्तवरमग्गेन, बोधिमूलमुपेहिति।। 74।।

74. "This pottage shall The Conqueror eat,
Beside the stream Nerañjarā,
And thence by road triumphal go
To where the Tree of Wisdom stands."

ततो पदक्खिणं कत्वा, बोधिमण्डं अनुत्तरो।
अस्सत्थरुक्खमूलम्हि, बुज्झिस्सति महायसो।। 75।।

75. "Then shall the Peerless, Glorious One
Walk to the right, round Wisdom's Throne,
And there The Buddhaship achieve,
While sitting at the fig-tree's root."

इमस्स जनिका माता, माया नाम भविस्सति।
पिता सुद्धोदनो नाम, अयं हेस्सति गोतमो।। 76।।

76. "The mother that shall bring him forth,
Shall Māyā called be by name;

Suddhodana his father's name;
His own name shall be Gotama."

अनासवा वीतरागा, सन्तचित्ता समाहिता।
कोलितो उपतिस्सो च, अग्गा हेस्सन्ति सावका।। 77।।

77. "Kolita, Upatissa[16] too, –
These shall his Chief Disciples be;
Both undepraved, both passion-free,
And tranquil and serene of mind."

आनन्दो नामुपट्ठाको, उपट्ठिस्सति तं जिनं।
खेमा उप्पलवण्णा च, अग्गा हेस्सन्ति साविका।। 78।।

78. "Ānanda shall be servitor
And on The Conqueror attend;
Khema and Uppalavaṇṇā
Shall female Chief Disciples be,"

अनासवा वीतरागा, सन्तचित्ता समाहिता।
बोधि तस्स भगवतो, अस्सत्थोति पवुच्चती'ति।। 79

79. "Both undepraved, both passion-free,
And tranquil and serene of mind.
The Bo-tree of this Blessed One
Shall be-the tree Assattha[17] called."

इदं सुत्वान वचनं, असमस्स महेसिनो।
आमोदिता नरमरू, बुद्धबीजं किर अयं।। 80।।

80. "Thus spake Th' Unequalled, Mighty Sage;
And all, when they had heard his speech,
Both men and gods rejoiced, and said:
"Behold a Buddha-scion here!"

उक्कुट्ठिसद्दा वत्तन्ति, अप्फाटेन्ति हसन्ति च।
कतञ्जली नमस्सन्ति, दससहस्सी सदेवका।। 81।।

81. "Now shouts were heard on every side,
The people clapped their arms and laughed.
Ten thousand worlds of men and gods
Paid me their homage then and said:"

यदिमस्स लोकनाथस्स, विरज्झिस्साम सासनं।
अनागतम्हि अद्धाने, हेस्साम सम्मुखा इमं।। 82।।

82. "If of our Lord Dīpaṁkara
The Doctrine now we fail to grasp,
We yet shall stand in time to come
Before this other face to face."

यथा मनुस्सा नदिं तरन्ता, पटिभित्थं विरज्झिय।
हेट्ठातित्थे गहेत्वान, उत्तरन्ति महानदिं।। 83।।

83. "Even as, when men a river cross,
And miss th' opposing landing-place,
A lower landing-place they find,
And there the river-bank ascend;"

'एवमेव मयं सब्बे, यदि मुञ्चामिमं जिनं।
अनागतम्हि अद्धाने, हेस्साम सम्मुखा इमं'।। 84।।

84. "Even so, we all, if we let slip
The present Conqueror that we have,
Yet still shall stand in time to come
Before this other, face to face."

दीपङ्करो लोकविदू, आहुतीनं पटिग्गहो।
मम कम्मं पकित्तेत्वा, दक्खिणं पादमुद्धरि।। 85।।

85. "Dīpaṁkara, Who All Worlds Knew,
Recipient of Offerings,
My future having prophesied,
His right foot raised and went his way."

ये तत्थासुं जिनपुत्ता, सब्बे पदक्खिणमकंसु मं।
नरा नागा च गन्धब्बा, अभिवादेत्वान पक्कमुं।। 86।।

86. "And all who were this Conqueror's sons,
Walked to the right around me then;
And serpents, men, and demigods,
Saluting me, departed thence."

दस्सनं मे अतिक्कन्ते, ससङ्घे लोकनायके।
हट्ठतुट्ठेन चित्तेन, आसना वुट्ठहिं तदा।। 87।।

87. "Now when The Leader of the World
Had passed from sight with all his train,
My mind with rapturous transport filled,
I raised me up from where I lay."

सुखेन सुखितो होमि, पामोज्जेन पमोदितो।
पीतिया च अभिस्सन्नो,पल्लङ्कं आभुजिं तदा।। 88।।

88. "Then overjoyed with joy was I,
Delighted with a keen delight;
And thus with pleasure saturate
I sat me down with legs across."

पल्लङ्केन निसीदित्वा, एवं चिन्तेसहं तदा।
वसीभूतो अहं झाने, अभिञ्ञासु पारमिं गतो।। 89।।

89. "And while cross-legged there I sat,
I thus reflected to myself:
Behold ! in trance am I adept,
And all the Powers High are mine."

सहस्सियम्हि लोकम्हि इसयो नत्थि मे समा।
असमो इद्धिधम्मेसु, अलभिं ईदिसं सुखं।। 90।।

90. "Nowhere throughout a thousand worlds
Are any seers to equal me;
Unequalled in the magic gifts
Have I this height of bliss attained."

पल्लङ्काभुजने मय्हं, दससहस्साधिवासिनो।
महानादं पवत्तेसुं, धुवं बुद्धो भविस्ससि।। 91।।

91. "Now while I sat with legs across,
The dwellers of ten thousand worlds
Boiled forth a glad and mighty shout:[18]
Surely a Buddha thou shalt be!"

या पुब्बे बोधिसत्तानं,पल्लङ्कवरमाभुजे।
निमित्तानि पदिस्सन्ति, तानि अज्ज पदिस्सरे।। 92।।

92. "The presages that erst were seen,
When Future Buddhas sat cross-legged,

These presages are seen today–
Surely a Buddha thou shalt be!"

सीतं ब्यपगतं होति, उण्हञ्च उपसम्मति।
तानि अज्ज पदिस्सन्ति, धुवं बुद्धो भविस्ससि।। 93।।

93. "All cold is everywhere dispelled,
And mitigated is the heat;
These presages are seen today–
Surely a Buddha thou shalt be!"

दससहस्सी लोकधातू, निस्सद्दा होन्ति निराकुला।
तानि अज्ज पदिस्सन्ति, धुवं बुद्धो भविस्ससि।। 94।।

94. "The system of ten thousand worlds
Is hushed to quiet and to peace;
These presages are seen today—
Surely a Buddha thou shalt be!"

महावाता न वायन्ति, न सन्दन्ति सवन्तियो।
तानि अज्ज पदिस्सन्ति, धुवं बुद्धो भविस्ससि।। 95।।

95. "The mighty winds then cease to blow,
Nor do the rivers onward glide;
These presages are seen today–
Surely a Buddha thou shalt be!"

थलजा दकजा पुप्फा, सब्बे पुप्फन्ति तावदे।
तेपज्ज पुप्फिता सब्बे, धुवं बुद्धो भविस्ससि।। 96।।

96. "All plants, be they of land or stream,
Do straightway put their blossoms forth;
Even so today they all have bloomed–
Surely a Buddha thou shalt be!"

लता वा यदि वा रुक्खा, फलभारा होन्ति तावदे।
तेपज्ज फलिता सब्बे, धुवं बुद्धो भविस्ससि।। 97।।

97. "And every tree, and every vine,
Is straightway laden down with fruit;
Even so today they're laden down-
Surely a Buddha thou shalt be!"

आकासट्ठा च भूमट्ठा, रतना जोतन्ति तावदे।
तेपज्ज रतना जोतन्ति, धुवं बुद्धो भविस्ससि।। 98।।

98. "In sky and earth doth straightway then
Full many a radiant gem appear;
Even so today they shine afar–
Surely a Buddha thou shalt be !"

मानुसका च दिब्बा च, तुरिया वज्जन्ति तावदे।
तेपज्जुभो अभिरवन्ति, धुवं बुद्धो भविस्ससि।। 99।।

99. "Then straightway music's heard to play
'Mongst men on earth and gods in heaven;
So all today in music join–
Surely a Buddha thou shalt be!"

विचित्तपुप्फा गगना, अभिवस्सन्ति तावदे।
तेपि अज्ज पवस्सन्ति, धुवं बुद्धो भविस्ससि।। 100।।

100. "There falleth straightway down from heaven
A rain of many-colored flowers;
Even so today these flowers are seen–
Surely a Buddha thou shalt be!"

महासमुद्दो आभुजति, दससहस्सी पकम्पति।
तेपज्जुभो अभिरवन्ति, धुवं बुद्धो भविस्ससि।। 101।।

101. "The mighty ocean heaves and roars,
And all the worlds ten thousand quake;
Even so is now this tumult heard-
Surely a Buddha thou shalt be!"

निरयेपि दससहस्से, अग्गी निब्बन्ति तावदे।
तेपज्ज निब्बुता अग्गी, धुवं बुद्धो भविस्ससि।। 102।।

102. "Straightway throughout the whole of hell
The fires ten thousand all die out;
Even so today have all expired–
Surely a Buddha thou shalt be!"

विमलो होति सूरियो, सब्बा दिस्सन्ति तारका।
तेपि अज्ज पदिस्सन्ति, धुवं बुद्धो भविस्ससि।। 103।।

103. "Unclouded then the sun shines forth,
And all the stars appear to view;
Even so today do they appear –
Surely a Buddha thou shalt be !"

अनोवट्ठेन उदकं, महिया उब्भिज्जि तावदे।
तम्पज्जुब्भिज्जते महिया, धुवं बुद्धो भविस्ससि।। 104।।

104. "Straightway, although no rain hath fallen,
Burst springs of water from the earth;
Even so today they gush in streams –
Surely a Buddha thou shalt be!"

तारागणा विरोचन्ति, नक्खत्ता गगनमण्डले।
विसाखा चन्दिमायुत्ता, धुवं बुद्धो भविस्ससि।। 105।।

105. "And bright then shine the starry hosts ,-
And constellations in the sky;
The moon in Libra now doth stand—
Surely a Buddha thou shalt be!"

बिलासया दरीसया, निक्खमन्ति सकासया।
तेपज्ज आसया छुद्धा, धुवं बुद्धो भविस्ससि।। 106।।

106. "All beasts that lurk in holes and clefts,
Then get them forth from out their lairs;
Even so today they 've left their dens –
Surely a Buddha thou shalt be!"

न होति अरति सत्तानं, सन्तुट्ठा होन्ति तावदे।
तेपज्ज सब्बे सन्तुट्ठा, धुवं बुद्धो भविस्ससि।। 107।।

107. "Straightway content is all the world,
And no unhappiness is known;
Even so today are all content –
Surely a Buddha thou shalt be!"

रोगा तदूपसम्मन्ति, जिघच्छा च विनस्सति।
तानिपज्ज पदिस्सन्ति, धुवं बुद्धो भविस्ससि।। 108।।

108. "Then every sickness vanishes,
And hunger likewise disappears;

These presages are seen today –
Surely a Buddha thou shalt be!"

रागो तदा तनु होति, दोसो मोहो विनस्सति।
तेपज्ज विगता सब्बे, धुवं बुद्धो भविस्ससि।। 109।।

109. "Then lust doth dwindle and grow weak,
And hate, infatuation too;
Even so today they disappear –
Surely a Buddha thou shalt be!"

भयं तदा न भवति, अज्जपेतं पदिस्सति।
तेन लिङ्गेन जानाम, धुवं बुद्धो भविस्ससि।। 110।।

110. "Then fear and danger are unknown;
All we are freed from them today;
And by this token we perceive –
'Surely a Buddha thou shalt be!'"

रजो नुद्धंसति उद्धं, अज्जपेतं पदिस्सति।
तेन लिङ्गेन जानाम, धुवं बुद्धो भविस्ससि।। 111।।

111. "No dust upwhirleth towards the sky;
Even so today this thing is seen;
And by this token we perceive –
'Surely a Buddha thou shalt be!'"

अनिट्ठगन्धो पक्कमति, दिट्ठगन्धो पवायति।
सोपज्ज वायति गन्धो, धुवं बुद्धो भविस्ससि।। 112।।

112. "All noisome odors drift away,
And heavenly fragrance fills the air;
Even so the winds now sweetness waft –
Surely a Buddha thou shalt be !"

सब्बे देवा पदिस्सन्ति, ठपयित्वा अरूपिनो।
तेपज्ज सब्बे दिस्सन्ति, धुवं बुद्धो भविस्ससि।। 113।।

113. "Then all the gods appear to view,
Save those that hold the formless realm;
Even so today these all are seen –
Surely a Buddha thou shalt be !"

यावता निरया नाम, सब्बे दिस्सन्ति तावदे।
तेपज्ज सब्बे दिस्सन्ति, धुवं बुद्धो भविस्ससि।। 114।।

114. "Then clearly seen are all the hells,
However many be their tale;
Even so today may all be seen–
Surely a Buddha thou shalt be!"

कुट्टा कवाटा सेला च, न होन्तावरणा तदा।
आकासभूता तेपज्ज, धुवं बुद्धो भविस्ससि।। 115।।

115. "Through walls, and doors, and mountain-rocks,
One finds an easy passage then;
Even so today they yield like air–
Surely a Buddha thou shalt be !"

चुती च उपपत्ति च, खणे तस्मिं न विज्जति।
तानिपज्ज पदिस्सन्ति, धुवंबुद्धो भविस्ससि। ।116।।

116. "Existence then forbears its round
Of death and rebirth for a time;
Even so today this thing is seen–
Surely a Buddha thou shalt be!"

'दहं पग्गण्ह वीरियं, मा निवत्त अभिक्कम।।
मयम्पेतं विजानाम, धुवं बुद्धो भविस्ससी'ति।। 117।।

117. "Do thou a strenuous effort make !
Do not turn back! Go on ! Advance!
Most certainly we know this thing :
'Surely a Buddha thou shalt be !'"

बुद्धस्स वचनं सुत्वा, दससहस्सीन चूभयं।
तुट्ठहट्ठो पमोदितो, एवं चिन्तेसहं तदा।। 118।।

118. "When I had heard The Buddha's speech,
And what the worlds ten thousand said,
Well-pleased, delighted, overjoyed,
I thus reflected to myself :"

अद्वेज्झवचना बुद्धा, अमोघवचना जिना।
वितथं नत्थि बुद्धानं, धुवं बुद्धो भवामहं।। 119।।

119. "The Buddhas never liars are;
A Conqueror's word ne'er yet was vain;
Nothing but truth The Buddhas speak–
Surely a Buddha I shall be!"

यथा खित्तं नभे लेड्डु धुवं पतति भूमियं।
तथेव बुद्धसेट्ठानं, वचनं धुवसस्सतं।। 120।।

120. "As clods thrown upward in the air
Fall surely back upon the earth,
So what the glorious Buddhas speak
Is sure and steadfast to the end.
Nothing but truth The Buddhas speak[19]–
Surely a Buddha I shall be !"

यथापि सब्बसत्तानं, मरणं धुवसस्सतं।
तथेव बुद्धसेट्ठानं, वचनं धुवसस्सतं।। 121।।

121. "As also for each living thing
The approach of death is ever sure,
So what the glorious Buddhas speak
Is sure and steadfast to the end.
Nothing but truth The Buddhas speak
Surely a Buddha I shall be"

यथा रत्तिक्खये पत्ते, सूरियुग्गमनं धुवं।
तथेव बुद्धसेट्ठानं, वचनं धुवस्सतं।। 122।।

122. "As at the waning of the night
The rising of the sun is sure,
So what the glorious Buddhas speak
Is sure and steadfast to the end.
Nothing but truth, etc."

यथा निक्खन्तसयनस्स, सीहस्स नदनं धुवं।।
तथेव बुद्धसेट्ठानं, वचनं धुवसस्सतं।। 123।।

123. "As, when he issues from his den,
The roaring of the lion's sure,
So what the glorious Buddhas speak
Is sure and steadfast to the end.
Nothing but truth, etc."

"तथा आपन्नसत्तानं, भारमोरोपनं धुवं।
तथेव बुद्धसेट्ठानं, वचनं धुवसस्सतं"न्ति।। 124।।

124. "As when a female has conceived,
Her bringing forth of young is sure,
So what the glorious Buddhas speak
Is sure and steadfast to the end.
Nothing but truth The Buddhas speak –
Surely a Buddha I shall be!"

हन्द बुद्धकरे धम्मे, विचिनामि इतो चितो।
उद्धं अधो दस दिसा, यावता धम्मधातुया।। 125।।

125. "Come now! I'll search that I may find
Conditions which a Buddha make –
Above, below, to all ten[20] points,
Where'er conditions hold their sway."

विचिनन्तो तदादक्खिं, पठमं दानपारमिं।
पुब्बकेहि महेसीहि, अनुचिण्णं महापथं।। 126।।

126. "And then I searched, and saw the First
Perfection, which consists in Alms,
That highroad great whereon of old
The former seers had ever walked."

इमं त्वं पठमं ताव, दळहं कत्वा समादिय।
दानपारमितं गच्छ, यदि बोधिं पत्तुमिच्छसि।। 127।।

127. "Come now! This one as first adopt,
And practise it determinedly;
Acquire perfection in thine Alms,
If thou to Wisdom wouldst attain."

यथापि कुम्भो सम्पुण्णो, यस्स कस्सचि अधोकतो।
वमतेवुदकं निस्सेसं, न तत्थ परिरक्खति।। 128।।

128. "As when a jar is brimming full,
And some one overturneth it,
The jar its water all gives forth,
And nothing for itself keeps back;"

तथेव याचके दिस्वा, हीनमुक्कट्ठमज्झिमे।
ददाहि दानं निस्सेसं, कुम्भो विय अधोकतो"ति।। 129।।

129. "So, when a suppliant thou dost see,
Of mean, or high, or middling rank,
Give all in Alms, in nothing stint,
E'en as the overturned jar."

न हेते एत्तकायेव, बुद्धधम्मा भविस्सरे।
अञ्ञेपि विचिनिस्सामि, ये धम्मा बोधिपाचना।। 130।।

130. "But now there must be more than these
Conditions which a Buddha make :
Still others will I seek to find
That shall in Buddhaship mature."

विचिनन्तो तदादक्खिं, दुतियं सीलपारमिं।
पुब्बकेहि महेसीहि, आसेवितनिसेवितं।। 131।।

131. "Perfection Second then I sought,
And lo! the Precepts came to view,
Which mighty seers of former times
Had practised and had follow'd."

इमं त्वं दुतियं ताव, दळ्हं कत्वा समादिय।
सीलपारमितं गच्छ, यदि बोधिं पत्तुमिच्छसि।। 132।।

132. "Come now! as second this adopt,
And practise it determinedly;
The Precepts to perfection keep,
If thou to Wisdom wouldst attain."

यथापि चमरी वालं, किस्मिञ्चिपटिलग्गितं।
उपेति मरणं तत्थ, न विकोपेति वालधिं।। 133।।

133. "As when a Yak cow's flowing tail
Is firmly caught by bush or thorn,
She thereupon awaits her death,
But will not tear and mar her tail;"[21]

"तथेव चतूसु, भूमीसु, सीलानि परिपूरय।
परिरक्ख सब्बदा सीलं, चमरी विय वालधि"न्ति।। 134।।

134. "So likewise thou in stages four,
Observe and keep the Precepts whole,
On all occasions guard them well,
As ever Yak cow does her tail."

न हेते एत्तकायेव, बुद्धधम्मा भविस्सरे।
अञ्ञेपि विचिनिस्सामि, ये धम्मा बोधिपाचना।। 135।।

135. "But now there must be more than these
Conditions which a Buddha make;
Still others will I seek to find
That shall in Buddhaship mature."

विचिनन्तो तदादक्खिं, ततियं नेक्खम्मपारमिं।
पुब्बकेहि महेसीहि, आसेवितनिसेवितं।। 136।।

136. "And then Perfection Third I sought,
Which is Renunciation called,
Which mighty seers of former times
Had practised and had follow'd."

इमं त्वं ततियं ताव, दळ्हं कत्वा समादिय।
नेक्खम्मपारमितं गच्छ, यदि बोधिं पत्तुमिच्छसि।। 137।।

137. "Come now! this one as third adopt,
And practise it determinedly;
Renounce, and in perfection grow,
If thou to Wisdom wouldst attain."

यथा अन्दुघरे पुरिसो, चिरवुत्थो दुखट्टितो।
न तत्थ रागं जनेति, मुत्तिमेव, गवेसति।। 138।।

138. "Even as a man who long has dwelt
In prison, suffering miserably,
No liking for the place conceives,
But only longeth for release;"

"तथेव त्वं सब्बभवे, पस्स अन्दुघरे विय।
नेक्खम्माभिमुखो होहि, भवतो परिमुत्तिया"ति।। 139।।

139. "So likewise thou must every mode
Of being as a prison view—

Renunciation be thy aim;
Thus from existence free thyself."

न हेते एत्तकायेव, बुद्धधम्मा भविस्सरे।
अञ्ञेपि विचिनिस्सामि, ये धम्मा बोधिपाचना।। 140।।

140. "But now there must be more than these
Conditions which a Buddha make;
Still others will I seek to find
That shall in Buddhaship mature."

विचिनन्तो तदादक्खि, चतुत्थं पञ्ञापारमिं।
पुब्बकेहि महेसीहि, आसेवितनिसेवितं।। 141।।

141. "And then I sought and found the Fourth
Perfection, which is Wisdom called,
Which mighty seers of former times
Had practised and had follow'd."

इमं त्वं चतुत्थं ताव, दळ्हं कत्वा समादिय।
पञ्ञापारमितं गच्छ, यदि बोधिं पत्तुमिच्छसि।। 142।।

142. "Come now! this one as fourth adopt,
And practise it determinedly;
Wisdom to its perfection bring,
If thou to Wisdom wouldst attain."

यथापि भिक्खु भिक्खन्तो, हीनमुक्कट्ठमज्झिमे।
कुलानि न विवज्जेन्तो, एवं लभति यापनं।। 143।।

143. "Just as a priest, when on his rounds,
Nor low, nor high, nor middling folk
Doth shun, but begs of every one,
And so his daily food receives;"

"तथेव त्वं सब्बकालं, परिपुच्छन्तो बुधं जनं।
पञ्ञापारमितं गन्त्वा, सम्बोधिं पापुणिस्ससी"ति।। 144।।

144. "So to the learned ay resort,
And seek thy Wisdom to increase;
And when this Fourth Perfection's gained,
A Buddha's Wisdom shall be thine."

न हेते एत्तकायेव, बुद्धधम्मा भविस्सरे।
अञ्ञेपि विचिनिस्सामि, ये धम्मा बोधिपाचना।। 145।।

145. "But now there must be more than these
Conditions which a Buddha make;
Still others will I seek to find
That shall in Buddhaship mature."

विचिनन्तो तदादक्खिं, पञ्चमं वीरियपारमिं।
पुब्बकेहि महेसीहि, आसेवितनिसेवितं।। 146।।

146. "And then I sought and found the Fifth
Perfection, which is Courage called,
Which mighty seers of former times
Had practised and had follow'd."

इमं त्वं पञ्चमं ताव, दळहं कत्वा समादिय।
वीरियपारमितं गच्छ, बोधिं पत्तुमिच्छसि।। 147।।

147. "Come now! this one as fifth adopt,
And practise it determinedly;
In Courage perfect strive to be,
If thou to Wisdom wouldst attain."

यथापि सीहो मिगराजा, निसज्जट्ठानचङ्कमे।
अलीनवीरियो होति, पग्गहितमनो सदा।। 148।।

148. "Just as the lion, king of beasts,
In crouching, walking, standing still,
With courage ever is instinct,
And watchful always, and alert;"

"तथेव त्वं सब्बभवे, पग्गण्ह वीरियं दळहं।
वीरियपारमितं गन्त्वा, सम्बोधिं पापुणिस्ससी"ति।। 149।।

149. "So thou in each repeated birth,
Courageous energy display;
And when this Fifth Perfection's gained,
A Buddha's Wisdom shall be thine."

न हेते एत्तकायेव, बुद्धधम्मा भविस्सरे।
अञ्ञेपि विचिनिस्सामि, ये धम्मा बोधिपाचना।। 150।।

150. "But now there must be more than these
Conditions which a Buddha make;
Still others will I seek to find
That shall in Buddhaship mature."

विचिनन्तो तदादक्खि, छट्ठमं खन्तिपारिमिं।
पुब्बकेहि महेसीहि, आसेवितनिसेवितं।। 151।।

151. "And then I sought and found the Sixth
Perfection, which is Patience called,
Which mighty seers of former times
Had practised and had follow'd."

इमं त्वं छट्ठमं ताव, दळ्हं कत्वा समादिय।
तत्थ अद्वेज्झमानसो, सम्बोधिं पापुणिस्ससि।। 152।।

152. "Come now ! this one as sixth adopt,
And practise it determinedly;
And if thou keep an even mood,
A Buddha's Wisdom shall be thine."

यथापि पथवी नाम, सुचिम्पि असुचिम्पि च।
सब्बं सहति निक्खेपं, न करोति पटिघं तया।। 153।।

153. "Just as the earth, whate'er is thrown
Upon her, whether sweet or foul,
All things endures, and never shows
Repugnance, nor complacency;"

"तथेव त्वम्पि सब्बेसं, सम्मानावमानक्खमो।
खन्तिपारमितं गन्त्वा, सम्बोधिं पापुणिस्ससी"ति।। 154।।

154. "E'en so, or honor thou, or scorn,
Of men, with patient mood must bear;
And when this Sixth Perfection's gained,
A Buddha's Wisdom shall be thine.""

न हेते एत्तकायेव, बुद्धधम्मा भविस्सरे।
अञ्ञेपि विचिनिस्सामि, ये धम्मा बोधिपाचना।। 155।।

155. "But now there must be more than these
Conditions which a Buddha make;

Still others will I seek to find
That shall in Buddhaship mature."

विचिनन्तो तदादक्खि, सत्तमं सच्चपारमिं।
पुब्बकेहि महेसीहि, आसेवितनिसेवितं।। 156।।

156. "And then I sought and found the Seventh
Perfection, which is that of Truth,
Which mighty seers of former times
Had practised and had follow'd."

इमं त्वं सत्तमं ताव, दळहं कत्वा समादिय।
तत्थ अद्वेज्झवचनो, सम्बोधिं पापुणिस्ससि।। 157।।

157. "Come now! this one as seventh adopt,
And practise it determinedly;
If thou art ne'er of double speech,
A Buddha's Wisdom shall be thine."

यथापि ओसधी नाम, तुलाभूता सदेवके।
समये उतुवस्से वा,न वोक्कमति वीथितो।। 158।।

158. "Just as the morning star on high
Its balanced course doth ever keep,
And through all seasons, times, and years,
Doth never from its pathway swerve;"

"तथेव त्वम्पि सच्चेसु, मा वोक्कमसि वीथितो।
सच्चपारमितं गन्त्वा, सम्बोधिं पापुणिस्ससी"ति।। 159।।

159. "So likewise thou in all thy speech
Swerve never from the path of truth;
And when this Seventh Perfection's gained,
A Buddha's Wisdom shall be thine."

न हेते एत्तकायेव, बुद्धधम्मा भविस्सरे।
अञ्ञेपि विचिनिस्सामि, ये धम्मा बोधिपाचना।। 160।।

160. "But now there must be more than these
Conditions which a Buddha make;
Still others will I seek to find
That shall in Buddhaship mature."

विचिनन्तो तदादक्खि, अट्ठमं अधिट्ठानपारमिं।
पुब्बकेहि महेसीहि, आसेवितनिसेवितं।। 161।।

161\. "And then I sought and found the Eighth
Perfection, Resolution called,
Which mighty seers of former times
Had practised and had follow'd."

इमं त्वं अट्ठमं ताव, दळ्हं कत्वा समादिय।
तत्थ त्वं अचलो हुत्वा, सम्बोधिं पापुणिस्ससि।। 162।।

162\. "Come now! this one as eighth adopt,
And practise it determinedly;
And when thou art immovable,
A Buddha's Wisdom shall be thine."

यथापि पब्बतो सेलो, अचलो सुप्पतिट्ठितो।
न कम्पति भुसवातेहि, सकट्ठानेव तिट्ठति।। 163।।

163\. "Just as a rocky mountain-peak,
Unmoved stands, firm-stablished,
Unshaken by the boisterous gales,
And always in its place abides;"

"तथेव त्वम्पि अधिट्ठाने, सब्बदा अचलो भव।
अधिट्ठानपारमितं गन्त्वा, सम्बोधिं पापुणिस्ससी"ति।। 164।।

164\. "So likewise thou must ever be
In Resolution firm intrenched;
And when this Eighth Perfection's gained,
A Buddha's Wisdom shall be thine."

न हेते एत्तकायेव, बुद्धधम्मा भविस्सरे।
अञ्ञेपि विचिनिस्सामि, ये धम्मा बोधिपाचना।। 165।।

165\. "But now there must be more than these
Conditions which a Buddha make;
Still others will I seek to find
That shall in Buddhaship mature."

विचिनन्तो तदादक्खि, नवमं मेत्तापारमिं।
पुब्बकेहि महेसीहि, आसेवितनिसेवितं।। 166।।

166. "And then I sought and found the Ninth
Perfection, which is called Good-will;
Which mighty seers of former times
Had practised and had follow'd."

इमं त्वं नवमं ताव, दळ्हं कत्वा समादिय।
मेत्ताय असमो होहि, यदि बोधिं पत्तुमिच्छसि।। 167।।

167. "Come now! this one as ninth adopt,
And practise it determinedly;
Unequalled be in thy Good-will,
If thou to Wisdom wouldst attain."

यथापि उदकं नाम, कल्याणे पापके जने।
समं फरति सीतेन, पवाहेति रजोमलं।। 168।।

168. "As water cleanseth all alike,
The righteous and the wicked, too,
From dust and dirt of every kind,
And with refreshing coolness fills;"

"तथेव त्वम्पि अहितहिते, समं मेत्ताय भावय।
मेत्तापारमितं गन्त्वा, सम्बोधिं पापुणिस्ससी"ति।। 169।।

169. "So likewise thou both friend and foe,
Alike with thy Good-will refresh,
And when this Ninth Perfection 's gained,
A Buddha's Wisdom shall be thine."

न हेते एत्तकायेव, बुद्धधम्मा भविस्सरे।
अञ्ञेपि विचिनिस्सामि, ये धम्मा बोधिपाचना।। 170।।

170. "But now there must be more than these
Conditions which a Buddha make;
Still others will I seek to find
That shall in Buddhaship mature."

विचिनन्तो तदादक्खिं, दसमं उपेक्खापारमिं।
पुब्बकेहि महेसीहि, आसेवितनिसेवितं।। 171।।

171. "And then I sought and found the Tenth
Perfection, called Indifference;

Which mighty seers of former times
Had practised and had follow'd."

इमं त्वं दसमं ताव, दळ्हं कत्वा समादिय।
तुलाभूतो दळ्हो हुत्वा, सम्बोधिं पापुणिस्ससि।। 172।।

172. "Come now'! this one as tenth adopt,
And practise it determinedly;
And when thou art of equal poise,
A Buddha's Wisdom shall be thine."

यथापि पथवी नाम, निक्खित्तं असुचिं सुचिं।
उपेक्खति उभोपेते, कोपानुनयवज्जिता।। 173।।

173. "Just as the earth, whate'er is thrown
Upon her, whether sweet or foul,
Indifferent is to all alike,
Nor hatred shows, nor amity;"

"तथेव त्वम्पि सुखदुक्खे, तुलाभूतो सदा भव।
उपेक्खापारमितं गन्त्वा, सम्बोधिं पापुणिस्ससी"ति।। 174।।

174. "So likewise thou in good or ill,
Must even-balanced ever be;
And when this Tenth Perfection's gained,
A Buddha's Wisdom shall be thine."

एत्तकायेव ते लोके, ये धम्मा बोधिपाचना।
ततुद्धं नत्थि अञ्ञत्र, दळ्हं तत्थ पतिट्ठह।। 175।।

175. "But earth no more conditions hath
That in The Buddhaship mature;
Beyond these are there none to seek;
So practise these determinedly."

इमे धम्मे सम्मसतो, सभावसरसलक्खणे।
धम्मतेजेन वसुधा, दससहस्सी पकम्पथ।। 176।।

176. "Now pondering these conditions ten,
Their nature, essence, character, –
Such fiery vigor had they all,
That all the worlds ten thousand quaked."

"चलती रवती पथवी, उच्छुयन्तंव पीळितं।
तेलयन्ते यथा चक्कं, एवं कम्पति मेदनी"ति।। 177।।

177. "Then shook and creaked the wide, wide earth,
As doth the sugar-mill at work;
Then quaked the ground, as doth the wheel
Of oil-mills when they 're made to turn."

यावता परिसा आसि, बुद्धस्स परिवेसने।
पवेधमाना सा तत्थ, मुच्छिता सेसि भूमियं।। 178।।

178. "Th' entire assemblage that was there,
And followed in The Buddha's train,
Trembled and shook in great alarm,
And fell astonied to the ground."

घटानेकसहस्सानि, कुम्भीनञ्च सता बहू।
सञ्चुण्णमथिता तत्थ, अञ्ञमञ्ञं पघट्टिता।। 179।।

179. "And many thousand waterpots,
And many hundred earthen jars,
Were one upon another dashed,
And crushed and pounded into dust."

उब्बिग्गा तसिता भीता, भन्ता ब्यधितमानसा।
महाजना समागम्म, दीपङ्करमुपागमुं।। 180।।

180. "Excited, trembling, terrified,
Confused, and sore oppressed in mind,
The multitudes together came,
And to Dīpaṁkara approached."

'किं भविस्सति लोकस्स, कल्याणमथ पापकं।
सब्बो उपद्दुतो लोको, तं विनोदेहि चक्खुम'।। 181।।

181. "Oh, tell us what these signs portend.
Will good or ill betide the world?
Lo! terror seizes hold on all.
Dispel our fears, All-Seeing One!"

तेसं तदा सञ्ञापेसि, दीपङ्करो महामुनि।
विस्सत्था होथ मा भाथ, इमस्मिं पथविकम्पने।। 182।।

182. "The Great Sage, then, Dīpaṁkara,
Allayed and pacified their fears: –
Be comforted; and fear ye not
For that the world doth quake and shake."

यमहं अज्ज ब्याकासिं, बुद्धो लोके भविस्सति।
एसो सम्मसति धम्मं, पुब्बकं जिनसेवितं।। 183।।

183. "Of whom today I made proclaim
'A glorious Buddha shall he be,' –
He now conditions pondereth,
Which former Conquerors fulfilled."

"तस्स सम्मसतो धम्मं, बुद्धभूमिं असेसतो।
तेनायं कम्पिता पथवी, दससहस्सी सदेवके"ति।। 184।।

184. "'T is while on these he is intent,
As basis for The Buddhaship,
The ground in worlds ten thousand shakes,
In all the realms of gods and men."

बुद्धस्स वचनं सुत्वा, मनो निब्बायि तावदे।
सब्बे मं उपसङ्कम्म, पुनापि अभिवन्दिसुं।। 185।।

185. "When thus they 'd heard The Buddha speak,
Their anxious minds received relief;
And all then drawing near to me,
Again they did me reverence."

"समादियित्वा बुद्धगुणं, दळहं कत्वान मानसं।
दीपङ्करं नमस्सित्वा, आसना वुट्ठहिं तदा"ति।। 186।।

186. "Thus on the road to Buddhaship,
And firm determined in my mind,
I raised me up from off my seat,
And reverenced Dīpaṁkara."

दिब्बं मानुसकं पुप्फं, देवा मानुसका उभो।
समोकिरन्ति पुप्फेहि, वुट्ठहन्तस्स आसना।। 187।।

187. "Then as I raised me from my seat,
Both gods and men in unison

Sweet flowers of heaven and flowers of earth
Profusely sprinkled on my head."

वेदयन्ति च ते सोत्थिं, देवा मानसुका उभो।
महन्तं पत्थितं तुय्हं, तं लभस्सु यथिच्छितं।। 188।।

188. "And gods and men in unison
Their great delight proclaimed aloud :–
A mighty prayer thou now hast made;
Succeed according to thy wish'."

सब्बीतियो विवज्जन्तु, सोको रोगो विनस्सतु।
भा ते भवन्त्वन्तराया, फुस खिप्पं बोधिमुत्तमं।। 189।।

189. "From all misfortunes be thou free,
Let every sickness disappear!
Mayst thou no hindrance ever know,
And highest Wisdom soon achieve !"

यथापि समये पत्ते, पुप्फन्ति पुप्फिनो दुमा।
तथेव त्वं महावीर, बुद्धञाणेन पुप्फस्सु।। 190।।

190. "As, when the time of spring has come,
The trees put forth their buds and flowers,
Likewise dost thou, O Hero Great,
With knowledge of a Buddha bloom."

यथा ये केचि सम्बुद्धा, पूरयुं दस पारमी।
तथेव त्वं महावीर, पूरय दस पारमी।। 191।।

191. "As all they who have Buddhas been,
The Ten Perfections have fulfilled,
Likewise do thou, O Hero Great,
The Ten Perfections strive to gain."

यथा ये केचि सम्बुद्धा, बोधिमण्डम्हि बुज्झरे।
तथेव त्वं महावीर, बुज्झस्सु जिनबोधियं।। 192।।

192. "As all they who have Buddhas been,
On Wisdom's Throne their insight gained,
Likewise do thou, O Hero Great,
On Conqueror's Throne thy insight gain."

यथा ये केचि सम्बुद्धा, धम्मचक्कं पवत्तयुं।
तथेव त्वं महावीर, धम्मचक्कं पवत्तय।। 193।।

193. "As all they who have Buddhas been,
Have made the Doctrine's Wheel to roll,
Likewise do thou, O Hero Great,
Make Doctrine's Wheel to roll once more."

पुण्णमासे यथा चन्दो, परिसुद्धो विरोचति।
तथेव त्वं पुण्णमनो, विरोच दससहस्सियं।। 194।।

194. "As on the mid-day of the month
The moon in full perfection shines,
Likewise do thou, with perfect mind,
Shine brightly in ten thousand worlds."

राहुमुत्तो यथा सूरियो, तापेन अतिरोचति।
तथेव लोका मुच्चित्वा, विरोच सिरिया तुवं।। 195।।

195. "As when the sun, by Rāhu freed,
Shines forth exceeding bright and clear.
So thou, when freed from ties of earth,
Shine forth in bright magnificence."

यथा या काचि नदियो, ओसरन्ति महोदधिं।
एवं सदेवका लोका, ओसरन्तु तवन्तिके।। 196।।

196. "Just as the rivers of all lands
Into the ocean find their way,
May gods and men from every world.
Approach and find their way to thee."

"तेहि थुतप्पसत्थो सो, दस धम्मे समादिय।
ते धम्मे परिपूरेन्तो, पवनं पाविसी तदा"ति।। 197।।

197. "Thus praised they me with glad acclaim;
And I, beginning to fulfil
The ten conditions of my quest,
Re-entered then into the wood."

NOTES AND REFERENCES

1. This entire story is related by The Buddha to his disciples, and describes how, in his long-ago existence as the Brāhmaṇa Sumedha, he first resolved to strive for the Buddhaship. In stanzas 12-16 he speaks of himself, that is, of Sumedha, in the third person, but elsewhere in the first.
2. Only six of the ten noises indicative of a flourishing town are here mentioned.'
3. Probably gold, silver, pearls, gems (such as sapphire and ruby), cat's-eye, diamond, and coral.
4. Lust, hatred, and infatuation.
5. The two eyes, ears, and so forth.
6. The, Himālaya mountains. *Himālaya* and *Himavant* are Sanskrit words of almost identical signification. The former means "snow-abode," and is a compound of *hima*, "snow," and *ālaya*, "settling-down place," or "abode." *Hima-vant* means "snowy."
7. Native gloss: Jātaka, vol. i., p. 7, 1. 14 (P.T.S) Exempted from the five defects: The following are the five defects in a walking-place : hardness and unevenness; trees in the midst; dense underbrush; excessive narrowness; excessive width. For if the walking-place be on hard and uneven ground, then any one who uses it hurts and blisters his feet, so 'that he fails of concentration of mind, and his meditation is broken up; while he who walks at ease on a soft and even surface succeeds in meditation. Therefore, hardness and unevenness of surface are to be reckoned as one defect. If a walking-place have trees in it, whether in the middle or at the end, then any one who uses it is liable, if not careful, to strike his forehead or his head against them. Therefore, trees in the midst are a second defect. If a walking-place be overgrown with a dense underbrush of grass, vines, and so forth, any one who uses it in the dark is liable to tread upon snakes and other creatures and kill them, or they may bite and injure him. Thus a dense underbrush is a third defect. If a walking-place be excessively narrow, say only a cubit or half a cubit wide, then any one who uses it is liable to stumble at the borders and stub his toes and break his toe-nails. Therefore, excessive narrowness is a fourth defect. If a walking-place be excessively wide, then any one who uses it is liable to have his mind wander and fail of concentration. Thus excessive width is a fifth defect. A walking-place should be a path a cubit and a half in breadth, with a margin of a cubit on either side, and it should be

sixty cubits in length, and it should have a surface soft and evenly sprinkled with sand.

8. *Ibidem*, 1. 30 (P.T.S). And having all the virtues eight: Having the eight advantages for a monk. The following are the eight advantages for a monk: it admits of no storing-up of treasure or grain; it favors only a blameless alms-seeking; there one can eat his alms in peace and quiet; there no annoyance is experienced from the reigning families when they oppress the kingdom with their levies of the precious metals or of leaden money; no passionate desire arises for furniture and implements; there is no fear of being plundered by robbers; no intimacies are formed with kings and courtiers; and one is not shut in in any of the four directions.
9. Native gloss : Jātaka, vol. i., p. 8, 1. 27(P.T.S): For cloaks possess the nine defects: . . . For one who retires from the world and takes up the life of an anchorite, there are nine defects inherent in garments of cloth. The great cost is one defect; the fact that it is got by dependence on others is another; the fact that it is easily soiled by use is another, for when it has been soiled it must be washed and dyed; the fact that when it is much worn it must needs be patched and mended is another; the difficulty of obtaining a new one when needed is another; its unsuitableness for an anchorite who has retired from the world is another; its acceptableness to one's enemies is another, for it must needs be guarded lest the enemy take it; the danger that it may be worn for ornament is another; the temptation it affords to load one's self down with it in travelling is another.
10. The bast, or inner bark of certain trees, was much used in India as cloth, to which indeed it bears a striking resemblance. -Native gloss : Jātaka, vol. i., p. 9, 1. 2 (P.T.S) : Which is with virtues twelve endued; Possessing twelve advantages. For there are twelve advantages in a dress of bark. It is cheap, good, and suitable; this is one advantage. You can make it yourself; this is a second. It gets dirty but slowly by use, and hence time is not wasted in washing it; this is a third. It never needs sewing, even when much used and worn; this is a fourth. But when a new one is needed, it can be made with ease; this is a fifth. Its suitableness for an anchorite who has retired from the world is a sixth. That it is of no use to one's enemies is a seventh. That it cannot be worn for ornament is an eighth. Its lightness is a ninth. Its conducing to moderation in dress is a tenth. The irreproachableness and blamelessness of searching for bark is an eleventh. And the unimportance of its loss is a twelfth.

11. Native gloss : Jātaka, vol. i., p. 9, 1.11(P.T.S) : My hut of leaves I then for sook, So crowded with the eight defects: . . . For there are eight evils connected with the use of a leaf-hut. The great labor involved in searching for materials and in the putting of them together is one evil. The constant care necessary to replace the grass, leaves, and bits of clay that fall down is a second. Houses may do for old men, but no concentration of mind is possible when one's meditation is liable to be interrupted; thus the liability to interruption is a third. The protection afforded against heat and cold renders the body delicate, and this is a fourth. In a house all sorts of evil deeds are possible; thus the cover it affords for disgraceful practices is a fifth. The taking possession, saying, "This is mine," is a sixth. To have a house is like having a com panion; this is a seventh. And the sharing of it with many others, as for instance with lice, bugs, and house-lizards, is an eighth.
12. *Ibidem*, p. 10, 1. 9 (P.T.S) : And at the foot of trees I lived, For such abodes have virtues ten: . . . The following are the ten virtues. The smallness of the undertaking is one virtue, for all that is necessary is simply to go to the tree. The small amount of care it requires is a second; for, whether swept or unswept, it is suitable for use. The freedom from interruption is a third. It affords no cover for disgraceful practices; wickedness there would be too public; thus the fact that it affords no cover for disgraceful practices is a fourth. It is like living under the open sky, for there is no feeling that the body is confined; thus the non-confinement of the body is a fifth. There is no taking possession; this is a sixth. The abandonment of all longings for household life is a seventh. When a house is shared with others, some one is liable to say, "I will look after this house myself. Begone !" Thus the freedom from eviction is an eighth. The happy contentment experienced by the occupant is a ninth. The little concern one need feel about lodgings, seeing that a man can find a tree no matter where he may be stopping, this is a tenth.
13. Translated from the prose of the Jātaka, vol. i., p. 10 (P.T.S) , last line but one : At his [Dīpaṁkara's] conception, birth, attainment of Buddhaship, and when he caused the Wheel of Doctrine to roll, the entire system of ten thousand worlds trembled, quivered, and shook, and roared with a mighty roar; also the Thirty-Two Prognostics appeared.
14. Native gloss: Jātaka, vol. i., p. 13,1. 31 (P.T.S): As he lay in the mud, he opened his eyes again, and gazing upon the Buddha-glory of Dīpaṁkara, The Possessor of the Ten Forces, he reflected

as follows: "If I so wished, I might burn up all my corruptions, and as novice follow with the congregation when they enter the city of Ramma; but I do not want to burn up my corruptions and enter Nirvāṇa unknown to any one. What now if I, like Dīpaṁkara, were to acquire the supreme wisdom, were to cause multitudes to go on board the ship of Doctrine and cross the ocean of the round of rebirth, and were afterwards to pass into Nirvāṇa! That would be something worthy of me!"

15. Native gloss : Jātaka, vol. i., p. 14,1. 20 (P.T.S) : For it is only a human being that can successfully wish to be a Buddha; a serpent, or a bird, or a deity cannot successfully make the wish. Of human beings it is only one of the male sex that can make the wish: it would not be successful on the part of a woman, or of a eunuch, or of a neuter, or of a hermaphrodite. Of men it is he, and only he, who is in a fit condition by the attainment of saintship in that same existence, that can successfully make the wish. Of those in a fit condition it is only he who makes the wish in the presence of a living Buddha that succeeds in his wish; after the death of a Buddha a wish made at a relic-shrine, or at the foot of a Bodhi-tree, will not be successful. Of those who make the wish in the presence of a Buddha it is he, and only he, who has retired from the world that can successfully make the wish, and not one who is a layman. Of those who have retired from the world it is only he who is possessed of the Five High Powers and is master of the Eight Attainments that can successfully make the wish, and no one can do so who is lacking in these excellences. Of those, even, who possess these excellences it is he, and only he, who has such firm resolve that he is ready to sacrifice his life for The Buddhas that can successfully make the wish, but no other. Of those who possess this resolve it is he, and only he, who has great zeal, determination, strenuousness, and endeavor in striving for the qualities that make a Buddha that is successful. The following comparisons will show the intensity of the zeal. If he is such a one as to think: "The man who, if all within the rim of the world were to become water, would be ready to swim across it with his own arms and get to the further shore, he is the one to attain the Buddhaship; or, in case all within the rim of the world were to become a jungle of bamboo, would be ready to elbow and trample his way through it and get to the further side,—he is the one to attain the Buddhaship; or, in case all within the rim of the world were to become a *terra firma* of thick-set javelins, would be ready to tread on them and go afoot to the further side, he is the one to attain the Buddhaship; or, in case

all within the rim of the world were to become live coals, would be ready to tread on them and so get to the further side, he is the one to attain the Buddhaship," if he deems not even one of these feats too hard for himself, but has such great zeal, determination, strenuousness, and power of endeavor that he would perform these feats in order to attain the Buddhaship, then, but not otherwise, will his wish succeed.

16. Better known as Moggallāna and Sāriputta, respectively.
17. *Ficus religiosa* (Aśvattha-Vṛkṣa).
18. There have been many beings who, like Sumedha here, were to become Buddhas, and who were therefore called Bodhisattvas or "Future Buddhas." The certainty of their ultimate "Illumination," or Buddhaship, was always foretokened by certain presages. The "dwellers of ten thousand worlds" describe in the following stanzas what these presages were, declare that they are reappearing now, and announce to Sumedha their prophetic inference that he will attain Buddhaship.
19. This refrain is added to these stanzas in the Buddha-Vaṁsa. In the Jātaka it is omitted.
20. The four cardinal points of the compass, the four intermediate points, the zenith and nadir.
21. As Fausböll observes, a very similar statement is made by Aelian, περὶ ξω'ω ν , xvi. 11. See also Visuddhi-Magga, chapter-i.

Chapter II

A LIST OF FORMER BUDDHAS

Translated from the Introduction to the Jātaka (i.43[28]).

खुद्दक निकाये जातक-अट्ठकथा

यस्मिं पन कप्पे दीपङ्करो दसबलो उदपादि, तस्मिं अञ्ञेपि तयो बुद्धा अहिसुं। तेसं सन्तिका बोधिसत्तस्स ब्याकरणं नत्थि, तस्मां ते इध न दस्सिता। अट्ठकथायं पन तम्हा कप्पा पट्ठाय सब्बेपि बुद्धे दस्सेतुं इदं वुत्तं-

Now in the same world-cycle that saw Dīpaṁkara, The One Possessing the Ten Forces, there were also three other Buddhas; but as none of them prophesied concerning the Future Buddha, I have not mentioned them. In the Commentary, however, all the Buddhas are mentioned from the beginning of that world-cycle on, as follows :–

तण्हङ्करो मेधङ्करो, अथोपि सरणङ्करो।
दीपङ्करो च सम्बुद्धो, कोण्डञ्ञो द्विपदुत्तमो।। 247।।

247. "Taṇhaṁkara, Medhaṁkara,
And also Saraṇaṁkara,
Dīpaṁkara, the Buddha great,
Koṇḍañña, of all men the chief,"

मङ्गलो च सुमनो च, रेवतो सोभितो मुनि।
अनोमदस्सी पदुमो, नारदो पदुमुत्तरो।। 248।।

248. "Maṅgala, and Sumana too,
Revata, Sobhita, the sage,

Anomadassi, Paduma,
Nārada, Padumuttara,"

सुमेधो च सुजातो च, पियदस्सी महायसो।
अत्थदस्सी धम्मदस्सी, सिद्धत्थो लोकनायको।। 249।।

249. "Sumedha, and Sujātā too,
Piyadassī, the glorious one,
Atthadassī, Dhammadassī,
Siddhattha, guide of every man,"

तिस्सो फुस्सो च सम्बुद्धो, विपस्सी सिखि वेस्सभू।
ककुसन्धो कोणागमनो, कस्सपो चाति नायको।। 250।।

250. "Tissa, Phussa, the Buddha great,
Vipassi, Sikhi, Vessabhū,
Kakusandha, Koṇāgamana,
Kassapa also, guide for men,"

"एते अहेसुं सम्बुद्धा, वीतरागा समाहिता।
सतरंसीव उप्पन्ना, महातमविनोदना।
जलित्वा अग्गिखन्धाव, निब्बुता ते ससावका"ति।। 251।।

251. "All these aforetime Buddhas were,
Tranquil, from every passion free.
And like the sun, the many-rayed,
They chased away the darkness dense,
And having flamed like tongues of fire,
Became extinct with all their train."

तत्थ अम्हाकं बोधिसत्तो दीपङ्करादीनं चतुवीसतिया बुद्धानं सन्तिके अधिकारं करोन्तो कप्पसतसहस्साधिकानि चत्तारि असङ्ख्ये- य्यानि आगतो। कस्सपस्स पन भगवतो ओरभागे ठपेत्वा इमं सम्मा- सम्बुद्धं अञ्ञो बुद्धो नाम नत्थि। इति दीपङ्करादीनं चतुवीसतिया बुद्धानं सन्तिके लद्धब्याकरणो पन बोधिसत्तो येनेन।

Our Future Buddha, in his passage through four immensities and a hundred thousand world-cycles to the present time, has made his wish under twenty-four of these Buddhas, beginning with Dīpaṁkara. But since Kassapa, The Blessed One, there has been no Supreme Buddha excepting our present one. Accordingly, our Future Buddha has received recognition at the hands of twenty-four Buddhas, beginning with Dīpaṁkara.

Chapter III

THE CHARACTERISTICS OF A FUTURE BUDDHA

Translated from the Introduction to the Jātaka (i.44[28])

खुद्दक निकाये जातक-अट्टकथा

"मनुस्सत्तं लिङ्गसम्पत्ति, हेतु सत्थारदस्सनं।
पब्बज्ञा गुणसम्पत्ति, अधिकारो च छन्दता।
अट्ठधम्मसमोधाना, अभिनीहारो समिज्झती"ति।।

(बुद्धवंस 2.59)

इमे अट्ठ धम्मे समोधानेत्वा दीपङ्करपादमूले कताभिनीहारेन "हन्द बुद्धकरे धम्मे, विचिनामि इतो चितो"ति उस्साहं कत्वा "विचिनन्तो तदादक्खिं, पठमं दानपारमि"न्ति दानपारमितादयो बुद्धकारकधम्मा दिट्ठा, ते पूरेन्तोयेव याव वेस्सन्तरत्तभावा आगमि। आगच्छन्तो च ये ते कताभिनीहारानं बोधिसत्तानं आनिसंसा संवण्णिता–

"A human being, male of sex,
Who saintship gains, a Teacher meets,
As hermit lives, and virtue loves,
Nor lacks resolve, nor fiery zeal,
Can by these eight conditions joined,
Make his most earnest wish succeed."

These eight conditions were all united in him when he made his earnest wish at the feet of Dīpaṁkara, saying, –

"Come now! I 'll search that I may find
Conditions which a Buddha make."

Thereupon, putting forth a strenuous effort, – as it is said :

"And then I searched, and found the First
Perfection, which consists in alms," –

he discovered, not only the perfection which is called alms, but also all the others that go to make a Buddha. And in fulfilling them he reached his Vessantara existence[22]. In so doing, all the blessings celebrated in the following stanzas as belonging to Future Buddhas who make the earnest wish were attained by him:-

एवं सब्बङ्गसम्पन्ना, बोधिया नियता नरा।
संसरं दीघमद्धानं, कप्पकोटिसतेहिपि।। 252।।

252. "Such men in every virtue trained,
And destined for the Buddhaship,
In all their weary rounds of birth,
Though cycle-millions come and go,"

अवीचिम्हि नुप्पज्जन्ति, तथा लोकन्तरेसु च।
निज्झामतण्हा खुप्पिपासा, न होन्ति कालकञ्जका।
न होन्ति खुद्दका पाणा, उप्पज्जन्तापि दुग्गतिं।। 253।।

253. "Are never born inside of hell,
Nor in the intermundane voids.
They never share the Manes' thirst,[23]
Their hunger or ferocity,"[24]
And though sometimes of low estate,
Are never of the insect class.

जायमाना मनुस्सेसु, जच्चन्धा न भवन्ति ते।
सोतवेकल्लता नत्थि, न भवन्ति मूगपक्खिका।। 254।।

254. "When they appear among mankind,
'T is not as blind from birth they come,

Deafness they never have to bear,
Nor dumbness have they to endure."

इत्थिभावं न गच्छन्ति, उभतोब्यञ्जनपण्डका।
न भवन्ति परियापन्ना, बोधिया नियता नरा।। 255।।

255. "They're never of the female sex,
Nor as hermaphrodites appear,
As eunuchs are they never classed,
Those destined for the Buddhaship."

मुत्ता आनन्तरिकेहि, सब्बत्थ सुद्धगोचरा।
मिच्छादिट्ठिं न सेवन्ति, कम्मकिरियदस्सना।। 256।।

256. "From all the five great crimes exempt,
And pure in all their walks in life,
They follow not vain heresy,
For well they know how *karma* works."

वसमानापि सग्गेसु, असञ्ञं नूपपज्जरे।
सुद्धावासेसु देवेसु, हेतु नाम न विज्जति।। 257।।

257. "Though in the heavens they may be born,
Yet ne'er 'mongst those perception-reft;
Nor are they destined to rebirth
'Amongst dwellers in the Pure Abodes."[24]

नेक्खम्मनिन्ना सप्पुरिसा, विसंयुत्ता भवाभवे।
चरन्ति लोकत्थचरियायो, पूरेन्ति सब्बपारमी"ति।। 258।।

258. "These pleasure-abnegating men
Live unattached in every birth,
And ever toil to help the world,
While all perfections they fulfil."

ते आनिसंसे अधिगन्त्वाव आगतो। पारमियो पूरेन्तस्स चस्स अकित्तिब्राह्मणकाले सङ्खब्राह्मणकाले धनञ्चयराजकाले महासुदस्सनकाले महागोविन्दकाले निमिमहाराजकाले चन्दकुमारकाले विसय्हसेट्ठिकाले सिविराजकाले वेस्सन्तरकालेति दानपारमिताय पूरितत्तभावानं परिमाणं नाम नत्थि। एकन्तेन पनस्स ससपण्डितजातके-

Now in accomplishing these Ten Perfections there was no limit to the number of existences in which he fulfilled the perfection of almsgiving; as when he was born as the Brāhmaṇa Akitti, the Brāhmaṇa Saṁkha, king Dhanañjaya, Mahā-Sudassana, Mahā-Govinda, king Nimi, prince Canda, Visayha the treasurer, king Sivi, and king Vessantara. But the acme was reached when as the Wise Hare[25] he said, –

"भिक्खाय उपगतं दिस्वा, सकत्तानं परिच्चजिं।
दानेन मे समो नत्थि, एसा मे दानपारमी"ति।। 259।।

259. "There came a beggar, asked for food;
Myself I gave that he might eat.
In alms there's none can equal me;
In alms have I perfection reached."

एवं अत्तपरिच्चागं करोन्तस्स दानपारमिता परमत्थपारमी नाम जाता। तथा सीलवराजकाले चम्पेय्यनागराजकाले भूरिदत्तनागराजकाले छद्दन्तनागराजकाले जयद्दिसराजपुत्तकाले अलीनसत्तुकुमारकालेति सीलपारमिताय पूरितत्तभावानं परिमाणं नाम नत्थि। एकन्तेन परस्स सङ्खपालजातके–

Thus, in this offering up of his own life, he acquired the perfection of almsgiving in its highest degree.

Likewise there was no limit to the number of existences in which he fulfilled the precepts; as when he was born as the elephant-king Sīlava, the snake-king Campeyya, the snake-king Bhūridatta, the elephant-king Chaddanta, and prince Alīnasattu, son of king Jayaddisa. But the acme was reached when, as related in the Saṁkhapāla Birth-Story, he said:

"सूलेहि विज्झियन्तोपि, कोट्टियन्तोपि सत्तिहि।
भोजपुत्ते न कुप्पामि, एसा मे सीलपारमी"ति।। 260।।

260. "They pierced me through with pointed stakes,
They hacked me with their hunting-knives;
Yet gainst these Bhojans raged I not,
But kept the precepts perfectly."

एवं अत्तपरिच्चागं करोन्तस्स सीलपारमिता परमत्थपारमी नाम जाता। तथा सोमनस्सकुमारकाले, हत्थिपालकुमारकाले, अयोघरपण्डित-कालेति महारज्जं पहाय नेक्खम्मपारमिताय पूरितत्तभावानं परिमाणं नाम नत्थि। एकन्तेन पनस्स चूळसुतसोमजातके–

Thus, in giving up his own life, he acquired perfection in the keeping of the precepts.

Likewise there was no limit to the number of existences in which he fulfilled the perfection of abnegation by abandoning his throne; as when he was born as prince Somanassa, prince Hatthipāla, and the paṇḍit Ayoghara. But the acme was reached when, as related in the Lesser Sutasoma Birth-Story, he said:

"महारज्जं हत्थगतं, खेळपिण्डंव छड्डयिं।
चजतो न होति लग्गं, एसा मे नेक्खम्मपारमी"ति॥ 261॥

261. "A kingdom dropped into my hands;
Like spittle vile I let it fall,
Nor for it felt the smallest wish,
And thus renunciation gained."

एवं निस्सङ्गताय रज्जं छड्डेत्वा निक्खमन्तस्स नेक्खम्मपारमिता परमत्थपारमी नाम जाता। तथा विधुरपण्डितकाले, महागोविन्द-पण्डितकाले, कुद्दालपण्डितकाले, अरकपण्डितकाले, बोधिपरिब्बा-जककाले, महोसधपण्डितकालेति, पञ्ञापारमिताय पूरितत्तभावानं परिमाणं नाम नत्थि। एकन्तेन पनस्स सत्तुभस्तजातके सेनकपण्डित-काले–

Thus, free from attachment, he renounced a kingdom and retired from the world, and by so doing acquired the perfection of abnegation in its highest degree.

Likewise there was no limit to the number of existences in which he fulfilled the perfection of knowledge; as when he was born as the paṇḍit Vidhūra, the paṇḍit Mahā-Govinda, the paṇḍit Kuddāla, the paṇḍit Araka, the wandering ascetic Bodhi, and the paṇḍit Mahosadha. But the acme was reached when, as the paṇḍit Senaka of the Sattubhatta Birth-Story, he said:

"पञ्ञाय विचिनन्तोहं, ब्राह्मणं मोचयिं दुखा।
पञ्ञाय मे समो नत्थि, एसा मे पञ्ञापारमी"ति।। 262।।

262. "With wisdom sifted I the case,
And freed the Brāhmaṇa from his woe;
In wisdom none can equal me :
In wisdom I 've perfection reached,"

अन्तोभस्त्तगतं सप्पं दस्सेन्तस्स पञ्ञापारमिता परमत्थपारमी नाम जाता। तथा वीरियपारमितादीनम्पि पूरितत्तभावानं परिमाणं नाम नत्थि। एकन्तेन पनस्स महाजनकजातके–

And displayed to all present the serpent which lay concealed in the bag, and in so doing acquired the perfection of wisdom in its highest degree.

Likewise there was no limit to the number of existences in which he fulfilled the perfection of courage. But the acme was reached when, as related in the Greater Janaka Birth-Story, he said:

"अतीरदस्सी जलमज्झे, हता सब्बेव मानुसा।
चित्तस्स अञ्ञथा नत्थि, एसा मे वीरियपारमी"ति।। 263।।

263. "Far out of sight of land were we,
The crew were all as dead of fright;
Yet still unruffled was my mind :
In courage I've perfection reached."

एवं महासमुद्दं तरन्तस्स पवत्ता वीरियपारमिता परमत्थपारमी नाम जाता। खन्तिवादिजातके–

Thus, it was in crossing the ocean he acquired the perfection of courage in its highest degree.

Likewise in the Khantivāda Birth-Story, where he said:

"अचेतनंव कोट्टेन्ते, तिण्हेन फरसुना ममं।
कासिराजे न कुप्पामि, एसा मे खन्तिपारमी"ति।। 264।।

264. "Like one insensible I lay,
While with his hatchet keen he backed,
Nor raged I gainst Benares' king :
In patience I've perfection reached,"

एवं अचेतनभावेन विय महादुक्खं अधिवासेन्तस्स खन्तिपारमिता परमत्थपारमी नाम जाता। महासुतसोमजातके–

In enduring great suffering, while appearing to be unconscious, he acquired the perfection of patience in its highest degree.

Likewise in the Greater Sutasoma Birth-Story, where he said:

"सच्चवाचं अनुरक्खन्तो, चजित्वा मम जीवितं।
मोचेसिं एकसतं खत्तिये, एसा मे सच्चपारमी"ति।। 265।।

265. "I kept the promise I had made,
And gave my life in sacrifice,
A hundred warriors set I free :
In truth have I perfection reached,"

एवं जीवितं चजित्वा सच्चमनुरक्खन्तस्स सच्चपारमिता परमत्थपारमी नाम जाता। मूगपक्खजातके–

in keeping his word at the sacrifice of his life, he acquired the perfection of truth in its highest degree.

Likewise in the Mūgapakkha Birth-Story, where he said:

"माता पिता न मे देस्सा, नपि मे देस्सं महायसं।
सब्बञ्ञुतं पियं मय्हं, तस्मा वतमधिट्ठहि"न्ति।। 266।।

266. "It is not that I my parents hate,
It is not that glory I detest,
But since omniscience I held dear,
Therefore I kept my firm resolve,"

एवं[20] जीवितम्पि चजित्वा वतं अधिट्ठहन्तस्स अधिट्ठानपारमिता परमत्थपारमी नाम जाता। एकराजजातके–

in resolving on a course of conduct that cost him his life, he acquired the perfection of resolution in its highest degree.

Likewise in the Ekarāja Birth-Story, where he said :–

"न मं कोचि उत्तसति, नपिहं भायामि कस्सचि।
मेत्ताबलेनुपत्थद्धो, रमामि पवने तदा"ति।। 267।।

267. "No fear has any one of me,
Nor have I fear of any one,
In my good-will to all I trust,
And love to dwell in lonely woods,"

एवं जीवितम्पि अनोलोकेत्वा मेत्तायन्तस्स मेत्तापारमिता परमत्थ-पारमी नाम जाता। लोमहंसजातके–

in the exercise of feelings of good-will, and in taking no thought for his life, he acquired the perfection of good-will in its highest degree.

Likewise in the Lomahaṁsa Birth-Story, where he said :

"सुसाने सेय्यं कप्पेमि, छवट्ठिकं उपधायहं।
गामण्डला उपागन्त्वा, रूपं दस्सेन्तिनप्पक"न्ति।। 268।।

268. "I laid me down among the dead,
A pillow of their bones I made;
While from the villages around,
Some came to mock, and some to praise,"

एवं गामदारकेसु निट्ठुभनादीहि चेव मालागन्धूपहारादीहि च सुखदुक्खं उप्पादेन्तेसुपि उपेक्खं अनतिवत्तन्तस्स उपेक्खापारमिता परमत्थपारमी नाम जाता। अयमेत्थ सङ्खेपो, वित्थारतो पनेस अत्थो चरियापिटकतो गहेतब्बो। एवं पारमियो पूरेत्वा वेस्सन्तरत्तभावे ठितो–

while village children flocked about him, and some spat and others showered fragrant garlands upon him, he was indifferent alike to pleasure and pain, and acquired the perfection of indifference in its highest degree.

The above is an abridgment, but the full account is given in the Cariyā-Piṭaka.

Having thus fulfilled all the perfections, he said, in his existence as Vessantara, –

"अचेतनायं पथवी, अविञ्ञाय सुखं दुखं।
सापि दानबला मय्हं, सत्तक्खत्तुं पकम्पथा"ति।। 269।।

269. "This earth, unconscious though she be,

And ignorant of joy or grief,
E'en she then felt alms' mighty power,
And shook and quaked full seven times."

एवं महापथविकम्पनादीनि महापुञ्ञानि कत्वा आयुपरियोसाने ततो चुतो तुसितभवने निब्बत्ति। इति दीपङ्करपादमूलतो पट्ठाय याव अयं तुसितपुरे निब्बत्ति, एत्तकं ठानं दूरेनिदानं नामाति वेदितब्बं।

And having thus caused the earth to quake by his mighty deeds of merit, at the end of that existence he died, and was reborn in the Tusita heaven.

Accordingly the period from the time when he fell at the feet of Dīpaṁkara to his birth in the city of the Tusita gods constitutes the Distant Epoch.

NOTES AND REFERENCES

22. The Vessantara Birth-Story is the last of the five hundred and fifty, and is not yet published.
23. I despair of giving in metre more than the general drift of these two lines. See Hardy, "Manual of The Life of the Buddha," chap. ii.
24. The thirty one Grades of Being, chapter IV. 59 (Translated from Abhidhammattha-Saṅgaha (V-2).
25. The story of the Future Buddha's existence as the Wise Hare is given further on under the caption, "The Hare-Mark in the Moon." It is the only one of the numerous Birth-Stories above-mentioned that is to be found in this book. The stanza quoted, however, is not taken from that account, but from another work called the Cariyā-Piṭaka, which is wholly in poetry. The Cariyā-Piṭaka consists of Birth-Stories, and, besides the Wise Hare, gives several others of those here mentioned. Some are also briefly alluded to in the ninth chapter of the Visuddhi-Magga; but of course the great treasure-house for Birth-Stories is the Jātaka itself.

Chapter IV

THE BIRTH OF THE BUDDHA

Translated from the Introduction to the Jātaka (i.47[26]).

खुद्दक निकाये जातक अट्ठकथा-1, अविदूरेनिदानकथा

तुसितपुरे वसन्तेयेव पन बोधिसत्ते बुद्धकोलाहलं नाम उदपादि। लोकस्मिञ्हि तीणिकोलाहलानि उप्पज्जन्ति-कप्पकोलाहलं, बुद्धकोलाहलं, चक्कवत्तिकोलाहलन्ति। तत्थ "वस्ससतसहस्सस्स अच्चयेन कप्पुट्ठानं भविस्सती"ति लोकब्यूहा नाम कामावचरदेवा मुत्तसिरा विकिण्णकेसा रुदमुखा अस्सूनि हत्थेहि पुञ्छमाना रत्तवत्थनिवत्था अतिविय विरूपवेसधारिनो हुत्वा मनुस्सपथे विचरन्ता एवं आरोचेन्ति "मारिसा इतो वस्सतसहस्सस्स अच्चयेन कप्पुट्ठानं भविस्सति, अयं लोको विनस्सिस्सति, महासमुद्दोपि सुस्सिस्सति, अयञ्च महापथवी सिनेरु च पब्बतराजा उड्ड्य्हिस्सन्ति विनस्सिस्सन्ति, याव ब्रह्मलोका लोकविनासो भविस्सति, मेत्तं मारिसा भावेथ, करुणं, मुदितं, उपेक्खं मारिसा भावेथ, मातरं उपट्ठहथ, पितरं उपट्ठहथ, कुले जेट्ठापचायिनो होथा"ति। इदं कप्पकोलाहलं नाम। वस्ससहस्सस्स अच्चयेन पन सब्बञ्ञुबुद्धो लोके उप्पज्जिस्सतीति लोकपालदेवता "इतो मारिसा वस्ससहस्सस्स अच्चयेन बुद्धो लोके उप्पज्जिस्सती"ति उग्घोसेन्ता आहिण्डन्ति। इदं बुद्धकोलाहलं नाम। वस्ससतस्स अच्चयेन चक्कवत्ती राजा उप्पज्जिस्सतीति देवता "इतो मारिसा वस्ससतस्स

अच्चयेन चक्कवत्ती राजा लोके उप्पज्जिस्सती"ति उग्घोसेन्तियो आहिण्डन्ति। इदं चक्कवत्तिकोलाहलं नाम। इमानि तीणि कोलाहलानि महन्तानि होन्ति।

तेसु बुद्धकोलाहलसद्दं सुत्वा सकलदससहस्सचक्कवाळदेवता एकतो सन्निपतित्वा "असुको नाम सत्तो बुद्धो भविस्सती"ति ञत्वा तं उपसङ्कमित्वा आयाचन्ति। आयाचमाना च पुब्बनिमित्तेसु उप्पन्नेसु आयाचन्ति। तदा पन सब्बापि देवता एकेकचक्कवाळे चतुमहाराज-सक्कसुयामसन्तुसितसुनिम्मितवसवत्तिमहाब्रह्मेहि सद्धिं एकचक्कवाळे सन्निपतित्वा तुसितभवने बोधिसत्तस्स सन्तिकं गन्त्वा "मारिसा तुम्हेहि दस पारमियो पूरेन्तेहि न सक्कसम्पत्तिं, न मारसम्पत्तिं, न ब्रह्मसम्पतिं, न चक्कवत्तिसम्पत्तिं पत्थेन्तेहि पूरिता, लोकनित्थरणत्थाय पन सब्बञ्ञुतं पत्थेन्तेहि पूरिता, सो वो इदानि कालो मारिसा बुद्धत्ताय समयो, मारिसा बुद्धत्ताय समयो"ति याचिंसु।

अथ महासत्तो देवतानं पटिञ्ञं अदत्वाव कालदीप-देसकुलजनेत्तिआयुपरिच्छेदवसेन पञ्चमहाविलोकनं नाम विलोकेसि। तत्थ "कालो नु खो, अकालो नु खो"ति पठमं कालं विलोकेसि। तत्थ वस्ससतसहस्सतो उद्धं वड्ढितआयुकालो कालो नाम न होति। कस्मा? तदा हि सत्तानं जातिजरामरणानि न पञ्ञायन्ति। बुद्धानञ्च धम्मदेसना तिलक्खणमुत्ता नाम नत्थि। तेसं "अनिच्चं, दुक्खं, अनत्ता"ति कथेन्तानं "किं नामेतं कथेन्ती"ति नेव सोतब्बं न सद्धातब्बं मञ्ञन्ति, ततो अभिसमयो न होति, तस्मिं असति अनिय्यानिकं सासनं होति। तस्मा सो अकालो। वस्ससततो ऊनआयुकालोपि कालो न होति। कस्मा? तदा सत्ता उस्सन्नकिलेसा होन्ति, उस्सन्नकिलेसानञ्च दिन्नो ओवादो ओवादट्ठाने न तिट्ठति, उदके दण्डराजि विय खिप्पं विगच्छति। तस्मा सोपि अकालो। वस्ससतसहस्सतो पन पट्ठाय हेट्ठा, वस्ससततो पट्ठाय उद्धं आयुकालो कालो नाम। तदा च वस्ससतकालो। अथ महासत्तो "निब्बत्तितब्बकालो"ति कालं पस्सि।

ततो दीपं विलोकेन्तो सपरिवारे चत्तारो दीपे ओलोकेत्वा "तीसु दीपेसु बुद्धा न निब्बत्तन्ति, जम्बुदीपेयेव निब्बत्तन्ती"ति दीपं पस्सि।

ततो "जम्बुदीपो नाम महा दसयोजनसहस्सपरिमाणो, कतरस्मिं नु खो पदेसे बुद्धा निब्बत्तन्ती"ति ओकासं विलोकेन्तो मज्झिमदेसं पस्सि। मज्झिमदेसो नाम–"पुरत्थिमाय दिसाय गजङ्गलं नाम निगमो, तस्स अपरेन महासालो, ततो परं पच्चन्तिमा जनपदा, ओरतो मज्झे। पुब्बदक्खिणाय दिसाय सल्लवती नाम नदी, ततो परं पच्चन्तिमा जनपदा, ओरतो मज्झे। दक्खिणाय दिसाय सेतकण्णिकं नाम निगमो, ततो परं पच्चन्तिमा जनपदा, ओरतो मज्झे। पच्छिमाय दिसाय थूणं नाम ब्राह्मणगामो, ततो परं पच्चन्तिमा जनपदा, ओरतो मज्झे। उत्तराय दिसाय उसीरद्धजो नाम पब्बतो, ततो परं पच्चन्तिमा जनपदा, ओरतो मज्झे"ति एवं विनये वुत्तो पदेसो। सो आयामतो तीणि योजनसतानि, वित्थारतो अड्ढतेय्यानि, परिक्खेपतो नव योजनसतानीति एतस्मिं पदेसे बुद्धा, पच्चेकबुद्धा, अग्गसावका, असीति महासावका, चक्कवत्तिराजा अञ्ञे च महेसक्खा खत्तियब्राह्मणगहपतिमहासाला उप्पज्जन्ति। इदञ्चेत्थ कपिलवत्थु नाम नगरं, तत्थ मया निब्बत्तितब्बन्ति निट्ठं अगमासि।

ततो कुलं विलोकेन्तो "बुद्धा नाम वेस्सकुले वा सुद्दकुले वा न निब्बत्तन्ति, लोकसम्मते पन खत्तियकुले वा ब्राह्मणकुलेवाति द्वीसुयेव कुलेसु निब्बत्तन्ति। इदानि च खत्तियकुलं लोकसम्मतं तत्थ निब्बत्तिस्सामि। सुद्धोदनो नाम राजा मे पिता भविस्सती"ति कुलं पस्सि।

ततो मातरं विलोकेन्तो "बुद्धमाता नाम लोला सुराधुत्ता न होति, कप्पसतसहस्सं पन पूरितपारमी जातितो पट्ठाय अखण्डपञ्चसीलायेव होति। अयञ्च महामाया नाम देवी एदिसी, अयं मे माता भविस्सति, कित्तकं पनस्सा आयूति दसन्नं मासानं उपरि सत्त दिवसानी"ति पस्सि।

इति इमं पञ्चमहाविलोकनं विलोकेत्वा "कालो मे मारिसा बुद्धभावाया"ति देवतानं सङ्गहं करोन्तो पटिञ्ञं दत्वा "गच्छथ, तुम्हे"ति ता देवता उय्योजेत्वा तुसितदेवताहि परिवुतो तुसितपुरे नन्दनवनं पाविसि। सब्बदेवलोकेसु हि नन्दनवनं अत्थियेव। तत्थ नं देवता "इतो चुतो सुगतिं गच्छ, इतो चुतो सुगतिं गच्छा"ति पुब्बे कतकुसलकम्मोकासं सारयमाना विचरन्ति। सो एवं देवताहि कुसलं सारयमानाहि परिवुतो तत्थ विचरन्तो चवित्वा महामायाय देविया कुच्छिस्मिं पटिसन्धिं गण्हि।

तस्स आविभावत्थं अयमनुपुब्बिकथा–तदा किर कपिलवत्थुनगरे आसाळ्हिनक्खत्तं सङ्घुट्ठं अहोसि, महाजनो नक्खत्तं कीळति। महामायापि देवी पुरे पुण्णमाय सत्तमदिवसतो पट्ठाय विगतसुरापानं मालागन्धविभूतिसम्पन्नं नक्खत्तकीळं अनुभवमाना सत्तमे दिवसे पातोव उट्ठाय गन्धोदकेन न्हायित्वा चत्तारि सतसहस्सानि विस्सज्जेत्वा महादानं दत्वा सब्बालङ्कारविभूसिता वरभेजनं भुञ्जित्वा उपोसथङ्गानि अधिट्ठाय अलङ्कतपटियत्तं सिरिगब्भं पविसित्वा सिरिसयने निपन्न निद्दं ओक्कममाना इमं सुपिनं अद्दस–'चत्तारो किर नं महाराजानो सयनेनेव सद्धिं उक्खिपित्व हिमवन्तं नेत्वा सट्ठियोजनिके मनोसिलातले सत्तयोजनिकस्स महासालरुक्खस्स हेट्ठा ठपेत्वा एकमन्तं अट्ठंसु। अथ नेसं देवियो आगन्त्वा देविं अनोतत्तदहं नेत्वा मनुस्समलहरणत्थं न्हापेत्वा दिब्बवत्थं निवासापेत्वा गन्धेहि विलिम्पापेत्वा दिब्बपुप्फानि पिळन्धापेत्वा ततो अविदूरे एको रजतपब्बतो अत्थि, तस्स अन्तो कनकविमानं अत्थि, तत्थ पाचीनसीसकं दिब्बसयनं पञ्ञापेत्वा निपज्जापेसुं। अथ बोधिसत्तो सेतवरवारणो हुत्वा ततो अविदूरे एको सुवण्णपब्बतो अत्थि, तत्थ विचरित्वा ततो ओरुय्ह रजतपब्बतं अभिरुहित्वा उत्तरदिसतो आगम्म रजतदामवण्णाय सोण्डाय सेतपदुमं गहेत्वा कोञ्चनादं नदित्वा कनकविमानं पविसित्वा मातुसयनं तिक्खत्तुं पदक्खिणं कत्वा दक्खिणपस्सं फालेत्वा कुच्छिं पविट्ठसदिसो अहोसीति। एवं उत्तरासाळ्हनक्खत्तेन पटिसन्धिं गण्हि।

पुनदिवसे पबुद्धा देवी तं सुपिनं रञ्ञो आरोचेसि। राजा चतुसट्ठिमत्ते ब्राह्मणपामोक्खे पक्कोसापेत्वा गोमयहरितूपलित्ताय लाजादीहि कतमङ्गलसक्काराय भूमिया महारहानि आसनानि पञ्ञापेत्वा तत्थ निसिन्नानं ब्राह्मणानं सप्पिमधुसक्खराभिसङ्खतस्स वरपायासस्स सुवण्णरजतपातियो पूरेत्वा सुवण्णरजतपातीहियेव पटिकुज्जित्वा अदासि, अञ्ञेहि च अहतवत्थकपिलगाविदानादीहि ते सन्तप्पेसि। अथ नेसं सब्बकामेहि सन्तप्पितानं सुपिनं आरोचापेत्वा "किं भविस्सती"ति पुच्छि। ब्राह्मणा आहंसु "मा चिन्तयि, महाराज, देविया ते कुच्छिम्हि गब्भो पतिट्ठितो, सो च[24] खो पुरिसगब्भो, न इत्थिगब्भो, पुत्तो ते भविस्सति। सो सचे अगारं अज्झावसिस्सति, राजा भविस्सति चक्कवत्ती; सचे अगारा निक्खम्म पब्बजिस्सति, बुद्धो भविस्सति लोके विवट्टच्छदो"ति।

बोधिसत्तस्स पन मातुकुच्छिम्हि पटिसन्धिग्गहणक्खणे एकप्पहारेनेव सकलदससहस्सी लोकधातु सङ्कम्पि सम्पकम्पि सम्पवेधि। बात्तिसपुब्बनिमित्तानि पातुरहेसुं–दससु चक्कवाळसहस्सेसु अप्पमाणो ओभासो फरि। तस्स तं सिरिं दट्ठुकामा विय अन्धा चक्खूनि पटिलभिंसु, बधिरा सद्दं सुणिंसु, मूगा समालपिंसु, खुज्जा उजुगत्ता अहेसुं, पङ्गुला पदसा गमनं पटिलभिंसु, बन्धनगता सब्बसत्ता अन्दुबन्धनादीहि मुच्चिंसु, सब्बनरकेसु अग्गि निब्बायि, पेत्तिविसये खुप्पिपासा वूपसमि, तिरच्छानानं भयं नाहोसि, सब्बसत्तानं रोगो वूपसमि, सब्बसत्ता पियंवदा अहेसुं, मधुरेनाकारेन अस्सा हसिंसु, वारणा गज्जिंसु, सब्बतूरियानि सकसकनिन्नादं मुञ्चिंसु, अघट्टितानियेव मनुस्सानं हत्थूपगादीनि आभरणानि विरविंसु, सब्बदिसा विप्पसन्ना अहेसुं, सत्तानं सुखं उप्पादयमानो मुदुसीतलवातो वायि, अकालमेघो वस्सि, पथवितोपि उदकं उब्भिज्जित्वा विस्सन्दि, पक्खिनो आकासगमनं विजहिंसु, नदियो असन्दमाना अट्ठंसु, महासमुद्दे मधुरं उदकं अहोसि, सब्बत्थकमेव पञ्चवण्णेहि पदुमेहि सञ्छन्नतलो अहोसि, थलजजलजादीनि सब्बपुप्फानि पुप्फिंसु, रुक्खानं खन्धेसु खन्ध

पदुमानि, साखासु साखापदुमानि, लतासु लतापदुमानि पुप्फिसु, थले सिलातलानि भिन्दित्वा उपरूपरि सत्त सत्त हुत्वा दण्डपदुमानि नाम निक्खमिंसु, आकासे ओलम्बकपदुमानि नाम निब्बत्तिंसु, समन्ततो पुप्फवस्सा वस्सिंसु, आकासे दिब्बतूरियानि वज्जिंसु, सकल-दससहस्सिलोकधातु वट्टेत्व विस्सट्ठमालागुळो विय, उप्पीळेत्वा बद्धमालाकलापो विय, अलङ्कतपटियत्तं मालासनं विय च एकमालामालिनी विप्फुरन्तवाळबीजनी पुप्फधूमगन्धपरिवासिता परमसोभग्गप्पत्ता अहोसि।

एवं गहितपटिसन्धिकस्स बोधिसत्तस्स पटिसन्धितो पट्ठाय बोधि सत्तस्स चेव बोधिसत्तमातुया च उपद्दवनिवारणत्थं खग्गहत्था चत्तारो देवपुत्ता आरक्खं गण्हिसु। बोधिसत्तमातु पन पुरिसेसु रागचित्तं नुप्पज्जि, लाभग्गयसग्गप्पत्ता च अहोसि सुखिनी अकिलन्तकाया। बोधिसत्तञ्च अन्तोकुच्छिगतं विप्पसन्ने मणिरतने आवुतपण्डुसुत्तं विय पस्सति। यस्मा च बोधिसत्तेन वसितकुच्छि नाम चेतियगब्भसदिसा होति, न सक्का अञ्ञेन सत्तेन आवसितुं वा परिभुञ्जितुं वा, तस्मा बोधि सत्तमाता सत्ताहजाते बोधिसत्ते कालं कत्वा तुसितपुरे निब्बत्तति। यथा च अञ्ञा इत्थियो दस मासे अपत्वापि अतिक्कमित्वापि निसिन्नापि निपन्नापि विजायन्ति, न एवं बोधिसत्तमाता। सा पन बोधिसत्तं दस मासे कुच्छिना परिहरित्वा ठिताव विजायति। अयं बोधिसत्तमातुधम्मता ।

महामायापि देवी पत्तेन तेलं विय दस मासे कुच्छिना बोधिसत्तं परिहरित्वा परिपुण्णगब्भा ञातिघरं गन्तुकामा सुद्धोदनमहाराजस्स आरोचेसि–"इच्छामहं, देव, कुलसन्तकं देवदहनगरं गन्तु"न्ति। राजा "साधू"ति सम्पटिच्छित्वा कपिलवत्थुतो याव देवदहनगरा मग्गं समं कारेत्वा कदलिपुण्णघटधजपटाकादीहि अलङ्कारापेत्वा देविं सुवण्णसिविकाय निसीदापेत्वा अमच्चसहस्सेन उक्खिपापेत्वा महन्तेन परिवारेन पेसेसि। द्विन्नं पन नगरानं अन्तरे उभयनगरवासीनम्पि लुम्बिनीवनं नाम मङ्गलसालवनं अत्थि, तस्मिं समये मूलतो पट्ठाय याव अग्गसाखा सब्बं एकपालिफुल्लं अहोसि, साखन्तरेहि चेव पुप्फन्तरेहि च पञ्चवण्णा

भमरगणा नानप्पकारा च सकुणसङ्घा मधुरस्सरेन विकूजन्ता विचरन्ति। सकलं लुम्बिनीवनं चित्तलतावन– सदिसं, महानुभावस्स रञ्ञो सुसज्जितं आपानमण्डलं विय अहोसि। देविया तं दिस्वा सालवनकीळं कीळितुकामताचित्तं उदपादि। अमच्चा देविं गहेत्वा सालवनं पविसिंसु। सा मङ्गलसालमूलं गन्त्वा सालसाखं गण्हितुकामा अहोसि, सालसाखा सुसेदितवेत्तग्गं विय ओनमित्वा देविया हत्थपथं उपगञ्छि। सा हत्थं पसारेत्वा साखं अग्गहेसि। तावदेव चस्सा कम्मजवाता चलिंसु। अथस्सा साणिं परिक्खिपित्वा महाजनो पटिक्कमि। सालसाखं गहेत्वा तिट्ठमानाय एवस्सा गब्भवुट्ठानं अहोसि। तङ्खणंयेव चत्तारो विसुद्धचित्ता महाब्रह्मानो सुवण्णजालं आदाय सम्पत्ता तेन सुवण्णजालेन बोधिसत्तं सम्पटिच्छित्वा मातु पुरतो ठपेत्वा "अत्तमना, देवि, होहि, महेसक्खो ते पुत्तो उप्पन्नो"ति आहंसु।

यथा पन अञ्ञे सत्ता मातुकुच्छितो निक्खमन्ता पटिकूलेन असुचिना मक्खिता निक्खमन्ति, न एवं बोधिसत्तो। सो पन धम्मासनतो ओतरन्तो धम्मकथिको विय, निस्सेणितो ओतरन्तो पुरिसो विय, च द्वे च हत्थे द्वे च पादे पसारेत्वा ठितकोव मातुकुच्छिसम्भवेन केनचि असुचिना अमक्खितो सुद्धो विसदो कासिकवत्थे निक्खित्तमणिरतनं विय जोतयन्तो मातुकुच्छितो निक्खमि। एवं सन्तेपि बोधिसत्तस्स च बोधिसत्तमातुया च सक्कारत्थं आकासतो द्वे उदकधारा निक्खमित्वा बोधिसत्तस्स च मातुया च सरीरे उतुं गाहापेसुं।

अथ नं सुवण्णजालेन पटिग्गहेत्वा ठितानं ब्रह्मानं हत्थतो चत्तारो महाराजानो मङ्गलसम्मताय सुखसम्फस्साय अजिनप्पवेणिया गण्हिंसु, तेसं हत्थतो मनुस्सा दुकूलचुम्बटकेन। मनुस्सानं हत्थतो मुच्चित्वा पथवियं पतिट्ठाय पुरत्थिमदिसं ओलोकेसि, अनेकानि चक्कवाळसहस्सानि एकङ्गणानि अहेसुं। तत्थ देवमनुस्सा गन्धमालादीहि पूजयमाना "महापुरिस, इध तुम्हेहि सदिसो अञ्ञे नत्थि, कुतेत्थ उत्तरितरो"ति आहंसु। एवं चतस्सो दिसा, चतस्सो अनुदिसा, हेट्ठा,

उपरीति दस दिसा अनुविलोकेत्वा अत्तना सदिसं कञ्चि अदिस्वा "अयं उत्तरादिसा"ति सत्तपदवीतिहारेन अगमासि, महाब्रह्मुना सेतच्छत्तं धारियमानो, सुयामेन वाळबीजनिं, अञ्ञाहि च देवताहि सेसराजककुधभण्डहत्थाहि अनुगम्ममानो। ततो सत्तमपदे ठितो "अग्गोहमस्मि लोकस्सा"ति आदिकं आसभिं वाचं निच्छारेन्तो सीहनादं नदि।

बोधिसत्तो हि तीसु अत्तभावेसु मातुकुच्छितो निक्खन्तमत्तोव वाचं निच्छारेसि महोसधत्तभावे, वेस्सन्तरत्तभावे, इमस्मिं अत्तभावेति। महोसधत्तभावे किरस्स मातुकुच्छितो निक्खन्तमत्तस्सेव सक्को देवराजा आगन्त्वा चन्दनसारं हत्थे ठपेत्वा गतो, सो तं मुट्ठियं कत्वाव निक्खन्तो। अथ नं माता "तात, किं गहेत्वा आगतोसी"ति पुच्छि। "ओसधं, अम्मा"ति। इति ओसधं गहेत्वा आगतत्ता "ओसधदारको" त्वेवस्स नामं अकंसु। तं ओसधं गहेत्वा चाटियं पक्खिपिंसु, आगतागतानं अन्धबधिरादीनं तदेव सब्बरोगवूपसमाय भेसज्जं अहोसि। ततो "महन्तं इदं ओसधं, महन्तं इदं ओसध"न्ति उप्पन्नवचनं उपादाय "महोसध ो"त्वेवस्स नामं जातं। वेस्सन्तरत्तभावे पन मातुकुच्छितो निक्खन्तो दक्खिणहत्थं पसारेत्वा "अत्थि नु खो, अम्म, किञ्चि गेहस्मिं, दानं दस्सामी"ति वदन्तो निक्खमि। अथस्स माता "सधने कुले निब्बत्तोसि, ताता"ति पुत्तस्स हत्थं अत्तनो हत्थतले कत्वा सहस्सत्थविकं ठपेसि। इमस्मिं पन अत्तभावे इमं सीहनादं नदीति एवं बोधिसत्तो तीसु अत्तभावेसु मातुकुच्छितो निक्खन्तमत्तोव वाचं निच्छारेसि। यथा च पटिसन्धिग्गहणक्खणे, जातक्खणेपिस्स द्वत्तिंस पुब्बनिमित्तानि पातुरहेसुं। यस्मिं पन समये अम्हाकं बोधिसत्तो लुम्बिनीवने जातो, तस्मिंयेव समये राहुलमाता देवी, आनन्दत्थेरो, छन्नो अमच्चो, काळुदायी अमच्चो, कण्डको अस्सराजा, महाबोधिरुक्खो, चतस्सो निधिकुम्भियो च जाता। तत्थ एका गावुतप्पमाणा, एका अड्ढयोजनप्पमाणा, एका तिगावुतप्पमाणा, एका योजनप्पमाणा अहोसीति। इमे सत्त सहजाता नाम ।

Now while the Future Buddha was still dwelling in the city of the Tusita gods, the "Buddha-Uproar," as it is called, took place. For there are three uproars which take place in the world, —the Cyclic-Uproar, the Buddha-Uproar, and the Universal-Monarch-Uproar. They occur as follows:

When it is known that after the lapse of a hundred thousand years the cycle is to be renewed, the gods called *Loka-vyūhas,* inhabitants of a heaven of sensual pleasure, wander about through the world, with hair let down and flying in the wind, weeping and wiping away their tears with their hands, and with their clothes red and in great disorder. And thus they make announcement:

"Sirs, after the lapse of a hundred thousand years, the cycle is to be renewed; this world will be destroyed; also the mighty ocean will dry up; and this broad earth, and Sineru, the monarch of the mountains, will be burnt up and destroyed, — up to the Brahma heavens will the destruction of the world extend. Therefore, sirs, cultivate friendliness; cultivate compassion, joy, and indifference; wait on your mothers; wait on your fathers; and honor your elders among your kinsfolk."

This is called the Cyclic-Uproar.

Again, when it is known that after a lapse of a thousand yepars an omniscient Buddha is to arise in the world, the guardian angels of the world wander about, proclaiming:

"Sirs, after the lapse of a thousand years a Buddha will arise in the world."

This is called the Buddha-Uproar.

And lastly, when they realize that after the lapse of a hundred years a Universal Monarch is to arise, the terrestrial deities wander about, proclaiming:

"Sirs, after the lapse of a hundred years a Universal Monarch is to arise in the world."

This is called the Universal-Monarch-Uproar. And these three are mighty uproars.

When of these three Uproars they hear the sound of the Buddha-Uproar, the gods of all ten thousand worlds come together into one place, and having ascertained what particular being is to be The Buddha, they approach him, and beseech him to become one. But it is not till after omens have appeared that they beseech him.

At that time, therefore, having all come together in one world, with the Cātum-Mahārājas, and with the Sakka, the Suyāma, the Santusita, the Paranimmita-Vāsavatti, and the Mahā-Brahma of each several world, they approached the Future Buddha in the Tusita heaven, and besought him, saying, –

"Sir, it was not to acquire the glory of a Sakka, or of a Māra, or of a Brahma, or of a Universal Monarch, that you fulfilled the Ten Perfections (*pāramitās*); but it was to gain omniscience in order to save the world, that you fulfilled them. Sir, the time and fit season for your Buddhaship has now arrived."

After having exercised 30 *Pāramitās* in another births the Boodhisattva destined to become an ommiscient Buddha was born in the Tusita heaven.

But the Great Being, before assenting to their wish, made what is called the five great observations. He observed, namely, the time, the continent, the country, the family, and the mother and her span of life.

In the first of these observations he asked himself whether it was the right time or no. Now it is not the right time when the length of men's lives is more than a hundred thousand years. And why is it not the right time? Because mortals then forget about birth, old age, and death. And if The Buddhas, who always include in their teachings the Three Characteristics, were to attempt at such a time to discourse concerning transitoriness, misery, and the lack of substantive reality, men would not think it worth while listening to them, nor would they give them credence. Thus, there would be no conversions made; and if there were no conversions, the dispensation would not conduce to salvation. This, therefore, is not the right time.

Also it is not the right time when men's lives are less than a hundred years. And why is it not the right time? Because mortals are then exceedingly corrupt; and an exhortation given to the exceedingly corrupt makes no impression, but, like a mark drawn with a stick on the surface of the water, it immediately disappears. This, therefore, also is not the right time.

But when the length of men's lives is between a hundred years and a hundred thousand years, then is it the right time. Now at that time men's lives were a hundred years; accordingly the Great Being observed that it was the right time for his birth.

Next he made the observation concerning the continent. Looking over the four continents with their attendant isles, he reflected: "In three of the continents the Buddhas are never born; only in the continent of India are they born." Thus, he decided on the continent.

Next he made the observation concerning the place. "The continent of India is large," thought he, "being ten thousand leagues around. In which of its countries are The Buddhas born?"Thus, he decided on the Middle Country.

The Middle Country is the country defined in the Vinaya as follows:

"It lies in the middle, on this side of the town Kajañgala on the east, beyond which is Mahā-Sāla, and beyond that the border districts. It lies in the middle, on this side of the river Salalavatī on the southeast, beyond which are the border districts. It lies in the middle, on this side of the town Setakaṇṇika on the south, beyond which are the border districts. It lies in the middle, on this side of the Brāhmaṇical town Thūṇa on the west, beyond which are the border districts. It lies in the middle, on this side of the hill Usīraddhaja on the north, beyond which are the border districts."

It is three hundred leagues in length, two hundred and fifty in breadth, and nine hundred in circumference. In this country are born The Buddhas, the Private Buddhas, the Chief Disciples, the Eighty Great Disciples, the Universal Monarch, and other eminent ones, magnates of the warrior caste, of the Brāhmaṇa caste, and the wealthy householders. "And in it is this city called Kapilavatthu," thought he, and concluded that there he ought to be born.

Then he made the observation concerning the family. "The Buddhas," thought he, "are never born into a family of the peasant caste, or of the servile caste; but into one of the warrior caste, or of the Brāhmaṇa caste, whichever at the time is the higher in public estimation. The warrior caste is now the higher in public estimation. I will be born into a warrior family, and king Śuddhodana shall be my father." Thus, he decided on the family. King of the Śākya clan.

Then he made the observation concerning the mother. "The mother of a Buddha," thought he, "is never a wanton, nor a drunkard, but is one who has fulfilled the perfections through a hundred thousand cycles, and has kept the five precepts unbroken from the day of her birth. Now this queen Mahā-Māyā is such a one; and she shall be my mother."

"But what shall be her span of life?"[26] continued he. And he perceived that it was to be ten months and seven days.

Having thus made the five great observations, he kindly made the gods the required promise, saying,—

"Sirs, you are right. The time has come for my Buddha-ship."

Then, surrounded by the gods of the Tuṣita heaven, and dismissing all the other gods, he entered the Nandana Grove of the Tuṣita'capital,— for in each of the heavens there is a Nandana Grove. And here the gods said, "Attain in your next existence your high destiny," and kept reminding him that he had already paved the way to it by his accumulated merit. Now it was while he was thus dwelling, surrounded by these deities, and continually reminded of his accumulated merit, that he died, and was conceived in the womb of queen Mahā-Māyā. And in order that this matter may be fully understood, I will give the whole account in due order.

It is related that at that time the Midsummer Festival had been proclaimed in the city of Kapilavatthu, and the multitude were enjoying the feast. And queen Mahā-Māyā, abstaining from strong drink, and brilliant with garlands and perfumes, took part in the festivities for the six days previous to the day of full moon. And when it came to be the day of full moon, she rose early, bathed in perfumed water, and dispensed four hundred thousand pieces of money in great largess. And decked in full gala attire, she ate of the choicest food; after which she took the eight vows and entered her elegantly furnished chamber of state. And lying down on the royal couch, she fell asleep and dreamed the following dream:

The four guardian angels came and lifted her up, together with her couch, and took her away to the Himālaya Mountains. There, in the Manosilā table-land, which is sixty leagues in extent, they laid her under a prodigious sāl-tree, seven leagues in height, and took up their positions respectfully at one side. Then came the wives of these guardian angels, and conducted her to Anotatta Lake, and bathed her, to remove every human stain. And after clothing her with divine garments, they anointed her with perfumes and decked her with divine flowers. Not far off was Silver Hill, and in it a golden mansion. There they spread a divine couch with its head towards the .east, and laid her down upon it. Now the Future Buddha had become a superb white elephant, and was wandering about at no great distance, on Gold Hill. Descending thence, he ascended Silver Hill, and approaching from the north, he plucked a white lotus with his silvery trunk, and trumpeting loudly, went into the golden mansion. And three times he walked round his mother's couch, with his right side towards it, and striking her on her right side, he seemed to enter her womb. Thus, the conception took place in the Midsummer Festival.

On the next day the queen awoke, and told the dream to the king. And the king caused sixty-four eminent Brāhmaṇas to be summoned, and spread costly seats for them on ground festively prepared with green leaves, Dalbergia flowers, and so forth. The Brāhmaṇas being seated, he filled gold and silver dishes with the best of milk-porridge compounded with ghee, honey, and treacle; and covering these dishes with others, made likewise of gold and silver, he gave the Brāhmaṇas to eat. And not only with food, but with other gifts, such as new garments, tawny cows, and so forth, he satisfied them completely. And when their every desire had been satisfied, he told them the dream and asked them what would come of it.

"Be not anxious, great king ! "said the Brāhmaṇas; "a child has planted itself in the womb of your queen, and it is a male child and not a female. You will have a son. And he, if he continue to live the household life, will become a Universal Monarch; but if he leave the household life and retire from the world, he will become a Buddha, and roll back the clouds of sin and folly of this world."

Now the instant the Future Buddha was conceived in the womb of his mother, all the ten thousand worlds suddenly quaked, quivered, and shook. And the Thirty-two Prognostics appeared, as follows: an immeasurable light spread through ten thousand worlds; the blind recovered their sight, as if from desire to see this his glory; the deaf received their hearing; the dumb talked; the hunchbacked became straight of body; the lame recovered the power to walk; all those in bonds were freed from their bonds and chains; the fires went out in all the hells; the hunger and thirst of the Manes was stilled; wild animals lost their timidity; diseases ceased among men; all mortals became mild-spoken; horses neighed and elephants trumpeted in a manner sweet to the ear; all musical instruments gave forth their notes without being played upon; bracelets and other ornaments jingled; in all quarters of the heavens the weather became fair; a mild, cool breeze began to blow, very refreshing to men; rain fell out of season; water burst forth from the earth and flowed in streams; the birds ceased flying through the air; the rivers checked their flowing; in the mighty ocean the water became sweet; the ground became everywhere covered with lotuses of the five different colors; all flowers bloomed, both those on land and those that grow in the water; trunk-lotuses bloomed on the trunks of trees, branch-lotuses on the branches, and vine-lotuses on the vines; on the ground, stalk-lotuses, as they are called, burst through the overlying rocks and came up by sevens; in the sky were produced others, called hanging-lotuses; a shower of flowers fell all about; celestial music was heard to play in the sky; and the whole ten thousand worlds became one mass of garlands of the utmost possible magnificence, with waving chowries, and saturated with the incense-like fragrance of flowers, and resembled a bouquet of flowers sent whirling through the air, or a closely woven wreath, or a superbly decorated altar of flowers.

From the time the Future Buddha was thus conceived, four angels with swords in their hands kept guard, to ward off all harm from both the Future Buddha and the Future Buddha's mother. No lustful thought sprang up in the mind of the Future Buddha's mother; having reached the pinnacle of good fortune and of glory, she felt comfortable and well, and experienced no exhaustion of body. And within her womb she could distinguish the Future Buddha, like a white thread passed through a transparent jewel. And whereas a womb that has been occupied by a Future Buddha is like the shrine of a temple, and can never be occupied or used again, therefore it was that the mother of the Future Buddha died when he was seven days old, and was reborn in the Tuṣita heaven.

Now other women sometimes fall short of and sometimes run over the term of ten lunar months, and then bring forth either sitting or lying down; but not so the mother of a Future Buddha. She carries the Future Buddha in her womb for just ten months, and then brings forth while standing up. This is a characteristic of the mother of a Future Buddha. So also queen Mahā-Māyā carried the Future Buddha in her womb, as it were oil in a vessel, for ten months; and being then far gone with child, she grew desirous of going home to her relatives, and said to king Śuddhodana, –

"Sire, I should like to visit my kinsfolk in their city Devadaha."

"So be it," said the king; and from Kapilavatthu to the city of Devadaha, he had the road made even, and garnished it with plantain-trees set in pots, and with banners, and streamers; and, seating the queen in a golden palanquin borne by a thousand of his courtiers, he sent her away in great pomp.

Now between the two cities, and belonging to the inhabitants of both, there was a pleasure-grove of sāl-trees, called Lumbini Grove. And at this particular time this grove was one mass of flowers from the ground to the topmost branches, while amongst the branches and flowers hummed swarms of bees of the five different colors, and flocks of various kinds of birds flew about warbling sweetly. Throughout the whole of Lumbini Grove the scene resembled the Cittalatā Grove in India's paradise, or the magnificently decorated banqueting1 of some potent king.

When the queen beheld it she became desirous of disporting herself therein, and the courtiers therefore took her into it. And going to the foot of the monarch sal-tree of the grove, she wished to take hold of one of its branches. And the sal-tree branch, like the tip of a – well-steamed reed, bent itself down within reach of the queen's hand. Then she reached out her hand, and seized hold of the branch, and immediately her pains came upon her. Thereupon the people hung a curtain about her, and retired. So her delivery took place while she was standing up, and keeping fast hold of the sal-tree branch.

At that very moment came four pure-minded Mahā-Brahma angels bearing a golden net; and, receiving the Future Buddha on this golden net, they placed him before his mother and said, –

"Rejoice, O queen! A mighty son has been born to you."

Now other mortals on issuing from the maternal womb are smeared with disagreeable, impure matter; but not so the Future Buddha. He issued from his mother's womb like a preacher descending from his preaching-seat, or a man coming down a stair, stretching out both hands and both feet, unsmeared by any impurity from his mother's womb, and flashing pure and spotless, like a jewel thrown upon a vesture of Benares cloth. Notwithstanding this, for the sake of honoring the Future Buddha and his mother, there came two streams of water from the sky, and refreshed the Future Buddha and his mother.

Then the Brahma angels, after receiving him on their golden net, delivered him to the four guardian angels, who received him from their hands on a rug which was made of the skins of black antelopes, and was soft to the touch, being such as is used on state occasions; and the guardian angels delivered him to men who received him on a coil of fine cloth, and the men let him out of their hands on the ground, where he stood and faced the east. There, before him, lay many thousands of worlds, like a great open court; and in them, gods and men, making offerings to him of perfumes, garlands, and so on, were saying, –

"Great Being! There is none your equal, much less your superior."

When he had in this manner surveyed the four cardinal points, and the four intermediate ones, and the zenith, and the nadir, in short, all the ten directions in order, and had nowhere discovered his equal, he exclaimed, "This is the best direction," and strode forward seven paces, followed by Mahā-Brahma holding over him the white umbrella, Suyāma bearing the fan, and other divinities having the other symbols of royalty in their hands. Then, at the seventh stride, he halted, and with a noble voice, he shouted the shout of victory, beginning, –

"The chief am I in all the world."

Now in three of his existences did the Future Buddha utter words immediately on issuing from his mother's womb: namely, in his existence as Mahosadha; in his existence as Vessantara; and in this existence.

As respects his existence as Mahosadha, it is related that just as he was issuing from his mother's womb, Sakka, the king of the gods, came and placed in his hand some choice sandal-wood, and departed. And he closed his fist upon it, and issued forth.

"My child," said his mother, "what is it you bring with you in your hand?"

"Medicine, mother," said he.

Accordingly, as he was born with medicine in his hand, they gave him the name of Osadha-Dāraka [Medicine-Child]. Then they took the medicine, and placed it in an earthenware jar; and it was a sovereign remedy to heal all the blind, the deaf, and other afflicted persons who came to it. So the saying sprang up, "This is a great medicine, this is a great medicine!" And thus he received the name of Mahosadha [Great Medicine-Man].

Again, in the Vessantara existence, as he was issuing from his mother's womb, he stretched out his right hand, and said, –

"Pray, mother, is there anything in the house? I want to give alms."

Then, after he had completely issued forth, his mother said, –

"It's a wealthy family, my son, into which you are born; "and putting his hand in her own, she had them place in his a purse containing a thousand pieces of money.

Lastly, in this birth he shouted the shout of victory above-mentioned.

Thus, in three of his existences did the Future Buddha utter words immediately on issuing from his mother's womb. And just as at the moment of his conception, so also at the moment of his birth appeared the Thirty-two Prognostics.

Now at the very time that our Future Buddha was born in Lumbini Grove there also came into existence the mother of Rāhula, and Channa the courtier, Kāḷudāyi the courtier, Kanthaka the king of horses, the Great Bodhi tree, and the four urns full of treasure. Of these last, one was a quarter of a league in extent, another a half-league, the third three quarters of a league, and the fourth a league. These seven[27] are called the Connate Ones.

Then the inhabitants of both cities took the Future Buddha, and carried him to Kapilavatthu.

NOTES AND REFERENCES

26. That is, "How long is she to live after conceiving me?" And the answer is," Ten lunar [that is, the nine calendar] months of my mother's;pregnancy, and seven days after my birth."
27. In making up this number the Future Buddha is to be counted as number 1, and the four urns of treasure together as number 7.

Chapter V

THE YOUNG GOTAMID PRINCE

Translated from the Introduction to the Jātaka (i.54)

खुद्दक निकाये जातक अट्ठकथा-1

उभयनगरवासिनो बोधिसत्तं गहेत्वा कपिलवत्थुनगरमेव अगमंसु। तं दिवसंयेव च "कपिलवत्थुनगरे सुद्धोदनमहाराजस्स पुत्तो जातो, अयं कुमारो बोधितले निसीदित्वा बुद्धो भविस्सती"ति तावतिंसभवने हट्ठतुट्ठा देवसङ्घा चेलुक्खेपादीनि पवत्तेन्ता कीळिंसु। तस्मि समये सुद्धोदनमहाराजस्स कुलूपको अट्ठसमापत्तिलाभी काळदेवीलो नाम तापसो भत्तकिच्चं कत्वा दिवाविहारत्थाय तावतिंसभवनं गन्त्वा तत्थ दिवाविहारं निसिन्नो ता देवता कीळमाना दिस्वा "किंकारणा तुम्हे एवं तुट्ठमानसा कीळथ, मय्हम्पेतं कारणं कथेथा"ति पुच्छि। देवता आहंसु "मारिस, सुद्धोदनरञ्ञो पुत्तो जातो, सो बोधितले निसीदित्वा बुद्धो हुत्वा धम्मचक्कं पवत्तेस्सति, तस्स अनन्तं बुद्धलीळं दट्ठुं धम्मञ्च सोतुं लच्छामाति इमिना कारणेन तुट्ठाम्हा"ति। तापसो तासं वचनं सुत्वा खिप्पं देवलोकतो ओरुय्ह राजनिवेसनं पविसित्वा पञ्ञत्तासने निसिन्नो "पुत्तो किर ते, महाराज, जातो, पस्सिस्सामि न"न्ति आह। राजा अलङ्कतपटियत्तं कुमारं आहरापेत्वा तापसं वन्दापेतुं अभिहरि, बोधिसत्तस्स पादा परिवत्तित्वा तापसस्स जटासु पतिट्ठहिंसु। बोधिसत्तस्स हि तेनत्तभावेन वन्दितब्बयुत्तको नाम अञ्ञो नत्थि। सचे हि अजानन्ता बोधिसत्तस्स सीसं तापसस्स पादमूले ठपेय्युं, सत्तधा तस्स

मुद्धा फलेय्य। तापसो "न मे अत्तानं नासेतुं युत्त"न्ति उट्ठायासना बोधिसत्तस्स अज्जलिं पग्गहेसि। राजा तं अच्छरियं दिस्वा अत्तनो पुत्तं वन्दि।

तापसो अतीते चत्तालीस कप्पे, अनागते चत्तालीसाति असीति कप्पे अनुस्सरति। बोधिसत्तस्स लक्खणसम्पत्तिं दिस्वा "भविस्सति नु खो बुद्धो, उदाहु नो"ति आवज्जेत्वा उपधारेन्तो "निस्संसयं बुद्धो भविस्सती"ति ञत्वा "अच्छरियपुरिसो अय"न्ति सितं अकासि। ततो "अहं इमं बुद्धभूतं दट्ठुं लभिस्सामि नु खो, नो"ति उपधारेन्तो "न लभिस्सामि, अन्तरायेव कालं कत्वा बुद्धसतेनपि बुद्धसहस्सेनपि गन्त्वा बोधेतुं असक्कुणेय्ये अरूपभवे निब्बत्तिस्सामी"ति दिस्वा "एवरूपं नाम अच्छरियपुरिसं बुद्धभूतं दट्ठुं न लभिस्सामि, महती वत मे जानि भविस्सती"ति परोदि।

मनुस्सा दिस्वा "अम्हाकं अय्यो इदानेव हसित्वा पुन परोदि। किं नु खो, भन्ते, अम्हाकं अय्यपुत्तस्स कोचि अन्तरायो भविस्सती"ति पुच्छिंसु। "नत्थेतस्स अन्तरायो, निस्संसयेन बुद्धो भविस्सती"ति। अथ "कस्मा परोदित्था"ति? "एवरूपं पुरिसं बुद्धभूतं दट्ठुं न लभिस्सामि, महती वत मे जानि भविस्सती'ति अत्तानं अनुसोचन्तो रोदामी"ति आह। ततो सो "किं नु खो मे ञातकेसु कोचि एतं बुद्धभूतं दट्ठुं लभिस्सति, न लभिस्सती"ति उपधारेन्तो अत्तनो भागिनेय्यं नाळकदारकं अद्दस। सो भगिनिया गेहं गन्त्वा "कहं ते पुत्तो नाळको"ति? "अत्थि गेहे, अय्या"ति। "पक्कोसाहि न"न्ति पक्कोसापेत्वा अत्तनो सन्तिकं आगतं कुमारं आह–"तात, सुद्धोदनमहाराजस्स कुले पुत्तो जातो, बुद्धङ्कुरो एस, पञ्चतिंस वस्सानि अतिक्कमित्वा बुद्धो भविस्सति, त्वं एतं दट्ठुं लभिस्ससि, अज्जेव पब्बजाही"ति। सत्तासीतिकोटिधने कुले निब्बत्तदारकोपि "न मं मातुलो अनत्थे नियोजेस्सती"ति चिन्तेत्वा तावदेव अन्तरापणतो कासायानि चेव मत्तिकापत्तञ्च आहरापेत्वा केसमस्सुं ओहारेत्वा कासायानि वत्थानि अच्छादेत्वा "यो लोके उत्तमपुग्गलो, तं उद्दिस्स मय्हं पब्बज्जा"ति बोधिसत्ताभिमुखं अज्जलिं पग्गय्ह पञ्चपतिट्ठितेन वन्दित्वा पत्तं थविकाय

पक्खिपित्वा अंसकूटे लग्गेत्वा हिमवन्तं पविसित्वा समणधम्मं अकासि। सो परमाभिसम्बोधिं पत्तं तथागतं उपसङ्कमित्वा नाळकपटिपदं कथापेत्वा पुन हिमवन्तं पविसित्वा अरहत्तं पत्वा उक्कट्ठपटिपदं पटिपन्नो सत्तेव मासे आयुं पालेत्वा एकं सुवण्णपब्बतं निस्साय ठितकोव अनुपादिसेसाय निब्बानधातुया परिनिब्बायि।

बोधिसत्तम्पि खो पञ्चमे दिवसे सीसं न्हापेत्वा "नामग्गहणं गण्हिस्सामा"ति राजभवनं चतुज्जातिकगन्धेहि विलिम्पित्वा लालापञ्चमकानि पुप्फानि विकिरित्वा असम्भिन्नपायासं पचापेत्वा तिण्णं वेदानं परङ्गते अट्ठसतब्राह्मणे निमन्तेत्वा राजभवने निसीदापेत्वा सुभोजनं भोजेत्वा महासक्कारं कत्वा "किं नु खो भविस्सती"ति लक्खणानि परिग्गहापेसुं। तेसु–

"रामो धजो लक्खणो चापि मन्ती, कोण्डञ्ञो च भोजो सुयामो सुदत्तो।

एते तदा अट्ठ अहेसुं ब्राह्मणा, छळङ्गवा मन्तं वियाकरिंसू"ति॥ 270॥

इमे अट्ठेव ब्राह्मणा लक्खणपरिग्गाहका अहेसुं। पटिसन्धिग्गहणदिवसे सुपिनोपि एतेहेव परिग्गहितो। तेसु सत्त जना द्वे अङ्गुलियो उक्खिपित्वा द्वेधा ब्याकरिंसु–"इमेहि लक्खणेहि समन्नागतो अगारं अज्झावसमानो राजा होति चक्कवती, पब्बजमानो बुद्धो"ति, सब्बं चक्कवत्तिरञ्ञो सिरिविभवं आचिक्खिंसु। तेसं पन सब्बदहरो गोत्ततो कोण्डञ्ञो नाम माणवो बोधिसत्तस्स वरलक्खणनिप्फत्तिं ओलोकेत्वा– "इमस्स अगारामज्झे ठानकारणं नत्थि, एकन्तेनेस विवट्टच्छदो बुद्धो भविस्सती"ति एकमेव अङ्गुलिं उक्खिपित्वा एकंसब्याकरणं ब्याकासि। अयञ्हि कताधिकारो पच्छिमभविकसत्तो पञ्ञाय इतरे सत्त जने अभिभवित्वा "इमेहि लक्खणेहि समन्नागतस्स अगारमज्झे ठानं नाम नत्थि, असंसयं बुद्धो भविस्सती"ति एकमेव गतिं अद्दस, तस्मा एकं अङ्गुलिं उक्खिपित्वा एवं ब्याकासि। अथस्स नामं गण्हन्ता सब्बलोकस्स अत्थसिद्धिकरत्ता "सिद्धत्थो"ति नाममकंसु।

अथ ते ब्राह्मणा अत्तनो घरानि गन्त्वा पुत्ते आमन्तयिंसु–"ताता, अम्हे महल्लका, सुद्धोदनमहाराजस्स पुत्तं सब्बञ्ञुतं पत्तं मयं सम्भवेय्याम वा नो वा, तुम्हे तस्मिं कुमारे सब्बञ्ञुतं पत्ते तस्स सासने पब्बजेय्याथा"ति। ते सत्तपि जना यावतायुकं ठत्वा यथाकम्मं गता, कोण्डञ्ञमाणवोव अरोगो अहोसि। सो महासत्ते वुड्ढिमन्वाय महाभिनिक्खमनं अभिनिक्खमित्वा अनुक्कमेन उरुवेलं गन्त्वा "रमणीयो, वत अयं भूमिभागो, अलं वतिदं कुलपुत्तस्स पधानत्थिकस्स पधानाया"ति चित्तं उप्पादेत्वा तत्थ वासं उपगते "महापुरिसो पब्बजितो"ति सुत्वा तेसं ब्राह्मणानं पुत्ते उपसङ्कमित्वा एवमाह "सिद्धत्थकुमारो किर पब्बजितो, सो निस्संसयं बुद्धो भविस्सति। सचे तुम्हाकं पितरो अरोगा अस्सु, अज्ज निक्खमित्वा पब्बजेय्युं। सचे तुम्हेपि इच्छेय्याथ, एथ, अहं तं पुरिसं अनुपब्बजिस्सामी"ति। ते सब्बे एकच्छन्दा भवितुं नासक्खिंसु, तयो जना न पब्बजिंसु। कोण्डञ्ञब्राह्मणं जेट्ठकं कत्वा इतरे चत्तारो पब्बजिंसु। ते पञ्चपि जना पञ्चवग्गियत्थेरा नाम जाता।

तदा पन राजा "किं दिस्वा मय्हं पुत्तो पब्बजिस्सती"ति पुच्छि। "चत्तारि पुब्बनिमित्तानी"ति। "कतरञ्च कतरञ्चा"ति? "जराजिण्णं, ब्याधितं, कालकतं, पब्बजित"न्ति। राजा "इतो पट्ठाय एवरूपानं मम पुत्तस्स सन्तिकं उपसङ्कमितुं मा अदत्थ, मय्हं पुत्तस्स बुद्धभावेन कम्मं नत्थि, अहं मम पुत्तं द्विसहस्सदीपपरिवारानं चतुन्नं महादीपानं इस्सरियाधिपच्चं रज्जं कारेन्तं छत्तिंसयोजनपरिमण्डलाय परिसाय परिवुतं गगनतले विचरमानं पस्सितुकामो"ति। एवञ्च पन वत्वा इमेसं चतुप्पकारानं निमित्तानं कुमारस्स चक्खुपथे आगमननिवारणत्थं चतूसु दिसासु गावुते आरक्खं ठपेसि। तं दिवसं पन मङ्गलट्ठाने सन्निपतितेसु असीतिया ञातिकुलसहस्सेसु एकेको एकमेकं पुत्तं पटिजानि–"अयं बुद्धो वा होतु राजा वा, मयं एकमेकं पुत्तं दस्साम। सचेपि बुद्धो भविस्सति, खत्तियसमणेहेव पुरक्खतपरिवारितो विचरिस्सति। सचेपि राजा भविस्सति, खत्तियकुमारेहेव पुरक्खत- परिवारितो विचरिस्सती"ति।

राजापि बोधिसत्तस्स उत्तमरूपसम्पन्न विगतसब्बदोसा धातियो पच्चुपट्ठापेसि। बोधिसत्तो अनन्तेन परिवारेन महन्तेन सिरिसोभग्गेन वड्ढति।

अथेकदिवसं रञ्ञो वप्पमङ्गलं नाम अहोसि। तं दिवसं सकलनगरं देवविमानं विय अलङ्करोन्ति। सब्बे दासकम्मकरादयो अहतवत्थनिवत्था गन्धमालादिपटिमण्डिता राजकुले सन्निपतन्ति। रञ्ञो कम्मन्ते नङ्गलसहस्सं योजीयति। तस्मिं पन दिवसे एकेनूनअट्ठसतनङ्गलानि सद्धिं बलिबद्दरस्मियोत्तेहि रजतपरिक्खतानि होन्ति, रञ्ञो आलम्बन-नङ्गलं पन रत्तसुवण्णपरिक्खतं होति। बलिबद्दानं सिङ्गरस्मिपतोदापि सुवण्णपरिक्खताव होन्ति। राजा महता परिवारेन निक्खन्तो पुत्तं गहेत्वा अगमासि। कम्मन्तट्ठाने एको जम्बुरुक्खो बहलपलासो सन्दच्छायो अहोसि। तस्स हेट्ठा कुमारस्स सयनं पञ्ञपापेत्वा उपरि सुवण्णतारकखचितं वितानं बन्धापेत्वा साणिपाकारेन परिक्खिपापेत्वा आरक्खं ठपापेत्वा राजा सब्बालङ्कारं अलङ्करित्वा अमच्चगणपरिवुतो नङ्गलकरणट्ठानं अगमासि। तत्थ राजा सुवण्णनङ्गलं गण्हाति, अमच्चा एकेनूनट्ठसतरजतनङ्गलानि, कस्सका सेसनङ्गलानि। ते तानि गहेत्वा इतो चितो च कसन्ति। राजा पन ओरतो वा पारं गच्छति, पारतो वा ओरं आगच्छति। एतस्मिं ठाने महासम्पत्ति अहोसि। बोधिसत्तं परिवारेत्वा निसिन्ना धातियो "रञ्ञो सम्पत्तिं पस्सिस्सामा"ति अन्तोसाणितो बहि निक्खन्ता। बोधिसत्तो इतो चितो च ओलोकेन्तो कञ्चि अदिस्वा वेगेन उट्ठाय पल्लङ्कं आभुजित्वा आनापाने परिग्गहेत्वा पठमज्झानं निब्बत्तेसि। धातियो खज्जभोज्जन्तरे विचरमाना थोकं चिरायिंसु। सेसरुक्खानं छाया निवत्ता, तस्स पन रुक्खस्स परिमण्डला हुत्वा अट्ठासि। धातियो "अय्यपुत्तो एकतो"ति वेगेन साणिं उक्खिपित्वा अन्तो पविसमाना बोधिसत्तं सयने पल्लङ्केन निसिन्नं तञ्च पाटिहारियं दिस्वा गन्त्वा रञ्ञो आरोचेसुं–"देव, कुमारो एवं निसिन्नो, अञ्ञेसं रुक्खानं छाया निवत्ता, जम्बुरुक्खस्स पन परिमण्डला ठिता"ति। राजा वेगेनागन्त्वा पाटिहारियं दिस्वा–"इदं ते, तात, दुतियं वन्दन"न्ति पुत्तं वन्दि।

अथ अनुक्कमेन बोधिसत्तो सोळसवस्सुद्देसिको जातो। राजा बोधिसत्तस्स तिण्णं उतूनं अनुच्छविके तयो पासादे कारेसि–एकं नवभूमकं, एकं सत्तभूमकं, एकं पञ्चभूमकं, चत्तालीससहस्सा च नाटकित्थियो उपट्ठापेसि। बोधिसत्तो देवो विय अच्छरासङ्घपरिवुतो, अलङ्कतनाटकपरिवुतो, निप्पुरिसेहि तूरियेहि परिचारियमानो महासम्पत्तिं अनुभवन्तो उतुवारेन तेसु पासादेसु विहरति। राहुलमाता पनस्स देवी अग्गमहेसी अहोसि।

तस्सेवं महासम्पत्तिं अनुभवन्तस्स एकदिवसं ञातिसङ्घस्स अब्भन्तरे अयं कथा उदपादि–"सिद्धत्थो कीळापसुतोव विचरति, किञ्चि सिप्पं न सिक्खति, सङ्गामे पच्चुपट्ठिते किं करिस्सती"ति। राजा बोधिसत्तं पक्कोसापेत्वा–"तात, तव ञातका सिद्धत्थो किञ्चि सिप्पं असिक्खित्वा कीळापसुतोव विचरती'ति वदन्ति, एत्थ किं पत्तकाले मञ्ञसी"ति। देव, मम सिप्पं सिक्खनकिच्चं नत्थि, नगरे मम सिप्पदस्सनत्थं भेरिं चरापेथ "इतो सत्तमे दिवसे ञातकानं सिप्पं दस्सेस्सामी"ति। राजा तथा अकासि। बोधिसत्तो अक्खणवेधिवालवेधिधनुग्गहे सन्निपातापेत्वा महाजनस्स मज्झे अञ्ञेहि धनुग्गहेहि असाधारणं ञातकानं द्वादसविधं सिप्पं दस्सेसि। तं सरभङ्गजातके आगतनयेनेव वेदितब्बं। तदास्स ञातिसङ्घो निक्कङ्खो अहोसि।

On this same day the happy and delighted hosts of the Heaven of the Thirty-three held a celebration, waving their cloaks and giving other signs of joy, because to king Śuddhodana in Kapilavatthu had been born a son who should sit at the foot of the Bo-tree, and become a Buddha.

Now it came to pass at that time that an ascetic named Kaladevala, who was an intimate friend of king Śuddhodana, and practised in the eight stages of meditation, went, after his daily meal, to the Heaven of the Thirty-three to take his noon-day rest. And as he was sitting there resting, he noticed these gods, and said,–

"Why do you frolic so joyously? Let me too know the reason."

"Sir," replied the gods, "it is because a son has been born to king Śuddhodana, who shall sit at the foot of the Bo-tree, and become a Buddha, and cause the Wheel of the Doctrine to roll; in him we shall be permitted to behold the infinite and masterful ease of a Buddha, and shall hear the Doctrine."

On hearing this, the ascetic descended from the world of the gods in haste, and entered the dwelling of the king; and having seated himself on the seat assigned to him, he said, –

"Great king, I hear that a son has been born to you. I would see him."

Then the king had the prince magnificently dressed, and brought in, and carried up to do reverence to the ascetic. But the feet of the Future Buddha turned and planted themselves in the matted locks of the ascetic. For in that birth there was no one worthy of the Future Buddha's reverence; and if these ignorant people had succeeded in causing the Future Buddha to bow, the head of the ascetic would have split in seven pieces.

"It is not meet that I compass my own death," thought the ascetic, and rose from his seat, and with joined hands did reverence to the Future Buddha. And when the king had seen this wonder, he also did reverence to his son.

Now the ascetic could look backward into the past for forty world-cycles, and forward into the future for forty world-cycles, – in all, eighty world-cycles. And, noting on the person of the Future Buddha all the lucky marks and characteristics, he began to reflect and consider whether or not they prophesied his Buddhaship. And perceiving that undoubtedly he would become a Buddha, he thought to himself, "What a marvellous personage he is! and smiled.

Next he considered in his mind whether he would live to see him attain the Buddhaship; and he perceived that he was not to have that opportunity. For he – would die before that time, and be reborn in the formless mode of existence, where it would be out of the power of even a hundred or a thousand Buddhas to come and enlighten him. And he thought, "It will not be mine to behold this so marvellous a personage when he has become a Buddha. My loss, alas, will be great," and wept.

The people noticed his behavior, and said to him, –

"Our good father smiled but a moment ago, and now has begun to weep. Reverend sir, is any misfortune to happen to our young master?"

"No misfortune is to happen to him. He will become a Buddha without any manner of doubt."

"Then why did you weep?"

"I wept at the thought of my own great loss; for, alas, I am not to have an opportunity of seeing this marvellous person after he has beco'me a Buddha."

Next he considered in his mind whether or not any of his relatives were to have the opportunity; and he saw that his sister's child Nālaka was to have it. And he went to his sister's house, and inquired, –

"Where is your son Nālaka?"

"Good father, he is in the house."

"Call him hither."

"My child," said he to the lad when he had come, "a son has been born in the family of Śuddhodana the king, who is the coming Buddha. Thirty-five years from now he will become a Buddha, and you will have an opportunity of seeing him. Retire from the world this very day."

And the child did so, although he belonged to a family possessing eight hundred and seventy millions of treasure; for he thought, "My uncle would not lay such a command upon me for any trifling reason." Sending to the bazāar, he procured some yellow garments, and an earthenware bowl, and cut off his hair and his beard, and put on the yellow garments. And stretching out his joined hands in the direction of the Future Buddha, he said, "I retire from the world to follow earth's greatest being." Then he prostrated himself, so that he touched the ground with the fivefold contact. Having thus done reverence, he placed the bowl in his script, slung the latter over his shoulder, and going to the Himālaya Mountains, he there performed the duties of a monk.

And after the Great Being had achieved the absolute and supreme wisdom, Nālaka came to him, and had him prescribe the Nālaka course of conduct.[28] Then, returning to the Himālaya Mountains, he attained to saintship, and adopted that excellent course. And keeping alive for seven months more, and being at the time near a certain Gold Hill, he passed out of existence by that final extinction in which none of the elements of being remain.

Now on the fifth day they bathed the Future Buddha's head, saying, "We will perform the rite of choosing a name for him." And they prepared the royal palace by anointing it with four kinds of perfumes, and by scattering Dalbergia blossoms and other flowers, five sorts in all. And making some porridge of whole rice-grains boiled in milk, they invited one hundred and eight Brāhmaṇas, men who had mastered the three Vedas. And having seated these Brāhmaṇas in the royal palace, and fed them with delicate food, and showed them every attention, they asked them to observe the marks and characteristics of the Future Buddha's person, and to prophesy his fortune.

Among the hundred and eight,—

270. "Rāma, Dhaja, Lakkhaṇa, also Manti,
Koṇḍañña, Bhoja, Suyāma, Sudatta,
These Brāhmaṇas eight were there with senses six subdued;
They from the magic books disclosed his fortune."

These eight Brāhmaṇas were the fortune-tellers, being the same[29] who had interpreted the dream of the night of the conception. Seven of these raised two fingers each, and gave a double interpretation, saying, "If a man possessing such marks and characteristics continue in the household life, he becomes a Universal Monarch; if he retire from the world, he becomes a Buddha." And then they set forth all the glory of a Universal Monarch.

But the youngest of them all, a youth whose clan-name was Koṇḍañña, after examining the splendid set of marks and characteristics on the person of the Future Buddha, raised only one finger, and gave but a single interpretation, saying, "There is here naught to make him stay in the household life. He will most undoubtedly become a Buddha, and remove the veil of ignorance and folly from the world." For this Koṇḍañña was one who had made an earnest wish under former Buddhas, and'was now in his last existence. Therefore it was that he outstripped the other seven in knowledge, and saw but one future; inasmuch as a person possessed of such marks and characteristics would never stay in the household life, but would undoubtedly become a Buddha. So he raised only one finger, and gave that interpretation.

Then the seven Brāhmaṇas went home and said to their sons, "Children, we are old, but whether we ourselves are alive or not when the son of Śuddhodana the king shall attain omniscience, you, at least, should then retire from the world under his dispensation."

And after these seven persons had lived out their term of life they passed away according to their deeds; but Koṇḍañña, being younger, was still alive and hale. And when the Great Being, after making the great retirement in pursuit of wisdom, had arrived at Uruvelā in his progress from place to place, he thought: "How pleasant indeed is this spot! How suitable for the struggles of a young man desirous of struggling!" and took up his abode there. Koṇḍañña heard the news that the Great Being had retired from the world, and drawing near to the sons of those seven Brāhmaṇas, he spoke to them as follows:

"I hear that prince Siddhāttha has retired from the world. Now he will unquestionably become a Buddha, and if your fathers were alive they would follow after him this very day. If you also would like to retire from the world, come with me. I mean to follow after that man in his retirement from the world."

But they could not all agree; and three of them did not

retire from the world. But the remaining four did so, and made the Brāhmaṇa Koṇḍañña their chief. And these five persons became known as the "Band of Five Elders."

Then said the king, "What shall my son see to make him retire from the world?"

"The four signs."

"What four?"

"A decrepit old man, a diseased man, a dead man, and a monk."

"From this time forth," said the king, "let no such persons be allowed to come near my son. It will never do for my son to become a Buddha. What I would wish to see is my son exercising sovereign rule and authority over the four great continents and the two thousand attendant isles, and walking through the heavens surrounded by a retinue thirty-six leagues in circumference." And when he had so spoken he placed guards for a distance of a quarter of a league in each of the four directions, in order that none of these four kinds of men might come within sight of his son.

On this same day, also, eighty thousand clansmen assembled together in the festival-hall, and each dedicated a son, saying, –

"Whether the young prince becomes a Buddha or a king, we will each one give a son : so that if he becomes a Buddha, he shall be followed and surrounded by monks of the warrior caste; and if he becomes a king, by nobles of the warrior caste."

And the king procured nurses for the Future Buddha, women of fine figure, and free from all blemish. And so the Future Buddha began to grow, surrounded by an immense retinue, and in great splendor.

Now on a certain day the king celebrated the Sowing Festival, as it was called. On that day they used to decorate the whole city, so that it looked like a palace of the gods; and all the slaves and other servants would put on new tunics; and, perfumed and garlanded, they would assemble together at the king's palace, where a thousand plows were yoked for the royal plowing.

On this occasion there were one hundred and eight plows, all save one ornamented with silver, as were also the reins for the oxen and the cross-bars of the plows. But the plow that was held by the king was ornamented with red gold, as also the horns, the reins, and the goads for the oxen. And the king issued forth with a large retinue, taking his son along with him. And in the field where the plowing was to be done was a solitary rose-apple tree of thick foliage and dense shade. Underneath this tree the king had a couch placed for the young prince, and spread over his head a canopy that was studded with gold stars; and he surrounded him with a screen, and appointed those that should watch by him; and then, decked with all his ornaments and surrounded by his courtiers, he proceeded to the place where they were to plow. On arriving there, the king took the gold plow, and the courtiers took the silver plows,– one hundred and eight save one, and the farmers the other plows; and then all plowed forward and back. The king went from the hither side to the farther side, and from the farther side back again; and the pomp and magnificence of the festival was at its climax.

Now the nurses who were sitting about the Future Buddha came out from behind the screen to behold the royal magnificence. And the Future Buddha, looking hither and thither and seeing no one, arose in haste and sat him down cross-legged, and mastering his inspirations and his expirations, entered on the first trance. The nurses delayed a little, being detained by the abundance of good things to eat. And the shadows of the other trees passed over to the east, but the shadow of the rose-apple tree remained steadily circular. Suddenly the nurses remembered that they had left their young master alone; and raising the screen, they entered and saw the Future Buddha sitting cross-legged on the couch, ind also noticed the miracle of the shadow. Then they went and announced to the king :

"Sire, thus and so is the prince sitting; and the shadows of the other trees have passed over to the east, but the shadow of the rose-apple tree remains steadily circular."

And the king came in haste, and seeing the miracle, he did obeisance to his son, saying, "This, dear child, is my second obeisance."

And thus, in due course, the Future Buddha attained to the age of sixteen years. And the king built three palaces for the Future Buddha, suited to the three seasons, —one of nine stories, another of seven stories, and another of five stories. And he provided him with forty thousand dancing girls. And the Future Buddha, with his gayly dressed dancers, was like a god surrounded by hosts of houris; and attended by musical instruments that sounded of themselves, and in the enjoyment of great magnificence, he lived, as the seasons changed, in each of these three palaces. And the mother of Rāhula was his principal queen.

Now while he was thus enjoying great splendor, one day there arose the following discussion among his relatives :

"Siddhāttha is wholly given over to pleasure, and is not training himself in any manly art. What could he do if war were to occur?"

The king sent for the Future Buddha, and said :

"My child, your relatives are saying that you are not training yourself, but are wholly given over to pleasure. Now what do you think we had best to do?"

"Sire, I do not need to train myself. Let the crier go about the city beating the drum, to announce that I will show my proficiency. On the seventh day from now I will show my proficiency to my relatives."

The king did so. And the Future Buddha assembled together bowmen that could shoot like lightning and at a hair's-breadth; and in the midst of the populace, and before his kinsfolk, he exhibited a twelvefold skill, such as none of the other bowmen could equal. All of which is to be understood after the manner related in the Sarabhaṅga Birth-Story. So the assembly of his kinsfolk doubted him no longer.

NOTES AND REFERENCES

28. The Nālaka course of conduct is given in the Nālaka Sutta of the Sutta-Nipāta, and consists of a number of precepts for leading the holy-life.
29. They presumably were the spokesmen for the sixty- four, as here for the one hundred and eight.

Chapter VI

THE GREAT RETIREMENT

Translated from the Introduction to the Jātaka (i.58[81])

खुद्दक निकाये जातक अट्ठकथा-1

अथेकदिवसं बोधिसत्तो उटयानभूमिं गन्तुकामो सारथिं आमन्तेत्वा "रथं योजेही"ति आह। सो "साधू"ति पटिस्सुणित्वा महारहं उत्तमरथं सब्बालङ्कारेन अलङ्करित्वा कुमुदपत्तवण्णे चत्तारो मङ्गलसिन्धवे योजेत्वा बोधिसत्तस्स पटिवेदेसि। बोधिसत्तो देवविमानसदिसं रथं अभिरुहित्वा उय्यानाभिमुखो अगमासि। देवता "सिद्धत्थकुमारस्स अभिसम्बुज्झन-कालो आसन्नो, पुब्बनिमित्तं दस्सेस्सामा"ति एकं देवपुत्तं जराजज्जरं खण्डदन्तं पलितकेसं वङ्कं ओभग्गसरीरं दण्डहत्थं पवेधमानं कत्वा दस्सेसुं। तं बोधिसत्तो चेव सारथि व पस्सन्ति। ततो बोधिसत्तो सारथिं-"सम्म, को नामेस पुरिसो, केसापिस्स न यथा अञ्ञेस"न्ति महापदाने आगतनयेन पुच्छित्वा तस्स वचनं सुत्वा "धीरत्थु वत भो जाति, यत्र हि नाम जातस्स जरा पञ्ञायिस्सती"ति संविग्गहदयो ततोव पट्निवत्तित्वा पासादमेव अभिरुहि। राजा "किं कारणा मम पुत्तो खिप्पं पटिनिवत्ती"ति पुच्छि। "जिण्णकं पुरिसं दिस्वा देवा"ति। "जिण्णकं दिस्वा पब्बजिस्सतीति आहंसु, कस्मा मं नासेथ, सीघं पुत्तस्स नाटकानि सज्जेथ, सम्पत्तिं अनुभवन्तो पब्बज्जाय सतिं न करिस्सती"ति वत्वा आरक्खं वड्ढेत्वा सब्बदिसासु अड्ढयोजने अड्ढयोजने ठपेसि।

पुनेकदिवसं बोधिसत्तो तथेव उय्यानं गच्छन्तो देवताहि निम्मितं ब्याधितं पुरिसं दिस्वा पुरिमनयेनेव पुच्छित्वा संविग्गहदयो निवत्तित्वा पसादं अभिरुहि। राजापि पुच्छित्वा हेट्ठा वुत्तनयेनेव संविदहित्वा पुन वड्ढेत्वा समन्ता तिगावुतप्पमाणे पदेसे आरक्खं ठपेसि। अपरं एकदिवसं बोधिसत्तो तथेव उय्यानं गच्छन्तो देवताहि निम्मितं कालकतं दिस्वा पुरिमनयेनेव पुच्छित्वा संविग्गहदयो पुन निवत्तित्वा पासादं अभिरुहि। राजापि पुच्छित्वा हेट्ठा वुत्तनयेनेव संविदहित्वा पुन वड्ढेत्वा समन्ता योजनप्पमाणे पदेसे आरक्खं ठपेसि। अपरं पन एकदिवसं उय्यानं गच्छन्तो तथेव देवताहि निम्मितं सुनिवत्थं सुपारुतं पब्बजितं दिस्वा "को नामेसो सम्मा"ति सारथिं पुच्छि। सारथि किञ्चापि बुद्धुप्पादस्स अभावा पब्बजितं वा पब्बजितगुणे वा न जानाति, देवतानुभावेन पन "पब्बजितो नामायं देवा"ति वत्वा पब्बज्जाय गुणे वण्णेसि। बोधिसत्तो पब्बज्जाय रुचिं उप्पादेत्वा तं दिवसं उय्यानं अगमासि। दीघभाणका पनाहु "चत्तारि निमित्तानि एकदिवसेनेव दिस्वा अगमासी"ति।

सो तत्थ दिवसभागं कीळित्वा मङ्गलपोंक्खरणियं न्हायित्वा अत्थङ्गते सूरिये मङ्गलसिलपट्टे निसीदि अत्तानं अलङ्कारापेतुकामो। अथस्स परिचारकपुरिसा नानावण्णानि दुस्सानि नानप्पकारा आभरणविकतियो मालागन्धविलेपनानि च आदाय समन्ता परिवारेत्वा अट्ठंसु। तस्मि खणे सक्कस्स निसिन्नासनं उण्हं अहोसि। सो "को नु खो मं इमम्हा ठाना चावेतुकामो"ति उपधारेन्तो बोधिसत्तस्स अलङ्कारेतुकामतं ञत्वा विस्सकम्मं आमन्तेसि "सम्म विस्सकम्म, सिद्धत्थकुमारो अज्ज अड्ढरत्तसमये महाभिनिक्खमनं निक्खमिस्सति, अयमस्स पच्छिमो अलङ्कारो, उय्यानं गन्त्वा महापुरिसं दिब्बालङ्कारेहि अलङ्करोही"ति। सो "साधू"ति पटिस्सुणित्वा देवतानुभावेन तङ्खणंयेव उपसङ्कमित्वा तस्सेव कप्पकसदिसो हुत्वा कप्पकस्स हत्थतो वेठनदुस्सं गहेत्वा बोधिसत्तस्स सीसं वेठेसि। बोधिसत्तो हत्थसम्फस्सेनेव "नायं मनुस्सो, देवपुत्तो एसो"ति अञ्ञासि। वेठनेन वेठितमत्ते सीसे मोळियं मणिरतनाकारेन दुस्ससहस्सं अब्भुग्गञ्छि। पुन वेठेन्तस्स दुस्ससहस्सन्ति

दसक्खत्तुं वेठेन्तस्स दस दुस्ससहस्सानि अब्भुग्गच्छिसु। "सीसं खुद्दकं, दुस्सानि बहूनि, कथं अब्भुग्गतानी"ति न चिन्तेतब्बं। तेसु हि सब्बमहन्तं आमलकपुप्फप्पमाणं, अवसेसानि कुसुम्बकपुप्फप्पमाणानि अहेसुं। बोधिसत्तस्स सीसं किञ्जक्खगवच्छितं विय कुय्यकपुप्फं अहोसि।

अथस्स सब्बालङ्कारपटिमण्डितस्स सब्बतालावचरेसु सकानि सकानि पटिभानानि दस्सयन्तेसु, ब्राह्मणेसु "जयनन्दा"तिआदिवचनेहि, सूतमागधादीसु नानप्पकारेहि मङ्गलवनचत्थुतिघोसेहि सम्भावेन्तेसु सब्बालङ्कारपटिमण्डितं रथवरं अभिरुहि। तस्मिं समये "राहुलमाता पुत्तं विजाता"ति सुत्वा सुद्धोदनमहाराजा "पुत्तस्स मे तुट्ठिं निवेदेथा"ति सासनं पहिणि। बोधिसत्तो तं सुत्वा "राहु जातो, बन्धनं जात"न्ति आह। राजा "किं मे पुत्तो अवचा"ति पुच्छित्वा तं वचनं सुत्वा "इतो पट्ठाय मे नत्ता राहुलकुमारोयेव नाम होतू"ति आह।

बोधिसत्तोपि खो रथवरं आरुय्ह यसेन अतिमनोरमेन सिरिसोभग्गेन नगरं पाविसि। तस्मिं समये किसागोतमी नाम खत्तियकञ्ञा उपरिपासादवरतलगता नगरं पदक्खिणं कुरुमानस्स बोधिसत्तस्स रूपसिरिं दिस्वा पीतिसोमनस्सजाता इदं उदानं उदानेति–

"निब्बुता नून सा माता, निब्बुतो नून सो पिता।
निब्बुता नून सा नारी, यस्सायं ईदिसो पती"ति।। 271।।

बोधिसत्तो तं सुत्वा चिन्तेसि "अयं एवमाह 'एवरूपं अत्तभावं पस्सन्तिया मातु हदयं निब्बायति, पितु हदयं निब्बायति, पजापतिया हदयं निब्बायती'ति! किस्मिं नु खो निब्बुते हदयं निब्बुतं नाम होती"ति? अथस्स किलेसेसु विरत्तमानसस्स एतदहोसि–रागग्गिम्हि निब्बुते निब्बुतं नाम होति, दोसग्गिम्हि निब्बुते निब्बुतं नाम होति, मोहग्गिम्हि निब्बुते निब्बुतं नाम होति, मानदिट्ठिआदीसु सब्बकिलेसदरथेसु निब्बुतेसु निब्बुतं नाम होति। अयं मे सुस्सवनं सावेसि, अहञ्हि निब्बानं गवेसन्तो चरामि, अज्जेव मया घरावासं छड्डेत्वा निक्खम्म पब्बजित्वा निब्बानं गवेसितुं वट्टति, अयं इमिस्सा आचरियभागो होतू"ति कण्ठतो ओमुञ्चित्वा किसागोतमिया

सतसहस्सग्घनकं मुत्ताहारं पेसेसि। सा "सिद्धत्थकुमारो मयि पटिबद्धचित्तो हुत्वा पण्णाकारं पेसेसी"ति सोमनस्सजाता अहोसि।

बोधिसत्तोपि महन्तेन सिरिसोभग्गेन अत्तनो पासादं अभिरुहित्वा सिरिसयने निपज्जि। तावदेव च नं सब्बालङ्कारपटिमण्डिता नच्चगीतादीसु सुसिक्खिता देवकञ्ञा विय रूपसोभग्गप्पत्ता इत्थियो नानातूरियानि गहेत्वा सम्परिवारयित्वा अभिरमापेन्तियो नच्चगीतवादि- तानि पयोजविंसु। बोधिसत्तो किलेसेसु विरत्तचित्तताय नच्चादीसु अनभिरतो मुहुत्तं निद्दं ओक्कमि। तापि इत्थियो "यस्सत्थाय मयं नच्चादीनि पयोजेम, सो निद्दं उपगतो, इदानि किमत्थं किलमामा"ति गहितग्गहितानि तूरियानि अज्झोत्थरित्वा निपज्जिंसु, गन्धतेलप्पदीपा झायन्ति। बोधिसत्तो पबुज्झित्वा सयनपिट्ठे पल्लङ्केन निसिन्नो अद्दस ता इत्थियो तूरियभण्डानि अवत्थरित्वा निद्दायन्तियो–एकच्चा पग्घरितखेळा, लालाकिलिन्नगत्ता, एकच्चा दन्ते खादन्तियो, एकच्चा काकच्छन्तियो, एकच्चा विप्पलपन्तियो, एकच्चा विवटमुखा, एकच्चा अपगतवत्था, पाकटबीभच्छसम्बाधट्ठाना। सो तासं तं विप्पकारं दिस्वा भिय्योसोमत्ताय कामेसु विरत्तचित्तो अहोसि। तस्स अलङ्कतपटियत्तं सक्कभवनसदिसम्पि तं महातलं अपविद्धनानाकुणपभरितं आमकसुसानं विय उपट्ठासि, तयो भवा आदित्तगेहसदिसा खायिंसु–"उपद्दुतं वत भो, उपस्सट्ठं वत भो"ति उदानं पवत्तेसि, अतिविय पब्बज्जाय चित्तं नमि।

सो "अज्जेव मया महाभिनिक्खमनं निक्खमितुं वट्टती"ति सयना उट्ठाय द्वारसमीपं गन्त्वा "को एत्था"ति आह। उम्मारे सीसं कत्वा निपन्नो छन्नो "अहं अय्यपुत्त छन्नो"ति आह। "अहं अज्ज महाभिनिक्खमनं निक्खमितुकामो, एकं मे अस्सं कप्पेही"ति आह। सो "साधु देवा"ति अस्सभण्डिकं महेत्वा अस्ससालं गन्त्वा गन्धतेलपदीपेसु जलन्तेसु सुमनपट्टवितानस्स हेट्ठा रमणीये भूमिभागे ठितं कण्डकं अस्सराजानं दिस्वा "अज्ज मया इममेव कप्पेतुं वट्टती"ति कण्डकं कप्पेसि। सो कप्पियमानोव अञ्ञासि "अयं कप्पना अतिगाळ्हा, अञ्ञेसु दिवसेसु

उय्यानकीळादिगमने कप्पना विय न होति, मय्हं अय्यपुत्तो अज्ज महाभिनिक्खमनं निक्खमितुकामो भविस्सती"ति। ततो तुट्ठमानसो महाहसितं हसि। सो सद्दो सकलनगरं पत्थरित्वा गच्छेय्य, देवता पन तं सद्दं निरुम्भित्वा न कस्सचि सोतुं अदंसु।

बोधिसत्तोपि खो छन्नं पेसेत्वाव "पत्तं ताव पस्सिस्सामी"ति चिन्तेत्वा निसिन्नपल्लङ्कतो उट्ठाय राहुलमाताय वसनट्ठानं गन्त्वा गब्भद्वारं विवरि। तस्मिं खणे अन्तोगब्भे गन्धतेलपदीपो झायति, राहुलमाता सुमनमल्लिकादीनं पुप्फानं अम्बणमत्तेन अभिप्पकिण्णसयने पुत्तस्स मत्थके हत्थं ठपेत्वा निद्दायति। बोधिसत्तो उम्मारे पादं ठपेत्वा ठितकोव ओलोकेत्वा "सचाहं देविया हत्थं अपनेत्वा मम पुत्तं गण्हिस्सामि, देवी पबुज्झिस्सति, एवं मे गमनन्तरायो भविस्सति, बुद्धो हुत्वाव आगन्त्वा पुत्तं पस्सिस्सामी"ति पासादतलतो ओतरि। यं पन जातकट्ठकथायं "तदा सत्ताहजातो राहुलकुमारो होती"ति वुत्तं, तं सेसट्ठकथासु नत्थि, तस्मा इदमेव गहेतब्बं।

एवं बाधिसत्तो पासादतला ओतरित्वा अस्ससमीपं गन्त्वा एवमाह–"तात कण्डक, त्वं अज्ज एकरत्तिं मं तारय, अहं तं निस्साय बुद्धो हुत्वा सदेवकं लोकं तारेस्सामी"ति। ततो उल्लङ्घित्वा कण्डकस्स पिट्ठिं अभिरुहि। कण्डको गीवतो पट्ठाय आयामन अट्ठारसहत्थो होति तदनुच्छविकेन उब्बेधेन समन्नागतो थामजवसम्पन्नो सब्बसेतो ध ोतसङ्खसदिसो। सो सचे हसेय्य वा पदसद्दं वा करेय्य, सद्दो सकलनगरं अवत्थरेय्य। तस्मा देवता अत्तनो आनुभावेन तस्स यथा न कोचि सुणाति, एवं हसितसद्दं सन्निरुम्भित्वा अक्कमन- अक्कमनपदवारे हत्थतलानि उपनामेसुं। बोधिसत्तो अस्सवरस्स पिट्ठिवेमज्झगतो छन्नं अस्सस्य वालधिं गाहापेत्वा अड्ढरत्तसमये महाद्वारसमीपं पत्तो। तदा पन राजा "एवं बोधिसत्तो याय कायचि वेलाय नगरद्वारं विवरित्वा निक्खमितुं न सक्खिस्सती"ति द्वीसु द्वारकवाटेसु एकेकं पुरिससहस्सेन विवरितब्बं कारापेसि। बोधिसत्तो थामबलसम्पन्नो, हत्थिगणनाय कोटिसहस्सहत्थीनं बलं धारेति, पुरिसगणनाय दसकोटिसहस्सपुरिसानं।

सो चिन्तेसि "सचे द्वारं न विवरीयति, अज्ज कण्डकस्स पिट्ठे निसिन्नोव वालधिं गहेत्वा ठितेन छन्नेन सद्धियेव कण्डकं ऊरूहि निप्पीळेत्वा अट्ठारसहत्थुब्बेधं पाकारं उप्पतित्वा अतिक्कमिस्सामी"ति। छन्नोपि चिन्तेसि "सचे द्वारं न विवरीयति, अहं अय्यपुत्तं खन्धे निसीदापेत्वा कण्डकं दक्खिणेन हत्थेन कुच्छियं परिक्खिपन्तो उपकच्छन्तरे कत्वा पाकारं उप्पतित्वा अतिक्कमिस्सामी"ति। कण्डकोपि चिन्तेसि "सचे द्वारं न विवरीयति, अहं अत्तनो सामिकं पिट्ठियं यथानिसिन्नमेव छन्नेन वालधिं गहेत्वा ठितेन सद्धियेव उक्खिपित्वा पाकारं उप्पतित्वा अतिक्कमिस्सामी"ति। सचे द्वारं न अवापुरीयित्थ, यथाचिन्तितमेव तेसु तीसु जनेसु अञ्ञतरो सम्पादेय्य। द्वारे अधिवत्था देवता पन द्वारं विवरि।

तस्मियेव खणे मारो "बोधिसत्तं निवत्तेस्सामी"ति आगन्त्वा आकासे ठितो आह—"मारिस, मा निक्खम, इतो ते सत्तमे दिवसे चक्करतनं पातुभविस्सति, द्विसहस्सपरित्तदीपपरिवारानं चतुन्नं महादीपानं रज्जं कारेस्ससि, निवत्त मारिसा"ति। "कोसि त्व"न्ति? "अहं वसवत्ती"ति। "मार, जानामहं मय्हं चक्करतनस्स पातुभावं, अनत्थिकोहं रज्जेन, दससहस्सिलोकधातुं उन्नादेत्वा बुद्धो भविस्सामी"ति आह। मारो "इतो दानि ते पट्ठाय कामवितक्कं वा ब्यापादवितक्कं वा विहिंसावितक्कं वा चिन्तितकाले जानिस्सामी"ति ओतारापेक्खो छाया विय अनपगच्छन्तो अनुबन्धि।

बोधिसत्तोपि हत्थगतं चक्कवत्तिरज्जं खेळपिण्डं विय अनपेक्खो छड्डेत्वा महन्तेन सक्कारेन नगरा निक्खमि आसाळ्हिपुण्णमाय उत्तरासाळ्हनक्खत्ते वत्तमाने। निक्खमित्वा च पुन नगरं ओलोकेतुकामो जातो। एवञ्च पनस्स चित्ते उप्पन्नमत्तेयेव "महापुरिस, न तया निवत्तित्वा ओलोकनकम्मं कत"न्ति वदमाना विय महापथवी कुलालचक्कं विय भिज्जित्वा परिवत्ति। बोधिसत्तो नगराभिमुखो ठत्वा नगरं ओलोकेत्वा तस्मिं पथविप्पदेसे कण्डकनिवत्तनचेतियट्ठानं दस्सेत्वा गन्तब्बमग्गाभिमुखं कण्डकं कत्वा पायासि महन्तेन सक्कारेन उळारेन

सिरिसोभग्गेन। तदा किरस्स देवता पुरतो सट्ठि उक्का- सहस्सानि धारयिंसु, पच्छतो सट्ठि, दक्खिणपस्सतो सट्ठि, वामपस्सतो सट्ठि, अपरा देवता चक्कवाळमुखचट्टियं अपरिभाणा उक्का धारयिंसु, अपरा देवता च नागसुपण्णादयो च दिब्बेहि गन्धेहि मालाहि चुण्णेहि धूमेहि पूजयमाना गच्छन्ति। पारिच्छत्तकपुप्फेहि चेव मन्दारवपुप्फेहि च घनमेघवुट्ठकाले धाराहि विय नभं निरन्तरं अहोसि, दिब्बानि संगीतानि पवत्तिसु, समन्ततो अट्ठसट्ठि तूरियसतसहस्सानि पवज्जिसु, समुद्दकुच्छियं मेघत्थनितकालो विय युगन्धरकुच्छियं सागरनिग्घोसकालो विय वत्तति।

इमिना सिरिंसोभग्गेन गच्छन्तो बोधिसत्तो एकरत्तेनेव तीणि रज्ञानि अतिक्कम्म तिंसयोजनमत्थके अनोमानदीतीरं पापुणि। "किं पन अस्सो ततो परं गन्तुं न सक्कोती"ति? "नो, न सक्को"ति। सो हि एकं चक्कवाळगब्भं नाभिया ठितचक्कस्स नेमिवट्टिं मद्दन्तो विय अन्तन्तेन चरित्वा पुरेपातरासमेव आगन्त्वा अत्तनो सम्पादितं भत्तं भुञ्जितुं समत्थो। तदा पन देवनागसुपण्णादीहि आकासे ठत्वा ओस्सट्ठेहि गन्धमालादीहि याव ऊरुप्पदेसा सञ्छन्नं सरीरं आकड्ढित्वा गन्धमालाजटं छिन्दन्तस्स अतिप्पञ्चो अहोसि, तस्मा तिंसयोजनमत्तमेव अगमासि। अथ बोधिसत्तो नदीतीरे ठत्वा छन्नं पुच्छि–"किन्नामा अयं नदी"ति? "अनोमा नाम, देवा"ति। "अम्हाकम्पि पब्बज्जा अनोमा भविस्सती"ति पण्हिया घट्टेन्तो अस्सस्स सञ्ञं अदासि। अस्सो उप्पतित्वा अट्ठसभवित्थाराय नदिया पारिमतीरे अट्ठासि।

बोधिसत्तो अस्सपिट्ठितो ओरुय्ह रजतपट्टसदिसे वालुकापुलिने ठत्वा छन्नं आमन्तेसि–"सम्म, छन्न, त्वं मय्हं आभरणानि चेव कण्डकञ्च आदाय गच्छ, अहं पब्बजिस्सामी"ति। "अहम्पि, देव, पब्बजिस्सामी"ति। बोधिसत्तो "न लब्भा तया पब्बजितुं, गच्छ त्व"न्ति तिक्खत्तुं पटिबाहित्वा आभरणानि चेव कण्डकञ्च पटिच्छापेत्वा चिन्तेसि "इमे मय्हं केसा समणसारुप्पा न होन्ती"ति। अञ्ञो बोधिसत्तस्स केसे छिन्दितुं युत्तरूपो नत्थि, ततो "सयमेव खग्गेन छिन्दिस्सामी"ति

दक्खिणेन हत्थेन असिं गण्हित्वा वामहत्थेन मोळिया सद्धिं चूळं गहेत्वा छिन्दि, केसा द्वङ्गुलमत्ता हुत्वा दक्खिणतो आवत्तमाना सीसं अल्लीयिंसु। तेसं यावजीवं तदेव पमाणं अहोसि, मस्सु च तदनुरूपं, पुन केसमस्सुओहारणकिच्चं नाम नाहोसि। बोधिसत्तो सह मोळिया चुळं गहेत्वा "सचाहं बुद्धो भविस्सामि, आकासे तिट्ठतु, नो चे, भूमियं पततू"ति अन्तलिक्खे खिपि। तं चूळामणिवेठनं योजनप्पमाणं ठानं गन्त्वा आकासे अट्ठासि। सक्को देवराजा दिब्बचक्खुना ओलोकेत्वा योजनियरतनचङ्कोटकेन सम्पटिच्छित्वा तावतिंसभवने चूळामणिचेतियं नाम पतिट्ठापेसि।

"छेत्वान मोळिं वरगन्धवासितं, वेहायसं उक्खिपि अग्गपुग्गलो।
सहस्सनेत्तो सिरसा पटिग्गहि, सुवण्णचङ्कोटवरेन वासवो" ति॥272॥

पुन बोधिसत्तो चिन्तेसि "इमानि कासिकवत्थानि मय्हं न समणसारुप्पानी"ति। अथस्स कस्सपबुद्धकाले पुराणसहायको घटीकारमहाब्रह्मा एकं बुद्धन्तरं जरं अपत्तेन मित्तभावेन चिन्तेसि–"अज्ज मे सहायको महाभिनिक्खमनं निक्खन्तो, समणपरिक्खारमस्स गहेत्वा गच्छिस्सामी"ति।

"तिचीवरञ्च पत्तो च, वासी सूचि च बन्धनं।
परिस्सावनेन अट्ठेते, युत्तयोगस्स भिक्खुनो"ति॥ 273॥

इमे अट्ठ समणपरिक्खारे आहरित्वा अदासि। बोधिसत्तो अरहद्धजं निवासेत्वा उत्तमपब्बज्जावेसं गण्हित्वा "छन्न, मम वचनेन मातापितूनं आरोग्यं वदेही"ति वत्वा उय्योजेसि। छन्नो बोधिसत्तं वन्दित्वा पदक्खिणं कत्वा पक्कामि। कण्डको पन छन्नेन सद्धिं मन्तयमानस्स बोधिसत्तस्स वचनं सुणन्तो ठत्वा "नत्थि दानि मय्हं पुन सामिनो दस्सन"न्ति चक्खुपथं विजहन्तो सोकं अधिवासेतुं असक्कोन्तो हदयेन फलितेन कालं कत्वा तावतिंसभवने कण्डको नाम देवपुत्तो हुत्वा निब्बति। छन्नस्स पठमं एकोव सोको अहोसि, कण्डकस्स पन कालकिरियाय दुतियेन सोकेन पीळितो रोदन्तो परिदेवन्तो नगरं अगमासि।

Now on a certain day the Future Buddha wished to go to the park, and told his charioteer to make ready the chariot. Accordingly the man brought out a sumptuous and elegant chariot, and adorning it richly, he harnessed to it four state-horses of the Sindhava breed, as white as the petals of the white lotus, and announced to the Future Buddha that everything was ready. And the Future Buddha mounted the chariot, which was like to a palace of the gods, and proceeded towards the park.

"The time for the enlightenment of prince Siddhāttha draweth nigh," thought the gods; "we must show him a sign:" and they changed one of their number into a decrepit old man, broken-toothed, gray-haired, crooked and bent of body, leaning on a staff, and trembling, and showed him to the Future Buddha, but so that only he and the charioteer saw him.

Then said the Future Buddha to the charioteer, in the manner related in the Mahāpadāna, –

"Friend, pray, who is this man? Even his hair is not like that of other men." And when he heard the answer, he said, "Shame on birth, since to every one that is born old age must come." And agitated in heart, he thereupon returned and ascended his palace.

"Why has my son returned so quickly?" asked the king.

"Sire, he has seen an old man," was the reply; "and because he has seen an old. man, he is about to retire from the world."

"Do you want to kill me, that you say such things? Quickly get ready some plays to be performed before my son. If we can but get him to enjoying pleasure, he will cease to think of retiring from the world." Then the king extended, the guard to half a league in each direction.

Again, on a certain day, as the Future Buddha was going to the park, he saw a diseased man whom the gods had fashioned; and having again made inquiry, he returned, agitated in heart, and ascended his palace.

And the king made the same inquiry and gave the same orders as before; and again extending the guard, placed them for three quarters of a league around.

And again on a certain day, as the Future Buddha was going to the park, he saw a dead man whom the gods had fashioned; and having again made inquiry, he returned, agitated in heart, and ascended his palace.

And the king made the same inquiry and gave the same orders as before; and again extending the guard, placed them for a league around.

And again on a certain day, as the Future Buddha was going to the park, he saw a monk, carefully and decently clad, whom the gods had fashioned; and he asked his charioteer, "Pray, who is this man?"

Now although there was no Buddha in the world, and the charioteer had no knowledge of either monks or their good qualities, yet by the power of the gods he was inspired to say, "Sire, this is one who has retired from the world;" and he thereupon proceeded to sound the praises of retirement from the world. The thought of retiring from the world was a pleasing one to the Future Buddha, and this day he went on until he came to the park. The repeaters of the Dīgha, however, say that he went to the park after having seen all the Four Signs on one and the same day.

When he had disported himself there throughout the day, and had bathed in the royal pleasure-tank, he went at sunset and sat down on the royal resting-stone with the intention of adorning himself. Then gathered around him his attendants 'with diverse-colored cloths, many kinds and styles of ornaments, and with garlands, perfumes, and ointments. At that instant the throne on which Sakka was sitting grew hot. And Sakka, considering who it could be that was desirous of dislodging him, perceived that it was the time of the adornment of a Future Buddha. And addressing Vissakamma, he said:

"My good Vissakamma, tonight, in the middle watch, prince Siddhāttha will go forth on the Great Retirement, and this is his last adorning of himself. Go to the park, and adorn that eminent man with celestial ornaments."

"Very well," said Vissakamma, in assent; and came on the instant, by his superhuman power, into the presence of the Future Buddha. And assuming the guise of a barber, he took from the real barber the turban-cloth, and began to wind it round the Future Buddha's head; but as soon as the Future Buddha felt the touch of his hand, he knew that it was no man, but a god.

Now once round his head took up a thousand cloths, and the fold was like to a circlet of precious stones; the second time round took another thousand cloths, and so on, until ten times round had taken up ten thousand cloths. Now let no one think, "How was it possible to use so many cloths on one small head?" for the very largest of them all had only the size of a sāma-creeper blossom, and the others that of kutumbaka flowers. Thus the Future Buddha's head resembled a kuyaka blossom twisted about with lotus filaments.

And having adorned himself with great richness,– while adepts in different kinds of tabors and tom-toms were showing their skill, and Brāhmaṇas with cries of victory and joy, and bards and poets with propitious words and shouts of praise saluted him,– he mounted his superbly decorated chariot.

At this juncture, Śuddhodana the king, having heard that the mother of Rāhula had brought forth a son, sent a messenger, saying, "Announce the glad news to my son."

On hearing the message, the Future Buddha said, "An impediment [Rāhula] has been born; a fetter has been born."

"What did my son say?" questioned the king; and when he had heard the answer, he said, "My grandson's name shall be prince Rāhula from this very day."

But the Future Buddha in his splendid chariot entered the

city with a pomp and magnificence of glory that enraptured all minds. At the same moment Kisā Gotamī, a virgin of the warrior caste, ascended to the roof of her palace, and beheld the beauty and majesty of the Future Buddha, as he circumambulated the city; and in her pleasure and satisfaction at the sight, she burst forth into this song of joy:

> 271. "Full happy now that mother is,
> Full happy now that father is,
> Full happy now that woman is,
> Who owns this lord so glorious!"

On hearing this, the Future Buddha thought, "In beholding a handsome figure the heart of a mother attains Nirvāṇa, the heart of a father attains Nirvāṇa, the heart of a wife attains Nirvāṇa. This is what she says. But wherein does Nirvāṇa consist?"And to him, whose mind was already averse to passion, the answer came: "When the fire of lust is extinct, that is Nirvāṇa; when the fires of hatred and infatuation are extinct, that is Nirvāṇa; when pride, false belief, and all other passions and torments are extinct, that is Nirvāṇa. She has taught me a good lesson. Certainly, Nirvāṇa is what I am looking for. It behooves me this very day to quit the household life, and to retire from the world in quest of Nirvāṇa.[30] I will send this lady a teacher's fee." And loosening from his neck a pearl necklace worth a hundred thousand pieces of money, he sent it to Kisā Gotamī. And great was her satisfaction at this, for she thought, "Prince Siddhāttha has fallen in love with me, and has sent me a present."

And the Future Buddha entered his palace in great splendor, and lay on his couch of state. And straightway richly dressed women, skilled in all manner of dance and song, and beautiful as celestial nymphs, gathered about him with all kinds of musical instruments, and with dance, song, and music they endeavored to please him. But the Future Buddha's aversion to passion did not allow him to take pleasure in the spectacle, and he fell into a brief slumber. And the women, exclaiming, "He for whose sake we should perform has fallen asleep. Of what use is it to weary ourselves any longer?"threw their various instruments on the ground, and lay down. And the lamps fed with sweet-smelling oil continued to burn. And the Future Buddha awoke, and seating himself cross-legged on his couch, perceived these women lying asleep, with their musical instruments scattered about them on the floor, – some with their bodies wet with trickling phlegm and spittle; some grinding their teeth, and muttering and talking in their sleep; some with their mouths open; and some with their dress fallen apart so as plainly to disclose their loathsome nakedness. This great alteration in their appearance still further increased his aversion for sensual pleasures. To him that magnificent apartment, as splendid as the palace of Sakka, began to seem like a cemetery filled with dead bodies impaled and left to rot; and the three modes of existence appeared like houses all ablaze. And breathing forth the solemn utterance, "How oppressive and stifling is it all!" his mind turned ardently to retiring from the world. "It hehooves me to go forth on the Great Retirement this very day," said he; and he arose from his couch, and coming near the door, called out, – "Who is there?"

"Master, it is I, Channa," replied the courtier who had been sleeping with his head on the threshold.[31]

"I wish to go forth on the Great Retirement today. Saddle a horse for me."

"Yes, sire." And taking saddle and bridle with him, the courtier started for the stable. There, by the light of lamps fed with sweet-smelling oils, he perceived the mighty steed Kanthaka in his pleasant quarters, under a canopy of cloth beautified with a pattern of jasmine flowers. "This is the one for me to saddle today," thought he; and he saddled Kanthaka.

"He is drawing the girth very tight," thought Kanthaka, whilst he was being saddled; "it is not at all as on other days, when I am saddled for rides in the park and the like. It must be that today my master wishes to issue forth on the Great Retirement." And in his delight he neighed a loud neigh. And that neigh would have spread through the whole town, had not the gods stopped the sound, and suffered no one to hear it.

Now the Future Buddha, after he had sent Channa on his errand, thought to himself, "I will take just one look at my son;" and, rising from the couch on which he was sitting, he went to the suite of apartments occupied by the mother of Rāhula, and opened the door of her chamber. Within the chamber was burning a lamp fed with sweet-smelling oil, and the mother of Rāhula lay sleeping on a couch strewn deep with jasmine and other flowers, her hand resting on the head of her son. When the Future Buddha reached the threshold, he paused, and gazed at the two from where he stood.

"If I were to raise my wife's hand from off the child's head, and take him up, she would awake, and thus prevent my departure. I will first become a Buddha, and then come back and see my son." So saying, he descended from the palace.

Now that which is said in the Jātaka Commentary, "At that time Rāhula was seven days old," is not found in the other commentaries. Therefore, the account above given is to be accepted. When the Future Buddha had thus descended from the palace, he came near to his horse, and said:

"My dear Kanthaka, save me now this one night; and then, when thanks to you I have become a Buddha, I will save the world of gods and men." And thereupon he vaulted upon Kanthaka's back.

Now Kanthaka was eighteen cubits long from his neck to his tail, and of corresponding height; he was strong and swift, and white all over like a polished conch-shell. If he neighed or stamped, the sound was so loud as to spread through the whole city; therefore the gods exerted their power, and muffled the sound of his neighing, so that no one heard it; and at every step he took they placed the palms of their hands under his feet.

The Future Buddha rode on the mighty back of the mighty

steed, made Channa hold on by the tail, and so arrived at midnight at the great gate of the city.

Now the king, in order that the Future Buddha should not at any time go out of the city without his knowledge, had caused each of the two leaves of the gate to be made so heavy as to need a thousand men to move it. But the Future Buddha had a vigor and a strength that was equal, when reckoned in elephant—power, to the strength of ten thousand million elephants, and reckoned in man-power, to the strength of a hundred thousand million men.

"If," thought he, "the gate does not open, I will straightway grip tight hold of Kanthaka with my thighs, and, seated as I am on Kanthaka's back, and with Channa holding on by the tail, I will leap up and carry them both with me over the wall, although its height be eighteen cubits."

"If," thought Channa, "the gate is not opened, I will place my master on my shoulder, and tucking Kanthaka under my arm by passing my right hand round him and under his belly, I will leap up and carry them both with me over the wall."

"If," thought Kanthaka, "the gate is not opened, with my master seated as he is on my back, and with Channa holding on by my tail, I will leap up and carry them both with me over the wall."

Now if the gate had not opened, verily one or another of these three persons would have accomplished that whereof he thought; but the divinity that inhabited the gate opened it for them.

At this moment came Māra,[32] with the intention of persuading the Future Buddha to turn back; and standing in the air he said,—

"Sir, go not forth! For on the seventh day from now the wheel of empire will appear to you, and you shall rule over the four great continents and their two thousand attendant isles. Sir, turn back!"

"Who are you?"

"I am Vasavatti."

"Māra, I knew that the wheel of empire was on the point of appearing to me; but I do not wish for sovereignty. I am about to cause the ten thousand worlds to thunder with my becoming a Buddha."

"I shall catch you," thought Māra, "the very first time you have a lustful, malicious, or unkind thought." And, like an ever-present shadow, he followed after, ever on the watch for some slip.

Thus the Future Buddha, casting away with indifference a universal sovereignty already in his grasp,—spewing it out as if it were but phlegm departed from the city in great splendor on the full-moon day of the month Āsālhi,[33] when the moon was in Libra. And when he had gone out from the city, he became desirous of looking back at it; but no sooner had the thought arisen in his mind, than the broad earth, seeming to fear lest the Great Being might neglect to perform the act of looking back, split and turned round like a potter's wheel.[34] When the Future Buddha had stood a while facing the city and gazing upon it, and had indicated in that place the spot for the "Shrine of the Turning Back of Kanthaka," he turned Kanthaka in the direction in which he meant to go, and proceeded on his way in great honor and exceeding glory.

For they say the deities bore sixty thousand torches in front of him, and sixty thousand behind him, and sixty thousand on the right hand, and sixty thousand on the left hand. Other deities, standing on the rim of the world, bore torches past all numbering; and still other deities, as well as serpents and birds, accompanied him, and did him homage with heavenly perfumes, garlands, sandal-wood powder, and incense. And the sky was as full of coral flowers as it is of pouring water at the height of the rainy season. Celestial choruses were heard; and on every side bands of music played, some of eight instruments, and some of sixty, sixty-eight hundred thousand instruments in all. It was as when the storm-clouds thunder on the sea, or when the ocean roars against the Yugandhara rocks.

Advancing in this glory, the Future Buddha in one night passed through three kingdoms, and at the end of thirty leagues he came to the river named Anomā.

But was this as far as the horse could go? Certainly not. For he was able to travel round the world from end to end, as it were round the rim of a wheel lying on its hub, and yet get back before breakfast and eat the food prepared for him. But on this occasion the fragrant garlands and other offerings which the gods and the serpents and the birds threw down upon him from the sky buried him up to his haunches; and as he was obliged to drag his body and cut his way through the tangled mass, he was greatly delayed. Hence it was that he went only thirty leagues.

And the Future Buddha, stopping on the river-bank, said to Channa,—

"What is the name of this river?"

"Sire, its name is Anomā [Illustrious]."

"And my retirement from the world shall also be called Anomā," replied the Future Buddha. Saying this, he gave the signal to his horse with his heel; and the horse sprang over the river, which had a breadth of eight usabhas,[35] and landed on the opposite bank. And the Future Buddha, dismounting and standing on the sandy beach that stretched away like a sheet of silver, said to Channa,

"My good Channa, take these ornaments and Kanthaka and go home. I am about to retire from the world."

"Sire, I also will retire from the world."

Three times the Future Buddha refused him, saying, "It is not for you to retire from the world. Go now!" and made him take the ornaments and Kanthaka.

Next he thought, "These locks of mine are not suited to a monk; but there is no one fit to cut the hair of a Future Buddha.

Therefore I will cut them off myself with my sword." And grasping a simitar with his right hand, he seized his top-knot with his left hand, and cut it off, together with the diadem. His hair thus became two finger-breadths in length, and curling to the right, lay close to his head. As long as he lived it remained of that length, and the beard was proportionate. And never again did he have to cut either hair or beard.

Then the Future Buddha seized hold of his top-knot and diadem, and threw them into the air, saying, –

"If I am to become a Buddha, let them stay in the sky; but if not, let them fall to the ground."

The top-knot and jewelled turban mounted for a distance of a league into the air, and there came to a stop. And Sakka, the king of the gods, perceiving them with his divine eye, received them in an appropriate jewelled casket, and established it in the Heaven of the Thirty-three as the "Shrine of the Diadem."

272. "His hair he cut, so sweet with many pleasant scents,
This Chief of Men, and high impelled it towards the sky;
And there god Vāsava, the god with thousand eyes,
In golden casket caught it, bowing low his head."

Again the Future Buddha thought, "These garments of mine, made of Benares cloth, are not suited to a monk."

Now the Mahā-Brahma god Ghaṭīkāra, who had been a friend of his in the time of the Buddha Kassapa, and whose affection for him had not grown old in the long interval since that Buddha, thought to himself, –

"To-day my friend has gone forth on the Great Retirement. I will bring him the requisites of a monk."

273. "Robes, three in all, the bowl for alms,
The razor, needle, and the belt,
And water-strainer, – just these eight
Are needed by th' ecstatic monk."

Taking the above eight requisites of a monk, he gave them to him.

When the Future Buddha had put on this most excellent vesture, the symbol of saintship and of retirement from the world, he dismissed Channa, saying–

"Channa, go tell my father and my mother from me that I am well."

And Channa did obeisance to the Future Buddha; and keeping his right side towards him, he departed.

But Kanthaka, who had stood listening to the Future Buddha while he was conferring with Channa, was unable to bear his grief at the thought, "I shall never see my master any more." And as he passed out of sight, his heart burst, and he died, and was reborn in the Heaven of the Thirty-three as the god Kanthaka.

At first the grief of Channa had been but single; but now he was oppressed with a second sorrow in the death of Kanthaka, and came weeping and wailing to the city.

NOTES AND REFERENCES

30. The Future Buddha puns upon the word "happy" in Kisā Gotamī's verses. The word in Pāli is *nibbuta,* and is in form a past passive participle of a verb which perhaps does not occur in Pāli in any finite form, but which appears in Sanskrit as *nirvṛ*. Now there is a Pāli verb of which the third person singular present indicative is *nibbāyati,* and from this verb is formed the verbal noun *nibbāna* (Sanskrit, *Nirvāṇa). Nibbuta* is constantly made to do duty as past passive participle to this verb, so that what would be the true form *(nibbāta)* is never found. The Future Buddha therefore puns when he pretends that Kisā Gotamī was using *nibbuta* as the participle of *nibbāyati,* and was urging him to Nirvāṇa.

    The verb *nibbāyati* means "to be extinguished," as the flame of a candle; and, when used as a metaphysical term, refers to the fires of lust, desire, etc. And as when fire is extinguished coolness results (a consummation devoutly to be wished in a hot climate like India), the verb acquires the further meaning of "be assuaged," "become happy." And in like manner the verbal noun Nirvāṇa (in Pāli *nibbāna),* meaning both literally and metaphorically "becoming extinguished," comes to stand for the *summum bonum.* I add a retranslation of the passage, to show the punning meanings given by the Future Buddha to the words, *nibbuta, nibbāyati,* and Nirvāṇa:

> "Nirvāṇa hath that mother gained,
> Nirvāṇa hath that father gained,
> 'Nirvāṇa hath that woman gained,
> Who owns this lord so glorious!"

On hearing this, the Future Buddha thought, "In beholding a handsome form the heart of a mother is made happy *(nibbāyati),* the heart of a father is made happy, the heart of a wife is made happy. This is what she says. But wherein does happiness *(nibbuta)* consist?"And to him whose mind was already averse to passion, the answer came: "When the fire of lust is assuaged *(nibbuta),* that is happiness *(nibbuta)*; when the fires of hatred and infatuation are assuaged, that is happiness; when pride, false belief, and all other passions and torments are assuaged, that is happiness. She has taught me a good lesson. Certainly, happiness (Nirvāṇa) is what I am looking for. It behooves me this very day to quit the household life and to retire from the world in quest of happiness. I will send this lady a teacher's fee."

31. In India it is customary to hang doors at the height of about two feet from the ground for the sake of coolness and ventilation. The threshold is thus exposed even when the door is shut.
32. The Buddhists recognize no real devil. Māra, the ruler of the sixth and highest heaven of sensual pleasure, approaches the nearest to our Satan. He stands for the pleasures of sense, and hence is The Buddha's natural enemy.
33. About the first of July.
34. I think the conception here is that a round portion of the earth, on which the Future Buddha stood, turned around like a modern rail road turn-table, thus detaching itself from the rest and turning the Future Buddha with it.
35. An *usabha* is 140 cubits.

Chapter VII

THE GREAT STRUGGLE

Translated from the Introduction to the Jātaka (i.65[29]).

खुद्दक निकाये जातक अट्ठकथा

बोधिसत्तोपि पब्बजित्वा तस्मियेव पदेसे अनुपियं नाम अम्बवनं अत्थि, तत्थ सत्ताहं पब्बज्जासुखेन वीतिनामेत्वा एकदिवसेनेव तिंसयोजनमग्गं पदसा गन्त्वा राजगहं पाविसि। पविसित्वा सपदानं पिण्डाय चरि। सकलनगरं बोधिसत्तस्स रूपदस्सनेन धनपालकेन पविट्ठराजगहं विय असुरिन्देन पविट्ठदेवनगरं विय च सङ्खोभं अगमासि। राजपुरिसा गन्त्वा "देव, एवरूपो नाम सत्तो नगरे पिण्डाय चरति, 'देवो वा मनुस्सो वा नागो वा सुपण्णो वा को नामेसो'ति न जानामा"ति आरोचेसुं। राजा पासादतले ठत्वा महापुरिसं दिस्वा अच्छरियब्भुतजातो पुरिसे आणापेसि–"गच्छथ भणे, वीमंसथ, सचे अमनुस्सो भविस्सति, नगरा निक्खमित्वा अन्तरधायिस्सति, सचे देवता भविस्सति, आकासेन गच्छिस्सति, सचे नागो भविस्सति, पथवियं निमुज्जित्वा गमिस्सति, सचे मनुस्सो भविस्सति, यथालद्धं भिक्खं परिभुञ्जिस्सती"ति।

महापुरिसोपि खो मिस्सकभत्तं संहरित्वा "अलं मे एत्तकं यापनाया"ति ञत्वा पविट्ठद्वारेनेव नगरा निक्खमित्वा पण्डव-पब्बतच्छायाय पुरत्थाभिमुखो निसीदित्वा आहारं परिभुञ्जितुं आरद्धो। अथस्स अन्तानि परिवत्तित्वा मुखेन निक्खमनाकारप्पत्तानि विय अहेसुं।

ततो तेन अत्तभावेन एवरूपस्स आहारस्स चक्खुनापि अदिट्ठपुब्बताय तेन पटिकूलाहारेन अट्टियमानो एवं अत्तनाव अत्तानं ओवदि "सिद्धत्थ, त्वं सुलभन्नपाने कुले तिवस्सिकगन्धसालिभोजनं नानग्गरसेहि भुञ्जनट्ठाने निब्बत्तित्वापि एकं पंसुकूलिकं दिस्वा कदा नु खो अहम्पि एवरूपो हुत्वा पिण्डाय चरित्वा भुञ्जिस्सामि, भविस्सति नु खो मे सो कालो'ति चिन्तेत्वा निक्खन्तो, इदानि किं नामेतं करोसी"ति। एवं अत्तनाव अत्तानं ओवदित्वा निब्बिकारो हुत्वा आहारं परिभुञ्जि।

राजपुरिसा तं पवत्तिं दिस्वा गन्त्वा रञ्ञो आरोचेसुं। राजा दूतवचनं सुत्वा वेगेन नगरा निक्खमित्वा बोधिसत्तस्स सन्तिकं गन्त्वा इरियापथस्मिंयेव पसीदित्वा बोधिसत्तस्स सब्बं इस्सरियं निय्यादेसि। बोधिसत्तो "मय्हं, महाराज, वत्थुकामेहि वा किलेसकामेहि वा अत्थो नत्थि, अहं परमाभिसम्बोधिं पत्थयन्तो निक्खन्तो"ति आह। राजा अनेकप्पकारं याचन्तोपि तस्स चित्तं अलभित्वा "अद्धा त्वं बुद्धो भविस्ससि, बुद्धभूतेन पन ते पठमं मम विजितं आगन्तब्ब"न्ति पटिञ्ञं गण्हिटि अयमेत्थ सङ्खेपो, विचारो पन "पब्बज्जं कित्तयि" स्समि, यथा पब्बजी चक्खुमा"ति इमं पब्बज्जासुत्तं (सुत्तनिपात, 407 आदयो) सद्धिं अट्ठकथाय ओकोकेत्वा वेदितब्बो।

बोधिसत्तोपि रञ्ञो पटिञ्ञं दत्वा अनुपुब्बेन चारिकं चरमानो आळारञ्च कालामं उदकञ्च रामपुत्तं उपसङ्कमित्वा समापत्तियों निब्बत्तेत्वा "नायं मग्गो बधाया"ति तम्पि समापत्तिभावनं अनलङ्करित्वा सदेवकस्स लोकस्स अत्तनो थामवीरियसन्दस्सनत्थं महापधानं पदहितुकामो उरुवेलं गन्त्वा "रमणीयो वनायं भूमिभागो"ति तत्थेव वासं उपगन्त्वा महापधानं पदहि। तेपि खो कोण्डञ्ञप्पमुखा पञ्च पब्बजिता गामनिगमराजधानीसु भिक्खाय चरन्ता तत्थ बोधिसत्तं सम्पापुणिंसु। अथ नं छब्बस्सानि महापधानं पदहन्तं "इदानि बुद्धो भविस्सति, इदानि बुद्धो भविस्सती"ति परिवेणसम्मज्जनादिकाय वत्तपटिपत्तिया उपट्ठहमाना सन्तिकावचरावस्स अहेसुं। बोधिसत्तोपि खो "कोटिप्पत्तं दुक्करकारियं करिस्सामी"ति

एकतिलतण्डुलादीहिपि वीतिनामेसि, सब्बसोपि आहारूपच्छेदं अकासि, देवतापि लोमकूपेहि ओजं उपसंहरमाना पटिक्खिपि।

अथस्स ताय निराहारताय परमकसिमानप्पत्तकायस्स सुवण्णवण्णो कायो काळवण्णो अहोसि। बात्तिंसमहापुरिसलक्खणानि पटिच्छन्नानि अहेसुं। अप्पेकदा अप्पाणकं झानं झायन्तो महावेदनाहि अभितुन्नो विसञ्ञीभूतो चङ्कमनकोटियं पतति। अथ नं एकच्चा देवता "कालकतो समणो गोतमो"ति वदन्ति, एकच्चा "विहारोवेसो अरहत"न्ति आहंसु। तत्थ यासं "कालकतो"ति अहोसि, ता गन्त्वा सुद्धोदनमहाराजस्स आरोचेसुं "तुम्हाकं पुत्तो कालकतो"ति। मम पुत्तो बुद्धो हुत्वा कालकतो, अहुत्वाति? बुद्धो भवितुं नासक्खि, पधानभूमियंयेव पतित्वा कालकतोति। इदं सुत्वा राजा "नाहं सद्दहामि, मम पुत्तस्स बोधिं अप्पत्वा कालकिरिया नाम नत्थी"ति पटिक्खिपि। कस्मा पन राजा न सद्दहतीति? काळदेवीलतापसस्स वन्दापनदिवसे जम्बुरुक्खमूले च पाटिहारियानं दिट्ठत्ता।

पुन बोधिसत्ते सञ्ञं पटिलभित्वा उट्ठिते ता देवता गन्त्वा "अरोगो ते महाराज पुत्तो"ति आरोचेन्ति। राजा "जानामहं पुत्तस्स अमरणभाव"न्ति वदति। महासत्तस्स छब्बस्सानि दुक्करकारियं करोन्तस्स आकासे गण्ठिकरणकालो विय अहोसि। सो "अयं दुक्करकारिका नाम बोधाय मग्गो न होती"ति ओळारिकं आहारं आहारेतुं गामनिगमेसु पिण्डाय चरित्वा आहारं आहरि, अथस्स बात्तिंसमहापुरिसलक्खणानि पाकतिकानि अहेसुं, कायो सुवण्णवण्णो अहोसि। पञ्चवग्गिया भिक्खू "अयं छब्बस्सानि दुक्करकारिकं करोन्तोपि सब्बञ्ञुतं पटिविज्झितुं नासक्खि, इदानि गामादीसु पिण्डाय चरित्वा ओळारिकं आहारं आहरियमानो किं सक्खिस्सति, बहुलिको एस पधानविब्भन्तो, सीसं न्हायितुकामस्स उस्सावबिन्दुतक्कनं विय अम्हाकं एतस्स सन्तिका विसेसतक्कनं, किं नो इमिना"ति महापुरिसं पहाय अत्तनो अत्तनो पत्तचीवरं गहेत्वा अट्ठारसयोजनमग्गं गन्त्वा इसिपतनं पविसिंसु।

Now the Future Buddha, having thus retired from the

world, in that place there was a mango-grove named Anu-piya, and here he first spent a week in the joy of having retired from the world, – in one day went on foot to Rājagaha, a distance of thirty leagues, and entering the city, he begged for food from house to house without passing any by. By the beauty of the Future Buddha, the whole city was thrown into a commotion, like that into which Rājagaha was thrown by the entrance of Dhanapālaka, or like that into which the heavenly city was thrown by the entrance of the chief of the Titans.

Then ran the king's men to the palace, and made announcement, –

"Sire, there is a being of such and such appearance going about the city begging for food. Whether he be a god, or a man, or a serpent, or a bird, we do not know."

Then the king, standing on the roof of his palace, and thence beholding the Great Being, became amazed and astonished, and commanded his men,

"Look ye now! Go and investigate this ! If this person be not a man, he will vanish from sight as soon as he leaves the city; if, namely, he be a god, he will depart by way of the air; if a serpent, he will sink into the ground. But if he be a human being, he will eat the food he has obtained in alms."

Now the Great Being, after collecting a number of scraps, sufficient, as he judged, for his sustenance, left the city by the same gate he had entered, and sitting down with his face to the east, in the shade of Paṇḍava rock, he attempted to eat his meal. But his stomach turned, and he felt as if his inwards were on the point of coming out by his mouth. Thereupon, in the midst of his distress at that repulsive food, – for in that existence he had never before so much as seen such fare, – he began to admonish himself, saying, "Siddhāttha, although you were born into a family having plenty to eat and drink, into a station in life where you lived on fragrant third season's rice[36] with various sauces of the finest flavors, yet when you saw a monk clad in garments taken from the rubbish heap, you exclaimed, 'Oh, when shall I be like him, and eat food which I have begged?

Will that time ever come? 'And then you retired from the world. And now that you have your wish, and have renounced all, what, pray, is this you are doing?" When he had thus admonished himself, his disgust subsided, and he ate his meal.

Then the king's men went and announced to the king what they had seen. And the king, on hearing the report of the messengers, issued hastily from the city, and approaching the Future Buddha, and being pleased with his deportment, he tendered him all his kingly glory.

"Great king," replied the Future Buddha, "I do not seek for the gratification of my senses or my passions, but have retired from the world for the sake of the supreme and absolute enlightenment."

"Verily," said the king, when his repeated offers had all been refused, "you are sure to become a Buddha; but when that happens, your first journey must be to my kingdom."

The above is an abridgment, but the full account, beginning with the lines, –

> "I sing the man of insight keen,
> And his retirement from the world,"

can be found by referring to the "Discourse on Retirement from the World," and its commentary.

Then the Future Buddha, having made the king the required promise, proceeded on his way; and coming to Āḷāra Kālāma and Uddaka, the disciple of Rāma, he acquired from them the eight stages of meditation. But becoming convinced that they did not lead to enlightenment, he ceased to practise them. And being desirous of making the Great Struggle, so as to show the world of gods and men his fortitude and heroism, he went to Uruvelā, and saying, "Truly, delightful is this spot," he there took up his abode, and began the Great Struggle.

And those five persons, Kondañña and the others, who since their retirement from the world, were wandering about for alms through villages, market-towns, and royal cities, here met with the Future Buddha. And during the six years of the Great Struggle, they swept his cell, and did all manner of service for him, and kept constantly at his beck and call, all the time saying, "Now he will become a Buddha, now he will become a Buddha."

And the Future Buddha, thinking, "I will carry austerity to the uttermost," tried various plans, such as living on one sesamum seed or on one grain of rice a day, and even ceased taking nourishment altogether, and moreover rebuffed the gods when they came and attempted to infuse nourishment through the pores of his skin. By this lack of nourishment his body became emaciated to the last degree, and lost its golden color, and became black, and his thirty-two physical characteristics as a great being became obscured. Now, one day, as he was deep in a trance of suppressed breathing, he was attacked by violent pains, and fell senseless to the ground, at one end of his walking-place.

And certain of the deities said, "The monk Gotama is dead;" but others said, "This is a practice of the saints." Then those who thought he was dead went to king Śuddhodana, and announced to him that his son was dead.

"Did he die after becoming a Buddha, or before?"asked the king.

"He was unable to become a Buddha, but in making the Struggle, he fell to the ground and died."

When the king heard this, he refused to credit it, saying, "I do not believe it. Death cannot come to my son before he attains to enlightenment."

But why would not the king believe it? Because of the miracles he had seen—the first when the ascetic Kāladevala had been compelled to do homage to the Future Buddha, and the other which happened to the rose-apple tree.

But the Future Buddha recovering his consciousness, and standing up, the deities went a second time to the king, and told him that his son was well again.

Said the king, "I knew that my son could not have died."

Now the six years which the Great Being thus spent in austerities were like time spent in endeavoring to tie the air into knots. And coming to the decision, "These austerities are not the way to enlightenment," he went begging through villages and market-towns for ordinary material food, and lived upon it. And his thirty-two physical characteristics as a great being again appeared, and the color of his body became like unto gold.

Then the band of five priests thought, "It is now six years that this man has been performing austerities without being able to attain to omniscience. And how much less can he be expected to do so in future, now that he has again taken to ordinary material food begged from town to town ! He has become luxurious, and given up the Struggle. For us to look for any benefit to come from that quarter would be as reasonable as if a man were to imagine he could bathe his head in a dew-drop. We will have nothing more to do with him." With that they took their bowls and robes, and left the Great Being, and going eighteen leagues off, entered Isipatana.

NOTE AND REFERENCE

36. A garment new, a new-built house, a new umbrella, and a bride.
    The new is good; but long-kept rice and long-kept servants men
    do praise.
    From the Sanskrit of the Nītipradīpa, 15, as given by Böhtlingk, Indische Sprüche, 3410.

Chapter VIII

THE ATTAINMENT OF BUDDHASHIP

Translated from the Introduction to the Jātaka (i.68[5]).

खुद्दक निकाये जातक अट्ठकथा

तेन खो पन समयेन उरुवेलायं सेनानिगमे सेनानिकुटुम्बिकस्स गेहे निब्बत्ता सुजाता नाम दारिका वयप्पत्ता एकस्मिं निग्रोधरुक्खे पत्थनं अकासि "सचे समजातिकं कुलघरं गन्त्वा पठमगब्भे पुत्तं लभिस्सामि, अनुसंवच्छरं ते सतसहस्सपरिच्चागेन बलिकम्मं करिस्सामी"ति। तस्सा सा पत्थना समिज्झि। सा महासत्तस्स दुक्करकारिकं करोन्तस्स छट्ठे वस्से परिपुण्णे विसाखपुण्णमायं बलिकम्मं कातुकामा हुत्वा पुरेतरं धेनुसहस्सं लट्ठिमधुकवने चरापेत्वा तासं खीरं पञ्च धेनुसतानि पायेत्वा तासं खीरं अड्ढतियानीति एवं याव सोळसन्नं धेनूनं खीरं अट्ठ धेनुयो पिवन्ति, ताव खीरस्स बहलतञ्च मधुरतञ्च ओजवन्ततञ्च पत्थयमाना खीरपरिवत्तनं नाम अकासि। सा विसाखपुण्णमदिवसे "पातोव बलिकम्मं करिस्सामी"ति रत्तिया पच्चूससमयं पच्चुट्ठाय ता अट्ठ धेनुयो दुहापेसि। वच्छका धेनूनं थनमूलं नागमिंसु, थनमूले पन नवभाजने उपनीतमत्ते अत्तनो धम्मताय

खीरधारा पवत्तिसु। तं अच्छरियं दिस्वा सुजाता सहत्थेनेव खीरं गहेत्वा नवभाजने पक्खिपित्वा सहत्थेनेव अग्गिं कत्वा पचितुं आरभि।

तस्मिं पायासे पच्चमाने महन्तमहन्ता बुब्बुळा उट्ठहित्वा दक्खिणावत्ता हुत्वा सञ्चरन्ति, एकफुसितम्पि बहि न पतति, उद्धनतो अप्पमत्तकोपि धूमो न उट्ठहति। तस्मिं समये चत्तारो लोकपाला आगन्त्वा उद्धने आरक्खं गण्हिंसु, महाब्रह्मा छत्तं धारेसि, सक्को अलातानि समानेन्तो अग्गिं जालेसि। देवता द्विसहस्सदीपपरिवारेसु चतूसु महादीपेसु देवानञ्च मनुस्सानञ्च उपकप्पनओजं अत्तनो देवानुभावेन दण्डकबद्धं मधुपटलं पीळेत्वा मधुं गण्हमाना विय संहरित्वा तत्थ पक्खिपिंसु। अञ्ञेसु हि कालेसु देवता कबळे कबळे ओजं पक्खिपन्ति, सम्बोधिदिवसे च पन परिनिब्बानदिवसे च उक्खलियंयेव पक्खिपन्ति। सुजाता एकदिवसेयेव तत्थ अत्तनो पाकटानि अनेकानि अच्छरियानि दिस्वा पुण्णं दासिं आमन्तेसि "अम्म पुण्णे, अज्ज अम्हाकं देवता अतिविय पसन्ना, मया एत्तके काले एवरूपं अच्छरियं नाम न दिट्ठपुब्बं, वेगेन गन्त्वा देवट्ठानं पटिजग्गाही"ति। सा "साधु, अय्ये"ति तस्सा वचनं सम्पटिच्छित्वा तुरिततुरिता रुक्खमूलं अगमासि।

बोधिसत्तोपि खो तस्मिं रत्तिभागे पञ्च महासुपिने दिस्वा परिग्गण्हन्तो "निस्संसयेनाहं अज्ज बुद्धो भविस्सामी"ति कतसन्निट्ठानो तस्सा रत्तिया अच्चयेन कतसरीरपटिजग्गनो भिक्खाचारकालं आगमयमानो पातोव आगन्त्वा तस्मिं रुक्खमूले निसीदि अत्तनो पभाय सकलरुक्खं ओभासयमानो। अथ खो सा पुण्णा आगन्त्वा अद्दस बोधिसत्तं रुक्खमूले पाचीनलोकधातुं ओलोकयमानं निसिन्नं, सरीरतो चरस निक्खन्ताहि पभाहि सकलरुक्खं सुवण्णवण्णं। दिस्वा तस्सा एतदहोसि–"अज्ज अम्हाकं देवता रुक्खतो ओरुय्ह सहत्थेनेव बलिकम्मं सम्पटिच्छितुं निसिन्ना मञ्ञे"ति उब्बेगप्पत्ता हुत्वा वेगेनागन्त्वा सुजाताय एतमत्थं आरोचेसि।

सुजाता तस्सा वचनं सुत्वा तुट्ठमानसा हुत्वा "अज्ज दानि

पट्ठाय मम जेट्ठधीतुट्ठाने तिट्ठाही"ति धीतु अनुच्छविकं सब्बालङ्कारं अदासि। यस्मा पन बुद्धभावं पापुणनदिवसे सतसहस्सग्घनिकं सुवण्णपातिं लद्धु वट्टति, तस्मा सा "सुवण्णपातियं पायासं पक्खिपिस्सामी"ति चित्तं उप्पादेत्वा सतसहस्सग्घनिकं सुवण्णपातिं नीहरापेत्वा तत्थ पायासं पक्खिपितुकामा पक्कभाजनं आवज्जेसि। 'सब्बो पायासो पदुमपत्ता उदकं विय विनिवत्तित्वा पातियं पतिट्ठासि, एकपातिपूरमत्तोव अहोसि'। सा तं पातिं अञ्ञाय सुवण्णपातिया पटि्कुज्जित्वा ओदातवत्थेन वेठेत्वा सब्बालङ्कारेहि अत्तभावं अलङ्करित्वा तं पातिं अत्तनो सीसे ठपेत्वा महन्तेन आनुभावेन निग्रोधरुक्खमूलं गन्त्वा बोधिसत्तं ओलोकेत्वा बलवसोमनस्सजाता "रुक्खदेवता"ति सञ्ञाय दिट्ठट्ठानतो पट्ठाय ओनतोनता गन्त्वा सीसतो पातिं ओतारेत्वा विवरित्वा सुवण्णभिङ्कारेन गन्धपुप्फवासितं उदकं गहेत्वा बोधिसत्तं उपगन्त्वा अट्ठासि। घटीकारमहाब्रह्मुना दिन्नो मत्तिकापत्तो एत्तकं अद्धानं बोधिसत्तं अविजहित्वा तस्मिं खणे अदस्सनं गतो, बोधिसत्तो पत्तं अपस्सन्तो दक्खिणहत्थं पसारेत्वा उदकं सम्पटिच्छि। सुजाता सहेव पातिया पायासं महापुरिसस्स हत्थे ठपेसि, महापुरिसो सुजातं ओलोकेसि। सा आकारं सल्लक्खेत्वा "अय्य, मया तुम्हाकं परिच्चत्तं, गण्हित्वा यथारुचिं गच्छथा"ति वन्दित्वा "यथा मय्हं मनोरथो निप्फन्नो, एवं तुम्हाकम्पि निप्फज्जतू"ति वत्सा सतसहस्स- ग्घनिकाय सुवण्णपातिया पुराणपण्णे विय अनपेक्खा हुत्वा पक्कामि।

बोधिसत्तोपि खो निसिन्नट्ठाना उट्ठाय रुक्खं पदक्खिणं कत्वा पातिं आदाय नेरञ्जराय तीरं गन्त्वा अनेकेसं बोधिसत्तसहस्सानं अभिसम्बुज्झनदिवसे ओतरित्वा न्हानट्ठानं सुप्पतिट्ठिततित्थं नाम अत्थि, तस्स तीरे पातिं ठपेत्वा ओतरित्वा न्हत्वा अनेकबुद्धसतसहस्सानं निवासनं अरहद्धजं निवासेत्वा पुरत्थाभिमुखो निसीदित्वा एकट्ठि-तालपक्कप्पमाणे एकूनपञ्ञास पिण्डे कत्वा सब्बं अप्पोदकं मधुपायासं परिभुञ्जि। सो एव हिस्स बुद्धभूतस्स सत्तसत्ताहं बोधिमण्डे एकूनपञ्ञास दिवसानि आहारो अहोसि। एत्तकं कालं नेव अञ्ञो आहारो अत्थि,

न न्हानं, न मुखधोवनं, न सरीरवळञ्जो, झानसुखेन मग्गसुखेन फलसुखेन च वीतिनामेसि। तं पन पायासं परिभुञ्जित्वा सुवण्णपातिं गहेत्वा "सचाहं, अज्ज बुद्धो भवितुं सक्खिस्सामि, अयं पाति पटिसोतं गच्छतु, नो चे सक्खिस्सामि, अनुसोतं गच्छतू"ति वत्वा नदीसोते पक्खिपि। सा सोतं छिन्दमाना नदीमज्झं गन्त्वा मज्झमज्झट्ठानेनेव जवसम्पन्नो अस्सो विय असीतिहत्थमत्तट्ठानं पटिसोतं गन्त्वा एकस्मिं आवट्टे निमुज्जित्वा काळनागराजभवनं गन्त्वा तिण्णं बुद्धानं परिभोगपातियो "किलि किली"ति रवं कारयमाना पहरित्वाव तासं सब्बहेट्ठिमा हुत्वा अट्ठासि। काळो नागराजा तं सद्दं सुत्वा "हिय्यो एको बुद्धो निब्बत्तो, पुन अज्ज एको निब्बत्तो"ति वत्वा अनेकेहि पदसतेहि थुतियो वदमानो उट्ठासि। तस्स किर महापथविया एकयोजनतिगावुतप्पमाणं नभं पूरेत्वा आरोहनकालो "अज्ज वा हिय्यो वा"ति सदिसो अहोसि।

बोधिसत्तोपि नदीतीरम्हि सुपुप्फितसालवने दिवाविहारं कत्वा सायन्हसमये पुप्फानं वण्टतो मुच्चनकाले देवताहि अलङ्कतेन अट्ठसभवित्थारेन मग्गेन सीहो विय विजम्भमानो बोधिरुक्खाभिमुखो पायासि। नागयक्खसुपण्णादयो दिब्बेहि गन्धपुप्फादीहि पूजयिंसु, दिब्बसङ्गीतादीनि पवत्तयसु, दससहस्सी लोकधातु एकगन्धा एकमाला एकसाधुकारा अहोसि। तस्मिं समये सोत्थियो नाम तिणहारको तिणं आदाय पटिपथे आगच्छन्तो महापुरिसस्स आकारं ञत्वा अट्ठ तिणमुट्ठियो अदासि। बोधिसत्तो तिणं गहेत्वा बोधिमण्डं आरुय्ह दक्खिणदिसाभागे उत्तराभिमुखो अट्ठासि। तस्मिं खणे दक्खिणचक्कवाळं ओसीदित्वा हेट्ठा अवीचिसम्पत्तं विय अहोसि, उत्तरचक्कवाळं उल्लङ्घित्वा उपरि भवग्गप्पत्तं विय अहोसि। बोधिसत्तो "इदं सम्बोधिं पापुणनट्ठानं न भविस्सति मञ्ञे"ति पदक्खिणं करोन्तो पच्छिमदिसाभागं गन्त्वा पुरत्थाभिमुखो अट्ठासि, ततो पच्छिमचक्कवाळं ओसीदित्वा हेट्ठा अवीचिसम्पत्तं विय अहोसि, पुरत्थिमचक्कवाळं उल्लङ्घित्वा उपरि भवग्गप्पत्तं विय अहोसि।

ठितट्ठितट्ठाने किरस्सं नेमिवट्टिपरियन्ते अक्कन्ते नाभिया पतिट्ठितमहासकटचक्कं विय महापथवी ओनतुन्नता अहोसि। बोधिसत्तो "इदम्पि सम्बोधिं पापुणनट्ठानं न भविस्सति मञ्ञे"ति पदक्खिणं करोन्तो उत्तरदिसाभागं गन्त्वा दक्खिणाभिमुखो अट्ठासि, ततो उत्तरचक्कवाळं ओसीदित्वा हेट्ठा अवीचिसम्पत्तं विय अहोसि, दक्खिणचक्कवाळं उल्लङ्घित्वा उपरि भवग्गप्पत्तं विय अहोसि। बोधिसत्तो "इदम्पि सम्बोधिं पापुणनट्ठानं न भविस्सति मञ्ञे"ति पदक्खिणं करोन्तो पुरत्थिमदिसाभागं गन्त्वा पच्छिमाभिमुखो अट्ठासि। पुरत्थिमदिसाभागे पन सब्बबुद्धानं, पल्लङ्कट्ठानं, तं नेव छम्भति, न कम्पति। महासत्तो "इदं सब्बबुद्धानं अविजहितं अचलट्ठानं किलेसपञ्जरविद्धंसनट्ठान"न्ति ञत्वा तानि तिणानि अग्गे गहेत्वा चालेसि, तावदेव चुद्दसहत्थो पल्लङ्को अहोसि। तानिपि खो तिणानि तथारूपेन सण्ठानेन सण्ठहिंसु, यथारूपं सुकुसलोपि चित्तकारो वा पोत्थकारो वा आलिखितुम्पि समत्थे नत्थि। बोधिसत्तो बोधिक्खन्ध पिट्ठितो कत्वा पुरत्थाभिमुखो दळहमानसो हुत्वा–

कामं तचो च नहारु च, अट्ठि च अवसिस्सतु।
उपसुस्सतु निस्सेसं, सरीरे मंसलोहितं।।

न त्वेवाहं सम्मासम्बोधिं अप्पत्वा इमं पल्लङ्कं भिन्दिस्सामीति असनिसतसन्निपातेनपि अभेज्जरूपं अपराजितपल्लङ्कं आभुजित्वा निसीदि।

तस्मिं समये मारो देवपुत्तो "सिद्धत्थकुमारो मय्हं वसं अतिक्कमितुकामो, न दानिस्स अतिक्कमितुं दस्सामी"ति मारबलस्स सन्तिकं गन्त्वा एतमत्थं आरोचेत्वा मारघोसनं नाम घोसापेत्वा मारबलं अदाय निक्खमि। सा मारसेना मारस्स पुरतो द्वादसयोजना होति, दक्खिणतो च वामतो च द्वादसयोजना, पच्छतो याव चक्कवाळपरियन्तं कत्वा ठिता, उद्धं नवयोजनुब्बेधा, यस्सा उन्नदन्तिया उन्नादसद्दो योजनसहस्सतो पट्ठाय पथविउन्द्रियनसद्दो विय सुय्यति। अथ मारो देवपुत्तो दियड्ढयोजनसतिकं गिरिमेखलं नाम हत्थिं अभिरुहित्वा बाहुसहस्सं मापेत्वा नानावुधानि अग्गहेसि। अवसेसायपि मारपरिसाय

द्वे जना एकसदिसं आवुधं न गण्हिसु, नानप्पकारवण्णा नानप्पकारमुखा हुत्वा महासत्तं अज्झोत्थरमाना आगमिंसु।

दससहस्सचक्कवाळदेवता पन महासत्तस्स थुतियो वदमाना अट्ठंसु। सक्को देवराजा विजयुत्तरसङ्खं धममानो अट्ठासि। सो किर सङ्खो वीसहत्थसतिको होति। सकिं वातं गाहापेत्वा धमन्तो चत्तारो मासे सद्दं करित्वा निस्सद्दो होति। महाकाळनागराजा अतिरेकपदसतेन वण्णं वदन्तो अट्ठासि महाब्रह्मा सेतच्छत्तं धारयमानो अट्ठासि। मारबले पन बोधिमण्डं उपसङ्कमन्ते तेसं एकोपि ठातुं नासक्खि, सम्मुखसम्मुखट्ठानेनेव पलायिंसु। काळो नागराजा पथवियं निमुज्जित्वा पञ्चयोजनसतिकं मञ्जेरिकनागभवनं गन्त्वा उभोहि हत्थेहि मुखं पिदहित्वा निपन्नो। सक्को विजयुत्तरसङ्खं पिट्ठियं कत्वा चक्कवाळ-मुखवट्टियं अट्ठासि। महाब्रह्मा सेतच्छत्तं चक्कवाळकोटियं अट्ठासि। महाब्रह्मा सेतच्छत्तं चक्कवाळकोटियां ठपेत्वा ब्रह्मलोकमेव अगमासि। एका देवतापि ठातुं समत्था नाहोसि, महापुरिसो एककोव निसीदि।

मारोपि अत्तनो परिसं आह "ताता सुद्धोदनपुत्तेन सिद्धत्थेन सदिसो अञ्ञो पुरिसो नाम नत्थि, मयं सम्मुखा युद्धं दातुं न सक्खिस्साम, पच्छाभागेन दस्सामा"ति। महापुरिसोपि तीणि पस्सानि ओलोकेत्वा सब्बदेवतानं पलातत्ता सुञ्ञानि अद्दस। पुन उत्तरपस्सेन मारबलं अज्झोत्थरमानं दिस्वा "अयं एत्तको जनो मं एककं सन्धाय महन्तं वायामं परक्कमं करोति, इमस्मिं ठाने मय्हं माता वा पिता वा भाता वा अञ्ञो वा कोचि ञातको नत्थि, इमा पन दस पारमियोव मय्हं दीघरत्तं पुट्ठपरिजनसदिसा, तस्मा पारमियोव फलकं कत्वा पारमिसत्थेनेव पहरित्वा अयं बलकायो मया विद्धंसेतुं वट्टती"ति दस पारमियो आवज्जमानो निसीदि।

अथ खो मारो देवपुत्तो "एतेनेव सिद्धत्थं पलापेस्सामी"ति वातमण्डलं समुट्ठापेसि। तङ्खणंयेव पुरत्थिमादिभेदा वाता समुट्ठहित्वा अड्ढयोजनएकयोजनद्वियोजनतियोजनप्पमाणानि पब्बतकूटानि पदालेत्वा वनगच्छरुक्खादीनि उम्मूलेत्वा समन्ता गामनिगमे चुण्णविचुण्णं कातुं

समत्थापि महापुरिसस्स पुञ्ञतेजेन विहतानुभावा बोधिसत्तं पत्वा चीवरकण्णमत्तम्पि चालेतुं नासक्खिंसु। ततो "उदकेन न अज्झोत्थरित्वा मारेस्सामी"ति महावस्सं समुट्ठापेसि। तस्सानुभावेन उपरूपरि सतपटलसहस्सपटलादिभेदा वलाहका उट्ठहित्वा वस्सिंसु। वुट्ठिध ारावेगेन पथवी छिद्दा अहोसि। वनरुक्खादीनं उपरिभागेन महामेघो आगन्त्वा महासत्तस्स चीवरे उस्सावबिन्दुट्ठानमत्तम्पि तेमेतुं नासक्खि। ततो पासाणवस्सं समुट्ठापेसि। महन्तानि महन्तानि पब्बतकूटानि ध ूमायन्तानि पज्जलन्तानि आकासेनागन्त्वा बोधिसत्तं पत्वा दिब्बमालागुळभावं आपज्जिंसु। ततो पहरणवस्सं समुट्ठापेसि। एकतोधारा उभतोध ाराअसिसत्तिखुरप्पादयो धूमायन्ता पज्जलन्ता आकासेनागन्त्वा बोधिसत्तं पत्वा दिब्बपुप्फानि अहेसुं। ततो अङ्गारवस्सं समुट्ठापेसि। किंसुकवण्णा अङ्गारा आकासेनागन्त्वा बोधिसत्तस्स पादमूले दिब्बपुप्फानि हुत्वा विकिरिंसु। ततो कुक्कुळवस्सं समुट्ठापेसि। अच्चुण्हो अग्गिवण्णो कुक्कुळो आकासेनागन्त्वा बोधिसत्तस्स पादमूले दिब्बचन्दनचुण्णं हुत्वा निपति। ततो वालुकावस्सं समुट्ठापेसि। अतिसुखुमवालुका धूमायन्ता पज्जलन्ता आकासेनागन्त्वा बोधिसत्तस्स पादमूले दिब्ब पुप्फानि हुत्वा निपतिंसु। ततो कललवस्सं समट्ठापेसि। तं कललं धूमायन्तं पज्जलन्तं आकासेनागन्त्वा बोधिसत्तस्स पादमूले दिब्बविलेपनं हुत्वा निपति। ततो "इमिना भिंसेत्वा सिद्धत्थं पला- पेस्सामी"ति अन्धकारं समुट्ठापेसि। तं चतुरङ्गसमन्नागतं विय महातमं हुत्वा बोधिसत्तं पत्वा सूरियप्पभविहतं विय अन्धकारं अन्तरधायि।

एवं मारो इमाहि नवहि वातवस्सपासाणपहरणअङ्गारकुक्कुळ- वालुकाकललअन्धकारवुट्ठीहि बोधिसत्तं पलापेतुं असक्कोन्तो "किं भणे, तिट्ठथ, इमं सिद्धत्थकुमार गण्हथ हनथ पलापेथा"ति परिसं आणापेत्वा सयम्पि गिरिमेखलस्स हत्थिनो खन्धे निसिन्नो चक्कावुध आदाय बोधिसत्तं उपसङ्कमित्वा "सिद्धत्थ उट्ठाहि एतस्मा पल्लङ्का, नायं तुय्हं पापुणाति, मय्हं एव पापुणाती"ति आह। महासत्तो तस्स वचनं सुत्वा अवोच–"मार, नेव तया दस पारमियो पूरिता, न

उपपारमियो, न परमत्थपारमियो, नापि पञ्च महापरिच्चागा परिच्चत्ता, न ञातत्थचरिया, न लोकत्थचरिया, न बुद्धचरिया पूरिता, सब्बा ता मयायेव पूरिता, तस्मा नायं पल्लङ्को तुय्हं पापुणाति,' मय्हेवेसो पापुणाती"ति।

मारो कुद्धो कोधवेगं असहन्तो महापुरिसस्स चक्कावुधं विस्सज्जेसि। तं तस्स दस पारमियो आवज्जेन्तस्स उपरिभागे मालावितानं हुत्वा अट्ठासि। तं किर खुरधारचक्कावुधं अञ्ञदा तेन कुद्धेन विस्सट्ठं एकघनपासाणत्थम्भे वंसकळीरे विय छिन्दन्तं गच्छति, इदानि पन तस्मिं मालावितानं हुत्वा ठिते अवसेसा मारपरिसा "इदानि पल्लङ्कतो वुट्ठाय पलायिस्सती"ति महन्तमहन्तानि सेलकूटानि विस्सज्जेसुं। तानिपि महापुरिसस्स दस पारमियो आवज्जेन्तस्स मालागुळभावं आपज्जित्वा भूमियं पतिंसु। देवता चक्कवाळमुखवट्टियं ठिता गीवं पसारेत्वा सीसं उक्खिपित्वा "नट्ठो वत सो सिद्धत्थकुमारस्स रूपग्गप्पत्तो अत्तभावो, किं नु खो करिस्सती"ति ओलोकेन्ति।

ततो महापुरिसो "पूरितपारमीनं बोधिसत्तानं अभिसम्बुज्झनदिवसे पत्तपल्लङ्को मय्हंव पापुणाती"ति वत्वा ठितं मारं आह – "मार तुय्हं दानस्स दिन्नभावे को सक्खी"ति। मारो "इमे एत्तका जना सक्खिनो"ति मारबलाभिमुखं हत्थं पसारेसि।

तस्मिं खणे मारपरिसाय "अहं सक्खी, अहं सक्खी"ति पवत्तसद्दो पथविउन्द्रियनसद्दसदिसो अहोसि। अय मारो महापुरिसं आह "सिद्धत्थ, तुय्हं दानस्स दिन्नभावे को सक्खी"ति। महापुरिसो "तुय्हं ताव दानस्स दिन्नभावे सचेतना, मय्हं पन इमस्मिं ठाने सचेतनो कोचि सक्खी नाम नत्थि, तिट्ठतु ताव मे अवसेसत्तभावेसु दिन्नदानं, वेस्सन्तरत्तभावे पन ठत्वा मय्हं सत्तसतकमहादानस्स दिन्नभावे अयं अचेतनापि घनमहापथवी सक्खी"ति चीवरगब्भन्तरतो दक्खिणहत्थं अभिनीहरित्वा "वेस्सन्तरत्तभावे ठत्वा मय्हं सत्तसतकमहादानस्स दिन्नभावे त्वं सक्खी न सक्खी"ति, महापथविअभिमुखं हत्थं पसारेसि।

महापथवी "अहं ते तदा सक्खी"ति विरवसतेन विरवसहस्सेन विरवसतसहस्सेन मारबलं अवत्थरमाना विय उन्नदि।

ततो महापुरिसे "दिन्नं ते सिद्धत्थ महादानं उत्तमदान"न्ति वेस्सन्तरदानं सम्मसन्ते दियड्ढयोजनसतिको गिरिमेखलहत्थी जण्णुकेहि पथवियं पतिट्ठासि, मारपरिसा दिसाविदिसा पलायि, द्वे एकमग्गेन गता नाम नत्थि, सीसाभरणानि चेव निवत्थवत्थानि च पहाय सम्मुखसम्मुखदिसाहियेव पलायिंसु। ततो देवसङ्घा पलायमानं मारबलं दिस्वा "मारस्स पराजयो जातो, सिद्धत्थकुमारस्स जयो, जयपूजं करिस्सामा"ति नागा नागानं, सुपण्णा सुपण्णानं, देवता देवतानं, ब्रह्मानो, ब्रह्मानं, उग्घोसेत्वा गन्धमालादिहत्था महापुरिसस्स सन्तिकं बोधिपल्लङ्कं अगमंसु।

एवं गतेसु च पन तेसु–

जयो हि बुद्धस्स सिरीमतो अयं, मारस्स च पापिमतो पराजयो।
उग्घोसयुं बोधिमण्डे पमोदिता, जयं तदा नागगणा महेसिनो।।274।।
जयो हि बुद्धस्स सिरीमतो अयं, मारस्स च पापिमतो पराजयो।
उग्घोसयुं बोधिमण्डे पमोदिता, सुपण्णसङ्घापि जयं महेसिनो।।275।।
जयो हि बुद्धस्स सिरीमतो अयं, मारस्स च पापिमतो पराजयो।
उग्धोसयुं बोधिमण्डे पमोदिता, जयं तदा देवगणा महेसिनो।।276।।
जयो हि बुद्धस्स सिरीमतो अयं, मारस्स च पापिमतो पराजयो।
उग्घोसयुं बोधिमण्डे पमोदिता, जयं तदा ब्रह्मगणापि तादिनो"ति।।277।।

अवसेसा दससु चक्कवाळसहस्सेसु देवता मालागन्धविलेपनेहि च पूजयमाना नानप्पकारा थुतियो च वदमाना अट्ठंसु। एवं अनत्थङ्गतेयेव सूरिये महापुरिसो मारबलं विधमेत्वा चीवरूपरि पतमानेहि बोधि रुक्खङ्कुरेहि रत्तपवाळपल्लवेहि विय पूजियमानो पठमयामे पुब्बेनिवासञाणं अनुस्सरित्वा, मज्झिमयामे दिब्बचक्खुं विसोधेत्वा, पच्छिमयामे पटिच्चसमुप्पादे ञाणं ओतारेसि। अथस्स द्वादसपदिकं

पच्चयाकारं वट्टविवट्टवसेन अनुलोमपटिलोमतो सम्मसन्तस्स दससहस्सी लोकधातु उदकपरियन्तं कत्वा द्वादसक्खत्तुं सम्पकम्पि।

महापुरिसे पन दससहस्सिलोकधातुं उन्नादेत्वा अरुणुग्गमनवेलाय सब्बञ्ञुतञ्ञाणं पटिविज्झन्ते सकलदससहस्सी लोकधातु अलङ्कतपटियत्ता अहोसि। पाचीनचक्कवालममुखवट्टियं उस्सापितानं धजानं पटाकानं रसियो पच्छिमचक्कवालमुखवट्ट यं पहरन्ति, तथा पच्छिमचक्कवालमुखवट्टियं उस्सापितानं पाचीनचक्कवाळ-मुखवट्ट्यिं, दक्खिणचक्कवाळमुखवट्ट्यिं उस्सापितानं उत्तरचक्क-वाळमुख्वट्टियं, उस्सापितानं दक्खिणचक्कवाळमुखवटियं पहरन्ति, पथवितले उस्सापितानं पन धजानं पट्टाकानं ब्रह्मलोकं आहच्च अट्ठंसु, ब्रह्मलोके बद्धानं पथवितले पतिट्ठहिंसु, दससहस्स- चक्कवाळेसु पुप्फूपगरुक्खा पुप्फं गण्हिंसु, फलूपगरुक्खा फलपिण्डीभारभरिता अहेसुं। खन्धेसु खन्धपदुमानि पुप्फिसु, साखासु साखापदुमानि, लतासु लतापदुमानि, आकासे ओलम्बकपदुमानि, सिलातलानि भिन्दित्वा उपरूपरि सत्त सत्त हुत्वा दण्डकपदुमानि उट्ठहिंसु। दससहस्सी उग्घोसयुं बोधिमण्डे पमोदिता, जयं तदा देवगणा महेसिनो।।

लोकधातु वट्ठेत्वा विस्सट्ठमालागुळा विय सुसन्थतपुप्फसन्थारो विय च अहोसि। चक्कवाळन्तरेसु अट्ठयोजनसहस्सलोकन्तरिका सत्तसूरियप्पभायपि अनोभासितपुब्बा एकोभासा अहेसुं, चतुरासी-तियोजनसहस्सगम्भीरो महासमुद्दो मधुरोदको अहोसि, नदियो नप्पवत्तिंसु, जच्चन्धा रूपानि पस्सिसु, जातिबधिरा सद्दं सुणिंसु, जातिपीठसप्पिनो पदसा गच्छिसु, अन्दुबन्धनादीनि छिज्जित्वा पतिंसु।

एवं अपरिमाणेन सिरिविभवेन पूजियमानो महापुरिसो अनेकप्प-कारेसु अच्छरियधम्मेसु पातुभूतेसु सब्बञ्ञुतञ्ञाणं पटिविज्झित्वा सब्बुद्धानं अविजहितं उदानं उदानेसि–

"अनेकजातिसंसार, सन्धाविस्सं अनिब्बिसं।
गहकारकं गवेसन्तो, दुक्खा जाति पुनप्पुनं।। 278।।

"गहकारक दिट्ठोसि, पुन गेहं न काहसि।
सब्बा ते फासुका भग्गा, गहकूटं विसङ्खतं।
विसङ्खारगतं चित्तं, तण्हानं खयमज्झगा"ति।। 279।।

'इति' तुसितपुरतो पट्ठाय याव अयं बोधिमण्डे सब्बञ्ञुतप्पत्ति, एत्तकं ठानं अविदूरेनिदानं नामाति वेदितब्बं अविनिदानकथा निट्ठिता

Now at that time there lived in Uruvelā a girl named Sujātā, who had been born in the family of the householder Senāni, in General's Town. On reaching maturity she made a prayer to a certain banyan-tree, saying, "If I get a husband of equal rank with myself, and my first-born is a son, I will make a yearly offering to you. of the value of a hundred thousand pieces of money." And her prayer had been successful.

And wishing to make her offering on the day of full moon of the month Visākhā, full six years after the Great Being commenced his austerities, she first pastured a thousand cows in Laṭṭhimadhu Wood, and fed their milk to five hundred cows, and the milk of these five hundred cows to two hundred and fifty, and so on down to feeding the milk of sixteen cows to eight. This "working the milk in and in," as it is called, was done to increase the thickness and the sweetness and the strength-giving properties of the milk. And when it came to be the full-moon day of Visākhā, she resolved to make her offering, and rose up early in the morning, just when night was breaking into day, and gave orders to milk the eight cows. The calves had not come at the teats of the cows; yet as soon as new pails were put under the udders, the milk flowed in streams of its own accord. When she saw this miracle, Sujātā took the milk with her own hands and placed it in a new vessel, and herself made a fire and began to cook it. While the milk-rice was cooking, immense bubbles arose, and turning to the right, went round together; but not a single drop ran over the edge, and not a particle of smoke went up from the fireplace. On this occasion the four guardian angels were present, and stood guard over the fireplace; Mahā-Brahma bore aloft the canopy of state, and Sakka raked the fire-brands together and made the fire blaze tip brightly. And just as a man crushes honey out of a honey-comb that has formed around a stick, so the deities by their superhuman power collected an amount of vital sap sufficient for the sustenance of the gods and men of all the four great continents and their two thousand attendant isles, and infused it into the milk-rice. At other times, to be sure, the deities infuse this sap into each mouthful; but on the day of the attainment of the Buddhaship, and on the day of decease, they place it in the kettle itself.

When Sujātā had seen so many miracles appear to her in one day, she said to her slave-girl Puṇṇā, –

"Puṇṇā, dear girl, the deity is very graciously disposed to us today. I have never before seen so many marvellous things happen in so short a time. Run quickly, and get everything ready at the holy place."

"Yes, my lady," replied the slave-girl, and ran in great haste to the foot of the tree.

Now that night the Future Buddha had five great, dreams, and on considering their meaning reached the conclusion, "Without doubt I shall become a Buddha this very day." And when night was over, and he had cared for his person, he came early in the morning to that tree, to await the hour to go begging. And when he sat down he illumined the whole tree with his radiance.

Then came Puṇṇā, and saw the Future Buddha sitting at the foot of the tree, contemplating the eastern quarter of the world. And when she beheld the radiance from his body lighting up the whole tree with a golden color, she became greatly excited, saying to herself, "Our deity, methinks, has come down from the tree today, and has seated himself, ready to receive our offering in person." And she ran in great haste, and told Sujātā of the matter.

When Sujātā heard this news, she was overjoyed; and

saying, "From this day forth be to me in the room of an eldest daughter," she decked Puṇṇā with all the ornaments appropriate to that position. And since a Future Buddha-on the day he attains the Buddhaship must needs receive a golden dish worth a hundred thousand pieces of money, therefore the idea occurred to her of putting the milk-rice in a golden dish. And bringing out a golden dish that was worth a hundred thousand, she took up the cooking-vessel and began to pour out the milk-rice. All the milk-rice rolled off like water from a lotus-leaf, and exactly filled the dish. Then, covering the dish with another, which was also made of gold, and wrapping it in a cloth, she adorned herself in all her ornaments, and with the dish on her head proceeded in state to the foot of the banyan-tree. As soon as she caught sight of the Future Buddha she was exceedingly overjoyed, supposing him to be the tree-god; and as she advanced she kept constantly bowing. And taking the pot from her head, she uncovered it, and with some flower-scented water in a golden vase, drew near and took up a position close to the Future Buddha. The earthenware bowl which the Future Buddha had kept so long, and which had been given him by Ghatīkāra., the Mahā-Brahma god, at that instant disappeared; and the Future Buddha, stretching out his right hand in an attempt to find his bowl, grasped the vase of water. Next Sujātā placed the dish of milk-rice in the hand of the Great Being. Then the Great Being looked at Sujātā; and she perceived that he was a holy man, and did obeisance, and said:

"Lord, accept my donation, and go whithersoever it seemeth to you good." And adding, "May your wishes prosper like mine own," she departed, caring no more for her golden dish worth a hundred thousand pieces of money than if it had been a dead leaf.

The Future Buddha rose from his seat and walked round the tree with his right side towards it; and taking the dish, he proceeded to the banks of the Nerañjarā and descended into its waters, just as many thousands of Future Buddhas before him had descended on the clay of their complete enlightenment. – The spot where he bathed is now a place of pilgrimage named Suppatiṭṭhita, and here he deposited the dish on the bank before descending into the water. – After bathing he dressed himself in that garb of saintship which had been the dress of many hundreds of thousands of Future Buddhas before him; and sitting down with his face to the east, he made the whole of the thick, sweet milk-rice into forty-nine pellets of the size of the fruit of the single-seeded palmyra-tree, and ate it. And he took no further nourishment until the end of the seven weeks, or forty-nine days, which he spent on the throne of wisdom after he had become a Buddha. During all that time he had no other nourishment; he neither bathed, nor rinsed his mouth, nor did he ease himself; but was wholly taken up by the delights of the Trances, of the Paths, and of the Fruits.

Now when he had consumed the milk-rice, he took the golden- dish; and saying, "If I am to succeed in becoming a Buddha today, let this dish go up-stream; but if not, let it go down-stream," he threw it into the water. And it swam, cleaving the stream, until it came to the middle of the river, and then, like a fleet horse, it ran up-stream for a distance of eighty cubits, keeping all the while in the middle of the stream. Then it dived into a whirlpool and went to the palace of the black snake-king, and hit, "click ! click !" against the dishes that had been used by the last three Buddhas, and took its place at the end of the row. When the black snake-king heard the noise, he exclaimed, –

"But yesterday a Buddha lived,
And now another has been born."

and so on, through several hundred laudatory verses. As a matter of only yesterday and today did the times of the snake-king's appearance above ground seem to him; and his body at such times towered up into the sky to a height of one and three quarters leagues.

Then the Future Buddha took his noonday rest on the banks of the river, in a grove of sāḷ-trees in full bloom. And at nightfall, at the time the flowers droop on their stalks, he rose up, like a lion when he bestirs himself, and went towards the Bodhi-tree, along a road which the gods had decked, and which was eight usabhas wide.

The snakes, the fairies, the birds, and other classes of beings did him homage with celestial perfumes, flowers, and other offerings, and celestial choruses poured forth heavenly music; so that the ten thousand worlds were filled with these perfumes, garlands, and shouts of acclaim.

Just then there came from the opposite direction a grass-cutter named Sotthiya, and he was carrying grass. And when he saw the Great Being, that he was a holy man, he gave him eight handfuls of grass. The Future Buddha took the grass, and ascending the throne of wisdom, stood on the southern side and faced the north. Instantly the southern half of the world sank, until it seemed to touch the Avīci hell, while the northern half rose to the highest of the heavens.

"Methinks," said the Future Buddha, "this cannot be the place for the attainment of the supreme wisdom; "and walking round-the tree with his right side towards it, he came to the "western side and faced the east. Then the western half of the world sank, until it seemed to touch the Avīci hell, while the eastern half rose to the highest of the heavens. Wherever, indeed, he stood, the broad earth rose and fell, as though it had been a huge cart-wheel lying on its hub, and some one were treading on the rim.

"Methinks," said the Future Buddha, "this also cannot be the place for the attainment of supreme wisdom;" and walking round the tree with his right side towards it, he came to the northern side and faced the south. Then the northern half of the world sank, until it seemed to touch the Avīci hell, while the southern half rose to the highest of the heavens.

"Methinks," said the Future Buddha, "this also cannot be the place for the attainment of supreme wisdom;" and walking round the tree with his right side towards it, he came to the eastern side and faced the west. Now it is on the eastern side of their Bodhi-trees that all The Buddhas have sat cross-legged, and that side neither trembles nor quakes.

Then the Great Being, saying to himself, "This is the immovable spot on which all The Buddhas have planted themselves ! This is the place for destroying passion's net!" took hold of his handful of grass by one end, and shook it out there. And straightway the blades of grass formed themselves into a seat fourteen cubits long, of such symmetry of shape as not even the most skilful painter or carver could design.

Then the Future Buddha turned his back to the trunk of the Bodhi-tree and faced the east. And making the mighty resolution, "Let my skin, and sinews, and bones become dry, and welcome! and let all the flesh and blood in my body dry tip! but never from this seat will I stir, until I have attained the supreme and absolute wisdom!" he sat himself down cross-legged in an unconquerable position, from which not even the descent of a hundred thunder-bolts at once could have dislodged him.

At this point the god Māra, exclaiming, "Prince Siddhāttha is desirous of passing beyond my control, but I will never allow it!" went and announced the news to his army, and sounding the Māra war-cry, drew out for battle. Now Māra's army extended in front of him for twelve leagues, and to the right and to the left for twelve leagues, and in the rear as far as to the confines of the world, and it was nine leagues high. And when it shouted, it made an earthquake like roaring and rumbling over a space of a thousand leagues. And the god Māra, mounting his elephant, which was a hundred and fifty leagues high, and had the name "Girded-with-mountains," caused a thousand arms to appear on his body, and with these he grasped a variety of weapons. Also in the remainder of that army, no two persons carried the same weapon; and diverse also in their appearances and countenances, the host swept on like a flood to overwhelm tne Great Being.

Now deities throughout the ten thousand worlds were busy

singing the praises of the Great Being. Sakka, the king of the gods, was blowing the conch-shell Vijayuttara. (This conch, they say, was a hundred and twenty cubits long, and when once it had been filled with wind, it would sound for four months before it stopped.) The great black snake-king sang more than a hundred laudatory verses. And Mahā-Brahma stood holding aloft the white umbrella. But as Māra's army gradually drew near to the throne of wisdom, not one of these gods was able to stand his ground, but each fled straight before him. The black snake-king dived into the ground, and coming to the snake-abode, Mañjerika, which was five hundred leagues in extent, he covered his face with both hands and lay down. Sakka slung his conch-shell Vijayuttara over his back, and took up his position on the rim of the world. Mahā-Brahma left the white umbrella at the end of the world, and fled to his Brahma-abode. Not a single deity was able to stand his ground, and the Great Being was left sitting alone.

Then said Māra to his followers –

"My friends, Siddhāttha, the son of Śuddhodana, is far greater than any other man, and we shall never be able to fight him in front. We will attack him from behind."

All the gods had now disappeared, and the Great Being looked around on three sides, and said to himself, "There is no one here." Then looking to the north, he perceived Māra's army coming on like a flood, and said—

"Here is this multitude exerting all their strength and power against me alone. My mother and father are not here, nor my brother, nor any other relative. But I have these Ten Perfections, like old retainers long cherished at my board. It therefore behooves me to make the Ten Perfections my shield and my sword, and to strike a blow with them that shall destroy this strong array." And he remained sitting, and reflected on the Ten Perfections.

Thereupon the god Māra caused a whirlwind, thinking, "By this will I drive away Siddhāttha." Straightway the east wind and all the other different winds began to blow; but although these winds could have torn their way through mountain-peaks half a league, or two leagues, or three leagues high, or have uprooted forest-shrubs and trees, or have reduced to powder and scattered in all directions, villages and towns, yet when they reached the Future Buddha, such was the energy of the Great Being's merit, they lost all power and were not able to cause so much as a fluttering of the edge of his priestly robe.

Then he caused a great rain-storm, saying, "With water will I overwhelm and drown him." And through his mighty power, clouds of a hundred strata, and clouds of a thousand strata arose, and also the other different kinds. And these rained down, until the earth became gullied by the torrents of water which fell, and until the floods had risen over the tops of every forest-tree. . But on coining to the Great Being, this mighty inundation was not able to wet his priestly robes as much as a dew-drop would have done.

Then he caused a shower of rocks, in which immense mountain-peaks flew smoking and flaming through the sky. But on reaching the Future Buddha they became celestial bouquets of flowers.

Then he caused a shower of weapons, in which single-edged, and double-edged swords, spears, and arrows flew smoking and flaming through the sky. But on reaching the Future Buddha they became celestial flowers.

Then he caused a shower of live coals, in which live coals as red as kiṁsuka flowers flew through the sky. But they scattered themselves at the Future Buddha's feet as a shower of celestial flowers.

Then he caused a shower of hot ashes, in which ashes that glowed like fire flew through the sky. But they fell at the Future Buddha's feet as sandal-wood powder.

Then he caused a shower of sand, in which very fine sand flew smoking and flaming through the sky. But it fell at the Future Buddha's feet as celestial flowers.

Then he caused a shower of mud, in which mud flew smoking and flaming through the sky. But it fell at the Future Buddha's feet as celestial ointment.

Then he caused a darkness, thinking, "By this will I frighten Siddhāttha, and drive him away." And the darkness became fourfold, and very dense. But on reaching the Future Buddha it disappeared like darkness before the light of the sun.

Māra, being thus unable with these nine storms of wind, rain, rocks, weapons, live coals, hot ashes, sand, mud, and darkness, to drive away the Future Buddha, gave command to his followers, "Look ye now! Why stand ye still? Seize, kill, drive away this prince ! "And, arming himself with a discus, and seated upon the shoulders of the elephant "Girded-with-mountains," he drew near the Future Buddha, and said:

"Siddhāttha, arise from this seat! It does not belong to you, but to me."

When the Great Being heard this he said–

"Māra, you have not fulfilled the Ten Perfections in any of their three grades; nor have you made the five great donations;[37] nor have you striven for knowledge, nor for the welfare of the world, nor for enlightenment. This seat does not belong to you, but to me."

Unable to restrain his fury, the enraged Māra now hurled his discus. But the Great Being reflected on the Ten Perfections, and the discus changed into a canopy of flowers, and remained suspended over his head. Yet they say that this keen-edged discus, when at other times Māra hurled it in anger, would cut through solid stone pillars as if they had been the tips of bamboo shoots. But on this occasion it became a canopy of flowers. Then the followers of Māra began hurling immense mountain-crags, saying, "This will make him get up from his seat and flee." But the Great Being kept his thoughts on the Ten Perfections, and the crags also became wreaths of flowers, and then fell to the ground.

Now the gods meanwhile were standing on the rim of the world, and craning their necks to look, saying:

"Ah, woe the day! the handsome form of prince Siddhāttha will surely be destroyed! What will he do to save himself?"

Then the Great Being, after his assertion that the seat which Future Buddhas had always used on the day of their complete enlightenment belonged to him, continued, and said:

"Māra, who is witness to your having given donations?" Said Māra, "All these, as many as you see here, are my witnesses;" and he stretched out his hand in the direction of his army. And instantly from Māra's army came a roar, "I am his witness! I am his witness !" which was like to the roar of an earthquake.

Then said Māra to the Great Being, – "Siddhāttha, who is witness to your having given donations?"

"Your witnesses," replied the Great Being, "are animate beings, and I have no animate witnesses present. However, not to mention the donations which I gave in other existences, the great seven-hundred-fold donation which I gave in my Vessantara existence shall now be testified to by the solid earth, inanimate though she be." And drawing forth his right hand from beneath his priestly robe, he stretched it out towards the mighty earth, and said, "Are you witness, or are you not, to my having given a great seven-hundred-fold donation in my Vessantara existence?"

And the mighty earth thundered, "I bear you witness !" with a hundred, a thousand, a hundred thousand roars, as if to overwhelm the army of Māra.

Now while the Great Being was thus calling to mind the donation he gave in his Vessantara existence, and saying to himself, "Siddhāttha, that was a great and excellent donation which you gave," the hundred-and-fifty-league-high elephant "Girded-with-mountains" fell upon his knees before the Great Being. And the followers of Māra fled away in all directions.

No two went the same way, but leaving their head-ornaments and their cloaks behind, they fled straight before them.

Then the hosts of the gods, when they saw the army of Māra flee, cried out, "Māra is defeated ! Prince Siddhāttha has conquered ! Let us go celebrate the victory !" And the snakes egging on the snakes, the birds the birds, the deities the deities, and the Brahma-angels the Brahma-angels, they came with perfumes, garlands, and other offerings in their hands to the Great Being on the throne of wisdom. And as they came, –

274. "The victory now hath this illustrious Buddha won!
The Wicked One, the Slayer, hath defeated been!"
Thus round the throne of wisdom shouted joyously
The bands of snakes their songs of victory for the Sage;

275. "The victory now hath this illustrious Buddha won !
The Wicked One, the Slayer, hath defeated been !"
Thus round the throne of wisdom shouted joyously
The flocks of birds their songs of victory for the Sage;

276. "The victory now hath this illustrious Buddha won !
The Wicked One, the Slayer, hath defeated been!"
Thus round the throne of wisdom shouted joyously
The bands of gods their songs of victory for the Sage;

277. "The victory now hath this illustrious Buddha won !
The Wicked One, the Slayer, hath defeated been!"
Thus round the throne of wisdom shouted joyously
The Brahma-angels songs of victory for the Saint.

And the remaining deities, also, throughout the ten thousand worlds, made offerings of garlands, perfumes, and ointments, and in many a hymn extolled him.

It was before the sun had set that the Great Being thus vanquished the army of Māra. And then, while the Bodhi-tree in homage rained red, coral-like sprigs upon his priestly robes, he acquired in the first watch of the night the knowledge of previous existences; in the middle watch of the night, the divine eye; and in the last watch of the night, his intellect fathomed Dependent Origination.

Now while he was musing on the twelve terms of Dependent Origination, forwards and backwards, round and back again, the ten thousand worlds quaked twelve times, as far as to their ocean boundaries. And when the Great Being, at the dawning of the day, had thus made the ten thousand worlds thunder with his attainment of omniscience, all these worlds became most gloriously adorned. Flags and banners erected on the eastern rim of the world let their streamers fly to the western rim of the world; likewise those erected on the western rim of the world, to the eastern rim of the world; those erected on the northern rim of the world, to the southern rim of the world; and those erected on the southern rim of the world, to the northern rim of the world; while those erected on the level of the earth let theirs fly until they beat against the Brahma-world; and those of the Brahma-world let theirs hang down to the level of the earth. Throughout the ten thousand worlds the flowering trees bloomed; the fruit trees were weighted down by their burden of fruit; trunk-lotuses bloomed on the trunks of trees; branch-lotuses on the branches of trees; vine-lotuses on the vines; hanging-lotuses in the sky; and stalk-lotuses burst through the rocks and came up by sevens. The system of ten thousand worlds was like a bouquet of flowers sent whirling through the air, or like a thick carpet of flowers; in the intermundane spaces the eight-thousand-league-long hells, which not even the light of seven suns had formerly been able to illumine, were now flooded with radiance; the eighty-four-thousand-league-deep ocean became sweet to the taste; the rivers checked their flowing; the blind from birth received their sight; the deaf from birth their hearing; the cripples from birth the use of their—limbs; and the bonds and fetters of captives broke and fell off.

When thus he had attained to omniscience, and was the centre of such unparalleled glory and homage, and so many prodigies were happening about him, he breathed forth that solemn utterance which has never been omitted by any of The Buddhas:

278. "Through birth and rebirth's endless round,
Seeking in vain, I hastened on,
To find who framed this edifice.
What misery ! – birth incessantly!

279. "O builder ! I 've discovered thee!
This fabric thou shalt ne'er rebuild!
Thy rafters all are broken now,
And pointed roof demolished lies !
This mind has demolition reached,
And seen the last of all desire!"

The period of time, therefore, from the existence in the Tuṣita Heaven to this attainment of omniscience on the throne of wisdom, constitutes the Intermediate Epoch.

Chapter IX

FIRST EVENTS AFTER THE ATTAINMENT OF BUDDHASHIP

Translated from the Māha-Vagga, and constituting the opening sections. Hail to that Blessed One, that Saint, and Supreme Buddha!

विनयपिटके महावग्गपालि, 1. महाक्खन्धकं, 1. बोधिकथा

तेन समयेन बुद्धो भगवा उरुवेलायं विहरति नज्जा नेरञ्जाय तीरे बोधिरुक्खमूले पठमाभिसम्बद्धो। अथ खो भगवा बोधिरुक्खमूले सत्ताहं एकपल्लङ्केन निसीदि विमुत्तिसुखपटिसंवेदी। अथ खो भगवा रत्तिया पठमं यामं पटिच्चसमुप्पादं अनुलोमपटिलोमं मनसाकासि अविज्ञापच्चया सङ्खारा, सङ्खारपच्चया विञ्ञाणं, विञ्ञाणपच्चया नामरूपं, नामरूपपच्चया सळायतनं, सळायतनपच्चया फस्सो, फस्सपच्चया वेदना, वेदनापच्चया तण्हा, तण्हापच्चया उपादानं, उपादानपच्चया भवो, भवपच्चया जाति, जातिपचच्चया जरामरणं, सोकपरिदेवदुक्खदोमनस्सुपायासा सम्भवन्ति–एवमेतस्स केवलस्स दुक्खक्खन्धस्स समुदयो होति।

"अविज्ञाय त्वेव असेसविरागनिरोधा सङ्गारनिरोधा विञ्ञाण-निरोधा, विञ्ञाणनिरोधाा नामरूपनिरोधा नामरूपनिरोधा सळायतन-निरोधो, सळायतननिरोधा फस्सनिरोधो, फस्सनिरोधा वेदनानिरोधो,

वेदनानिरोधा तण्हानिरोधो, तण्हानिरोधा उपादाननिरोधो, उपादाननिरोधा भवनिरोधो, भवनिरोधा जातिनिरोधा, जातिनिरोधा जरामरणं सोकपरिदेवदुक्खदोमनस्सुपायासा निरुज्झन्ति–एवमेतस्स केवलस्स दुक्खक्खन्धस्स निरोधो होती"ति।

अथ खो भगवा एतमत्थं विदित्वा तायं वेलायं इमं उदानं उदानेसि–

"यदा हवे पातुभवन्ति धम्मा आतापिनो झायतो ब्राह्मणस्स।
अथस्स कङ्खा वपयन्ति सब्बा यतो पजानाति सहेतुधम्मं"ति।।

2. अथ खो भगवा रत्तिया मज्झिमं यामं पटिच्चसमुप्पादं अनुलोमपटिलोमं मनसाकासि–"अविज्जापच्चया सङ्खारा, सङ्खारपच्चया विञ्ञाणं, विञ्ञाणपच्चया नामरूपं....पे॰....एवमेतस्स केवलस्स दुक्खक्खन्धस्स समुदयो होति।....पे॰....निरोधो होती"ति।

अथ खो भगवा एतमत्थं विदित्वा तायं वेलायं इमं उदानं उदानेसि–

"यदा हवे पातुभवन्ति धम्मा आतापिनो झायतो ब्राह्मणस्स।
अथस्स कङ्खा वपयन्ति सब्बा यतो खयं पच्चयानं अवेदी"ति।।

3. अथ खो भगवा रत्तिया पच्छिमं यामं पटिच्चसमुप्पादं अनुलोमपटिलोमं मनसाकासि–"अविज्जापच्चया सङ्खारा, सङ्खारपच्चया विञ्ञाणं, विञ्ञाणपच्चया नामरूपं....पे॰....एवमेतस्स केवलस्स दुक्खक्खन्धस्स समुदयो होति।....पे॰....निरोधो होती"ति।

अथ खो भगवा एतमत्थं विदित्वा तायं वेलायं इमं उदानं उदानेसि–

"यदा हवे पातुभवन्ति धम्मा आतापिनो झायतो ब्राह्मणस्स।
विधूपयं तिट्ठति मारसेनं सुरियो व ओभासयमन्तलिक्खं"ति।।

बोधिकथा निट्ठिता :

अजपालकथा

अथ खो भगवा सत्ताहस्स अच्चयेन तम्हा समाधिम्हा वुट्ठहित्वा

बोधिरुक्खमूला येन अजपालनिग्रोधो तेनुपसङ्कमि, उपसङ्कमित्वा अजपालनिग्रोधमूले सत्ताहं एकपल्लङ्केन निसीदि विमुत्तिसुखपटिसंवेदी। अथ खो अञ्ञतरो हुंहुङ्कजातिको ब्राह्मणो येन भगवा तेनुपसङ्कमि, उपसङ्कमित्वा भगवता सद्धिं सम्मोदि, सम्मोदनीयं कथं सारणीयं वीतिसारेत्वा एकमन्तं अट्ठासि। एकमन्तं ठितो खो सो ब्राह्मणो भगवन्तं एतदवोच–

"कित्तावता नु खो, मे भो गोतम, ब्राह्मणो होति, कतमे च पन ब्राह्मणकारका[5] धम्मा"ति? अथ खो भगवा एतमत्थं विदित्वा

तायं वेलायं इमं उदानं उदानेसि–
"यो ब्राह्मणो बाहितपापधम्मो
निहुंहुङ्को निक्कसावो यतत्तो।
वेदन्तगू वुसितब्रह्मचरियो
धम्मेन सो ब्रह्मवादं वदेय्य।
यस्सुस्सदा नत्थि कुहिञ्चि लोके"ति।।
अजपालकथा निट्ठिता।

मुचलिन्दकथा

अथ खो भगवा सत्ताहस्स अच्चयेन तम्हा समाधिम्हा वुट्ठहित्वा अजपालनिग्रोधमूला येन मुचलिन्दो तेनुपसङ्कमि, उपसङ्कमित्वा मुचलिन्दमूले सत्ताहं एकपल्लङ्केन निसीदि विमुत्तिसुखपटिसंवेदी। तेन खो पन समयेन महा अकालमेघो उदपादि, सत्ताहवद्दलिका सीतवातदुद्दिनी। अब खो मुचलिन्दो नागराजा सकभवना निक्खमित्वा भगवतो कायं सत्तक्खत्तुं भोगेहि परिक्खिपित्वा उपरिमुद्धनि महन्तं फणं करित्वा अट्ठासि–"मा भगवन्तं सीतं, मा भगवन्तं उण्हं, मा भगवन्तं डंसमकसवातातपसरीसपसम्फस्सो"ति। अथ खो मुचलिन्दो नागराजा सत्ताहस्स अच्चयेन विद्धं विगतवलाहकं देवं विदित्वा भगवतो काया भोगे विनिवेठेत्वा सकवण्णं पटिसंहरित्वा माणवकवण्णं

अभिनिम्मिनित्वा भगवतो पुरतो अट्ठासि पञ्जलिको भगवन्तं नमस्समानो। अथ खो भगवा एतमत्थं विदित्वा तायं वेलायं इमं उदानं उदानेसि–

"सुखो विवेको तुट्ठस्स सुतधम्मस्स पस्सतो।
अब्यापज्जं सुखं लोके पाणभूतेसु संयमो॥
सुखा विरागता लोके कामानं समतिक्कमो।
अस्मिमानस्स यो विनयो एतं वे परमं सुखं"ति ॥

मुचलिन्दकथा निट्ठिता।

At that time The Buddha, The Blessed One, was dwelling at Uruvelā at the foot of the Bodhi-tree on the banks of the river Nerañjarā, having just attained the Buddhaship. Then The Blessed One sat cross-legged for seven days together at the foot of the Bodhi-tree experiencing the bliss of emancipation.

Then The Blessed One, during the first watch of the night, thought over Dependent Origination both forward and back:

On ignorance depends *karma*;
On *karma* depends consciousness;
On consciousness depend name and form;
On name and form depend the six organs of sense;
On the six organs of sense depends contact;
On contact depends sensation;
On sensation depends desire;
On desire depends attachment;
On attachment depends existence;
On existence depends birth;
On birth depend old age and death, sorrow, lamentation, misery, grief, and despair.

Thus does this entire aggregation of misery arise. But on the complete fading out and cessation of ignorance ceases *karma*; on the cessation of *karma* ceases consciousness; on the cessation of consciousness cease name and form; on the cessation of name and form cease the six organs of sense; on the cessation of the six organs of sense ceases contact; on the cessation of contact ceases sensation; on the cessation of sensation ceases desire; on the cessation of desire ceases attachment; on the cessation of attachment ceases existence; on the cessation of existence ceases birth; on the cessation of birth cease old age and death, sorrow, lamentation, misery, grief, and despair. Thus does this entire aggregation of misery cease.

Then The Blessed One, concerning this, on that occasion, breathed forth this solemn utterance:

> "When to the strenuous, meditative Brāhmaṇa
> There come to light the elements of being,
> Then vanish all his doubts and eager questions,
> What time he knows The Elements have Causes."

Then The Blessed One, during the middle watch of the night, thought over Dependent Origination both forward and back: On ignorance depends *karma*. . . . Thus does this entire aggregation of misery arise. But on the complete fading out and cessation of ignorance ceases *karma*. . . . Thus does this entire aggregation of misery cease.

Then The Blessed One, concerning this, on that occasion, breathed forth this solemn utterance:

> "When to the strenuous, meditative Brāhmaṇa
> There come to light the elements of being,
> Then vanish all his doubts and eager questions,
> "What time he knows How Causes have an Ending."

Then The Blessed One, during the last watch of the night, thought over Dependent Origination both forward and back: On ignorance depends *karma*. . . . Thus, does this entire aggregation of misery arise. But on the complete fading out and cessation of ignorance ceases *karma*. . . . Thus does this entire aggregation of misery cease.

Then The Blessed One, concerning this, on that occasion, breathed forth this solemn utterance,

"When to the strenuous, meditative Brahman There come to light the elements of being, Then scattereth he the hordes of Māra's army; Like to the sun that lightens all the heavens."

End of the account of what took place under the Bodhi-tree.

Then The Blessed One, after the lapse of seven days, arose from that state of exalted calm, and leaving the foot of the Bo-tree, drew near to where the Ajapāla (that is, the Goatherd's) banyan-tree was; and having drawn near, he sat cross-legged at the foot of the Ajapāla banyan-tree, for seven days together, experiencing the bliss of emancipation.

Then a certain Brāhmaṇa, who was of a proud and contemptuous disposition, drew near to where The Blessed One was; and having drawn near, he exchanged greetings with The Blessed One. And having passed with him the greetings of friendship and civility, he stood respectfully at one side. And standing respectfully at one side, the Brāhmaṇa spoke to The Blessed One as follows:

"Gotama, what is it constitutes a Brahman? and what are the Brahman-making qualities?"

Then The Blessed One, concerning this, on that occasion, breathed forth this solemn utterance:

> "The Brāhmaṇa who his evil traits hath banished,
> Is free from pride, is self-restrained and spotless,
> Is learned, and the holy life hath followed,
> It is he alone may claim the name of Brahman;
> With things of earth he hath no point of contact."

End of the account of what took place under the Ajapāla-tree.

Then The Blessed One, after the lapse of seven days, arose from that state of exalted calm, and leaving the foot of the Ajapāla banyan-tree, drew near to where the Mucalinda tree was; and having drawn near, he sat cross-legged at the foot of the

Mucalinda tree for seven days together, experiencing the bliss of emancipation.

Now at that time a great cloud appeared out of season, and for seven days it was rainy, cloudy weather, with a cold wind. Then issued Mucalinda, the serpent-king, from his abode, and enveloping the body of The Blessed One seven times with his folds, spread his great hood above his head, saying:

"Let neither cold nor heat, nor gnats, flies, wind, sunshine, nor creeping creatures come near The Blessed One !"

Then, when seven days had elapsed, and Mucalinda, the serpent-king, knew that the storm had broken up, and that the clouds had gone, he unwound his coils from the body of The Blessed One. And changing his natural appearance into that of a young man, he stood before The Blessed One, and with his joined hands to his forehead did reverence to The Blessed One.

Then The Blessed One, concerning this, on that occasion, breathed forth this solemn utterance:

> "How blest the happy solitude
> Of him who hears and knows the truth!
> How blest is harmlessness towards all,
> And self-restraint towards living things!
> How blest from passion to be free,
> All sensuous joys to leave behind!
> Yet far the highest bliss of all
> To quit th' illusion false – 'I am.' "

End of the account of what took place under the Mucalinda-tree.

NOTE AND REFERENCE

37. These are the five donations great:
The gift of treasure, gift of child,
The gift of wife, of royal rule,
And last, the gift of life and limb.

From the *Abhidhānappadīpikā,* 421.

Chapter X

THE CONVERSION OF SĀRIPUTTA AND MOGGALLĀNA[38]

Translated from the Māha-Vagga (i.23[1]).

विनयपिटके महावग्गो, सारिपुत्तमोग्गल्लानपब्बज्ज्ञाकथा

तेन खो पन समयेन सञ्जयो परिब्बाजको राजगहे पटिवसति महतया परिब्बाजकपरिसाय सद्धिं अड्ढतेय्येहि परिब्बाजकसतेहि। तेन खो पन समयेन सारिपुत्तमोग्गल्लाना सञ्जये परिब्बाजके ब्रह्मचरियं चरन्ति। तेहि कतिका कता होति–यो पठमं अमतं अधिगच्छति, सो इतरस्स आरोचेतू ति। अथ खो आयस्मा अस्सजि पुब्बण्हसमयं निवासेत्वा पत्तचीवरमादाय राजगहं पिण्डाय पाविसि पासादिकेन अभिक्कन्तेन पटिक्कन्तेन आलोकितेन विलोकितेन सम्मिञ्जितेन पसारितेन, ओक्खित्तचक्खु इरियापथसम्पन्नो। अद्दसा खो सारिपुत्ती परिब्बाजको आयस्मन्तं अस्सजिं राजगहे पिण्डाय चरन्तं पासादिकेन अभिक्कन्तेन....पे0....ओक्खित्तचक्खुं इरियापथसम्पन्नं। दिस्वानस्स एतदहोसि–"ये वत लोके अरहन्तो वा अरहत्तमग्गं वा समापन्ना, अयं तेसं भिक्खु अञ्ञतरो। यन्नूनाहं इमं भिक्खुं उपसङ्कमित्वा पुच्छेय्यं "कंसि त्वं, आवुसो, उद्दिस्स पब्बजितो, को वा ते सत्था, कसस वा

त्वं धम्मं रोचेसी"ति? अथ खो सारिपुत्तस्स परिब्बाजकस्स एतदहोसि–"अकालो खो इमं भिक्खुं पुच्छितुं, अन्तरघरं पविट्ठो पिण्डाय चरति। यन्नूनाहं इमं भिक्खुं पिट्ठितो पिट्ठितो अनुबन्धेय्यं, अत्थिकेहि उपञ्ञातं मग्गं"ति। अथ खो आयस्मा अस्सजि राजगहे पिण्डाय चरित्वा पिण्डपातं आदाय पटिक्कमि। अथ खो सारिपुत्तो पि परिब्बाजको येनायस्मा अस्सजि तेनुपसङ्कमि, उपसङ्कमित्वा आयस्मता अस्सजिना सद्धिं सम्मोदि, सम्मोदनीयं कथं सारणीयं वीतिसारेत्वा एकमन्तं अट्ठासि। एकमन्तं ठितो खो सारिपुत्तो परिब्बाजको आयस्मन्तं अस्सजिं एतदवोच–"विप्पसन्नानि खो ते, आवुसो, इन्द्रियानि, परिसुद्धो छविवण्णो परियोदातो। कंसि त्वं, आवुसो, उद्दिस्स पब्बजितो, को वा ते सत्था, कस्स वा त्वं धम्मं रोजेसी"ति? अत्थावुसो, महासमणो सक्यपुत्तो सक्यकुला पब्बजितो, ताहं भगवन्तं उद्दिस्स पब्बजितो सो च मे भगवा सत्था, तस्स चाहं भगवतो धम्मं रोचेमी ति। किंवादी पनायस्मतो सत्था, किमक्खायी ति? अहं खो, आवुसो, नवो अचिरपब्बजितो, अधुनागतो इमं धम्मविनयं, न ताहं सक्कोमि वित्थारेन धम्मं देसेतुं, अपि च ते सङ्खित्तेन अत्थं वक्खामी ति। अथ खो सारिपुत्तो परिब्बाजको आयस्मन्तं अस्सजिं एतदवोच–"होतु आवुसो–"

"अप्पं बा बहुं वा भासस्सु अत्थं मे ब्रूहि।
अत्थेनेव मे अत्थो किं काहसि ब्यञ्जनं बहुं"ति॥

अथ खो आयस्मा अस्सजि सारिपुत्तस्स परिब्बाजकस्स इमं धम्मपरियायं अभासि–

"ये धम्मा हेतुप्पभवा तेसं हेतुं तथागतो आह।
तेसं च यो निरोधो एवंवादी महासमणो"ति॥

अथ खो सारिपुत्तस्स परिब्बाजकस्स इमं धम्मपरियायं सुत्वा विरजं वीतमलं धम्मचक्खुं उदपादि–यं किञ्चि समुदयधम्मं, सब्बं तं निरोधधम्मं ति।

"एसेव धम्मो यदि तावदेव पच्चब्यत्थ पदमसोकं।

अदिट्ठ अब्भतीतं बहुकेहि कप्पनहुतेही ति।।"

अथ खो सारिपुत्तो परिब्बाजको येन मोग्गल्लानो परिब्बाजको तेनुपसङ्कमि। अद्दसा खो मोग्गल्लानो परिब्बाजको सारिपुत्तं परिब्बाजकं दूरतो व आगच्छन्तं, दिस्वान सार रिपुत्तं परिब्बाजकं एतदवोच– "विप्पसन्नानि खो ते, आवुसो, इन्द्रियानि, परिसुद्धो छविवण्णो परियोदातो। कच्चि नु त्वं, आवुसो, अमतं अधिगतो"ति? आमावुसो, अमतं अधिगतो ति। यथा कथं पनत्वं, आवुसो, अमतं अधिगतो ति? इधाहं, आवुसो, अद्दसं अस्सजिं भिक्खुं राजगहे पिण्डाय चरन्तं पासादिकेन अभिक्कन्तेन....पे॰....इरियापथसम्पन्नं। दिस्वान मे एतदहोसि–"ये वत लोके अरहन्तो वा अरहत्तमग्गं वा समापन्ना, अयं तेसं भिक्खु अञ्ञतरो। अयन्नुनाहं इमं भिक्खुं उपसङ्कमित्वा पुच्छेय्यं–'कंसि त्वं, आवुसो....पे॰....धम्मं रोचेसी'" ति। तस्य मय्हं, आवुसो, एतदहोसि–"अकालो खो इमं भिक्खुं पुच्छितुं....पे॰.... अत्थिकेहि उपञ्ञातं मग्गं"ति। अथ खो, आवुसो, अस्सजि भिक्खु राजगहे पिण्डाय चरित्वा पिण्डपातं अदाय पटिक्कमि। अथ ख्वाहं, आवुसो, येन अस्सजि भिक्खु तेनुपसङ्कमिं, उपसङ्कमित्वा अस्सजिना भिक्खुना सद्धिं सम्मोदिं, सम्मोदनीयं कथं सारणीयं वीतिसारेत्वा एकमन्तं अट्ठासिं। एकमन्तं ठितो खो अहं, आवुसो, अस्सजिं भिक्खुं एतदवोचं–"विप्पसन्नापि खो ते, आवुसो, इन्द्रियानि, परिसुद्धो छविवण्णो परियोदातो। कंसि त्वं, आवुसो, ...पे॰....धम्मं रोचेसी"ति? अत्थावुसो, महासमणो सक्यपुत्तो सक्यकुला पब्बजितो, ताहं भगवन्तं उद्दिस्स पब्बजितो ....पे॰....किं काहसि व्यज्जनं बहुं ति। अथ खो, आवुसो, अस्सजि भिक्खु इमं धम्मपरियायं अभासि–

"ये धम्मा हेतुप्पभवा तेसं हेतुं तथागतो आह।
तेसं च यो निरोधो एवंवादी महासमणो"ति।।

अथ खो मोग्गल्लानस्स परिब्बाजकस्स इमं धम्मपरियायं सुत्वा विरजं वीतमलं धम्मचक्खुं उदपादि–यं किञ्चि समुदयधम्मं, सब्बं तं निरोधधम्मं ति।

एसेव धम्मो यदि तावदेव पच्चब्यत्थ पदमसोकं।
अदिट्ठ अब्भतीतं बहुकेहि कप्पनहुतेही ति।।

Now at that time, Sañjaya, the wandering ascetic, was dwelling at Rājagaha in company with a large following of wandering ascetics, two hundred and fifty in number; and at that time Sāriputta and Moggallāna were leading the religious life under Sañjaya, the wandering ascetic. And they had made this compact: "That one of us who shall first attain to the deathless is to tell it to the other."

Then the venerable Assaji, having put on his tunic in the morning and taken his bowl and his robes, entered Rājagaha for alms, winning the minds of men with his advancing and his retiring, with his looking and his gazing, with his drawing in his arms and his stretching out his arms, and having his eyes cast down, and perfect in his deportment. And Sāriputta, the wandering ascetic, saw the venerable Assaji going the rounds of Rājagaha for alms, winning the minds of men with his advancing and his retiring, with his looking and his gazing, with his drawing in his arms and his stretching out his arms, and having his eyes cast down, and perfect in his deportment. And when he had seen him, it occurred to him as follows:

"This must be a priest who is either a saint already, or has entered the path which conducts to saintship. What if now I draw near to this priest, and ask him, 'To follow whom, brother, did you retire from the world? Who is your teacher? and whose doctrine do you approve?'"

Then it occurred to Sāriputta, the wandering ascetic, as follows:

"It is not a fit time to ask this priest questions while he is inside the city, and going the rounds for alms. What if now I follow in the wake of this priest in the manner approved of for those who have requests to prefer?"

Then the venerable Assaji, after he had gone the rounds of Rājagaha and obtained alms, issued from the city; and Sāriputta, the wandering ascetic, drew near to where the vener able Assaji was; and having drawn near, he exchanged greetings with the venerable Assaji; and having passed with him the greetings of friendship and civility, he stood respect fully at one side. And standing respectfully at one side, Sāriputta, the wandering ascetic, spoke to the venerable Assaji as follows :

"Placid, brother, are all your organs of sense; clear and bright is the color of your skin. To follow whom, brother, did you retire from the world? Who is your teacher? and whose doctrine do you approve?"

"Brother, there is a great Sākyaputta "monk, one who has retired from the world out of the Sākya clan. To follow this Blessed One have I retired from the world, and this Blessed One is my teacher, and the Doctrine of this Blessed One do I approve."

"But what, venerable sir, is your teacher's doctrine? and what does he proclaim?"

"Brother, I am a novice and a new-comer, and the time is but short since I retired from the world under this Doctrine and Discipline. I am not able to expound to you the Doctrine at any great length, but I can tell you the substance of it in brief."

Then Sāriputta, the wandering ascetic, spoke to the venerable Assaji as follows :

"So be it, brother. Whether little or much, tell it me. Tell me only the substance; it is the substance I want. Why should you make a long matter of it?"

Then the venerable Assaji recited to Sāriputta, the wandering ascetic, the following exposition of the Doctrine :

"The Buddha hath the causes told
Of all things springing from a cause;
And also how things cease to be –
'T is this the Mighty Monk proclaims."

On hearing this exposition of the Doctrine, there arose in the mind of Sāriputta, the wandering ascetic, a clear and distinct perception of the Doctrine that whatever is subject to origination is subject also to cessation. "If this is the Doctrine," said he, "then, indeed, have you reached the sorrow-less state lost sight of and neglected for many myriads of world-cycles."

Then Sāriputta, the wandering ascetic, drew near to where Moggallāna, the wandering ascetic, was. And Moggallāna, the wandering ascetic, saw Sāriputta, the wandering ascetic, approaching from afar; and when he had seen him, he spoke to Sāriputta, the wandering ascetic, as follows:

"Placid, brother, are all your organs of sense; clear and bright is the color of your skin. Brother, have you attained to the deathless?"

"Yea, brother, I have attained to the deathless."

"But how, brother, did you attain to the deathless?"

"Brother, just now I saw Assaji the priest going the rounds of Rājagaha for alms, winning the minds of men with his advancing and his retiring, with his looking and his gazing, with his drawing in his arms and his stretching out his arms, and having his eyes cast down, and perfect in his deportment; and when I had seen him, it occurred to me as follows:

"This must be a priest who is either a saint already, or has entered the path which conducts to saintship. What if now I were to draw near to this priest, and ask him, 'To follow whom, brother, did you retire from the world? Who is your teacher? and whose doctrine do you approve?' Then, brother, it occurred to me as follows: 'It is not a fit time to ask this priest questions while he is inside the city and going the round for alms. What if now I follow in the wake of this priest in the manner approved of for those who have requests to prefer?' Then, brother, Assaji the priest, after he had gone the rounds of Rājagaha and obtained alms, issued from the city; and I, brother, drew near to where Assaji the priest was; and having drawn near, I exchanged greetings with the venerable Assaji; and having passed with him the greetings of friendship and civility, I stood respectfully at one side. And standing respectfully at one side, I spoke, brother, to the venerable Assaji as follows : 'Placid, brother, are all your organs of sense; clear and bright is the color of your skin. To follow whom, brother, did you retire from the world? Who is your teacher? and whose doctrine do you approve?' 'Brother, there is a great Sākyaputta monk, one who has retired from the world out of the Sākya clan. To follow this Blessed One have I retired from the world, and this Blessed One is my teacher, and the Doctrine of this Blessed One do I approve.' 'But what, venerable sir, is your teacher's doctrine? and what does he proclaim?' 'Brother, I am a novice and a new-comer, and the time is but short since I retired from the world under the Doctrine and Discipline. I am not able to expound to you the Doctrine at any great length, but I can tell you the substance of it in brief.' 'So be it, brother. Whether little or much, tell it me. Tell me only the substance; it is the substance I want. Why should you make a long matter of it?' Then, brother, Assaji the priest recited to me the following exposition of the Doctrine:

"'The Buddha hath the causes told
Of all things springing from a cause;
And also how things cease to be–
It is this the Mighty Monk proclaims.' "

On hearing this exposition of the Doctrine, there arose in the mind of Moggallāna, the wandering ascetic, a clear and distinct perception of the Doctrine that whatever is subject to origination is subject also to cessation. "If this is the Doctrine," said he, "then, indeed, have you reached the sorrowless state lost sight of and neglected for many myriads of world-cycles."

NOTES AND REFERENCES

38. Sāriputta and Moggallāna after their conversion became the two chief disciples of The Buddha. See the Story of Sumedha, verse 77.

Chapter XI

THE BUDDHA'S DAILY HABITS

Translated from the Sumaṅgala-Vilāsinī (i.45[10]), Buddhaghosa's Commentary on the Dīgha-Nikāya.

दीघनिकाये सुमङ्गलविलासिनी (पठमो भागो)

ब्रह्मणलसुत्तवण्णना, परिब्बाजककथावण्णना

पच्छिमयामकिच्चं, किच्चञ्च नामेतं सात्थकं, निरत्थकन्ति दुविधं होति। तत्थ निरत्थककिच्च भगवता बोधिपल्लङ्केयेव अरहत्तमग्गेन समुग्घातं कतं। सात्थकंयेव पन भगवतो किच्चं होति। तं पञ्चविधं– पुरेभत्तकिच्चं, पच्छाभत्तकिच्चं, पुरिमयामकिच्चं, मज्झिमयामकिच्चं, पच्छिमयामकिच्चन्ति।

तत्रिदं पुरेभत्तकिच्चं–

भगवा हि पातोव उट्ठाय उपट्ठाकानुग्गहत्थं सरीरफासुकत्थञ्च मुखधोवनादिसरीरपरिकम्मं कत्वा याव भिक्खाचारवेला ताव विवित्तासने वीतिनामेत्वा, भिक्खाचारवेलायं निवासेत्वा कायबन्धनं बन्धित्वा चीवरं पारुपित्वा पत्तमादाय कदाचि एकको, कदाचि भिक्खुसङ्घपरिवुततो, गामं वा निगमं वा पिण्डाय पविसति; कदाचि पकतिया, कदाचि अनेकेहि पाटिहारियोहि वत्तमानेहि। सेय्यथिदं, पिण्डाय पविसतो लोकनाथस्स पुरतो पुरतो गन्त्वा मुदुगतवाता पथविं सोधेन्ति, वलाहका उदकफुसितानि मुञ्चन्ता मग्गे रेणु वूपसमेत्वा उपरि वितानं हुत्वा

तिट्ठन्ति, अपरे वाता पुपफानि उपसंहरित्वा मग्गे ओकिरन्ति, उन्नता भूमिप्पदेसा ओनमन्ति, ओनता उन्नमन्ति, पादनिक्खेपसमये समाव भूमि होति, सुखसम्फस्सानि पदुमपुप्फानि वा पादे सम्पटिच्छन्ति। इन्छखीलस्स अन्तो ठपितमत्ते दक्खिणपादे सरीरतो छब्बण्णरस्मियो निक्खमित्वा सुवण्णरसपिञ्जरानि विय चित्रपटपरिक्खित्तानि विय च पासादकूटागारादीनि अलङ्करोन्तियो इतो चितो च धावन्ति, हत्थिअस्सविहङ्गादयो सकसकट्ठानेसु ठितायेव मधुरनाकारेन सद्दं करोन्ति, तथा भेरिवीणादीनि तूरियानि मनुस्सानञ्च कायूपगानि आभरणानि। तेन सञ्ञाणेन मनुस्सा जानन्ति–"अज्ज भगवा इध पिण्डाय पविट्ठो'ति। ते सुनिवत्था सुपारुता गन्धपुप्फादीनि आदाय घरा निक्खमित्वा अन्तरवीथिं पटिपज्जित्वा भगवन्तं गन्धपुप्फादीहि सक्कच्चं पूजेत्वा वन्दित्वा–"अम्हाकं, भन्ते, दस भिक्खू, अम्हाकं वीसति, पञ्ञासं...पे०....सतं देथा"ति याचित्वा भगवतोपि पत्तं गहेत्वा आसनं पञ्ञपेत्वा सक्कच्चं पिण्डपातेन पटिमानेन्ति। भगवा कतभत्तकिच्चो तेसं सत्तानं चित्तसन्तानानि ओलोकेत्वा तथा धम्मं देसेति, यथा केचि सरणगमनेसु पतिट्ठहन्ति, केचि पञ्चसु सीलेसु, केचि सोतापत्तिसकदागामिअनागामिफलानं अञ्ञतरस्मिं; केचि पब्बजित्वा अग्गफले अरहत्तेति। एवं महाजनं अनुग्गहेत्वा उट्ठायासना विहारं गच्छति। तत्थ गन्त्वा मण्डलमाळे पञ्ञत्तवरबुद्धासने निसीदति, भिक्खूनं भत्तकिच्चपरियोसानं आगम- यमानो। ततो भिक्खूनं भत्तकिच्चपरियोसाने उपट्ठाको भगवतो निवेदेति। अथ भगवा गन्धकुटिं पविसति। इदं ताव पुरेभत्तकिच्चं।

अथ भगवा एवं कतपुरेभत्तकिच्चो गन्धकुटिया उपट्ठाने निसीदित्वा पादे पक्खालेत्वा पादपीठे ठत्वा भिक्खुसङ्घं ओवदति– "भिक्खवे, अप्पमादेन सम्पादेथ, दुल्लभो बुद्धुप्पादो लोकस्मिं, दुल्लभो मनुस्सत्तपटिलाभो, दुल्लभा सम्पत्ति, दुल्लभा पब्बज्जा, दुल्लभं सद्धम्मस्सवन"न्ति। तत केचि भगवन्तं कम्मट्ठानं पुच्छन्ति। भगवापि तेसं चरियानुरूपं कम्पट्ठानं देति। ततो सब्बेपि भगवन्तं वन्दित्वा

अत्तनो अत्तनो रत्तिट्ठानदिवाट्ठानानि गच्छन्ति। केचि अरञ्ञं, केचि रुक्खमूलं, केचि पब्बतादीनं अञ्ञतरं, केचि चातुमहाराजिक- भवनं. ..पे०...केचि वसवत्तिभवन्ति। ततो भगवा गन्धकुटिं पविसित्वा सचे आकङ्खति, दक्खिणेन पस्सेन सतो सम्पजानो मुहुत्तं सीहसेय्यं कप्पेति। अथ समस्सासितकायो वुट्ठहित्वा दुतियभागे लोकं वोलोकेति। ततियभागे यं गामं वा निगमं वा उपनिस्साय विहरति तत्थ महाजनो पुरेभत्तं दानं दत्वा पच्छाभत्तं सुनिवत्थो सुपारुतो गन्धपुप्फादीनि आदाय विहारे सन्निपतति। ततो भगवा सम्पत्तपरिसाय अनुरूपेन पाटिहारियेन गन्त्वा धम्मसभायं पञ्ञत्तवरबुद्धासने निसज्ज धम्मं देसेति कालयुत्तं समययुत्तं, अथ कालं विदित्वा परिसं उय्योजेति, मनुस्सा भगवन्तं वन्दिता पक्कमन्ति। इदं पच्छाभत्तकिच्चं।

सो एवं निट्ठितपच्छाभत्तकिच्चो सचे गत्तानि ओसिञ्चितुकामो होति, बुद्धासना वुट्ठाय न्हानकोट्ठकं पविसित्वा उपट्ठाकेन पटियादितउदकेन गत्तानि उतुं गण्हापेति। उपट्ठाकोपि बुद्धासनं आनेत्वा गन्धकुटिपरिवेणे पञ्ञपेति। भगवा सुरत्तदुपट्टं निवासेत्वा कायबन्धनं बन्धित्वा उत्तरासङ्गं, एकंसं करित्वा तत्थ गन्त्वा निसीददति एककोव मुहुत्तं पटिसल्लीनो, अथ भिक्खू ततो ततो आगम्म भगवतो उपट्ठानं आगच्छन्ति। तत्थ एकच्चे पञ्हं पुच्छन्ति, एकच्चे कम्मट्ठानं, एकच्चे धम्मस्सवनं याचन्ति। भगवा तेसं अधिप्पायं सम्पादेन्तो पुरिमयामं वीतिनामेति। इदं पुरिमयामकिच्चं।

पुरिमयामकिच्चपरियोसाने पन भिक्खूसु भगवन्तं वन्दिता पक्कन्तेसु सकलदससहस्सिलोकधातुदेवतायो ओकासं लभमाना भगवन्तं उपसङ्कमित्वा पञ्हं पुच्छन्ति, यथाभिसङ्खतं अन्तमसो चतुरक्खरम्पि। भगवा तासं देवतानं पञ्हं विस्सज्जेन्तो चज्झिमयामं वीतिनामेति। इदं मज्झिमयामकिच्चं।

पच्छिमयामं पन तयो कोट्ठासे कत्वा पुरेभत्ततो पट्ठाय निसज्जाय पीळितस्स सरीरस्स किलासुभावमोचनत्थं एकं कोट्ठासं चङ्कमेन वीतिनामेति। दुतियकोट्ठासे गन्धकुटिं पविसित्वा दक्खिणेन पस्सेन

सतो सम्पजानो सीहसेय्यं कप्पेति। ततियकोट्ठासे पच्चुट्ठाय निसीदित्वा पुरिमबुद्धानं सन्तिके दानसीलादिवसेन कताधिकारपुग्गलदस्सनत्थं बुद्धचक्खुना लोकं वोलोकेति। इदं पच्छिमयामकिच्चं।

Habits are of two kinds, the profitable, and the unprofitable. Of these, the unprofitable habits of The Blessed One had been extirpated by his attainment of saintship at the time he sat cross-legged under the Bodhi-tree. Profitable habits, however, remained to The Blessed One.

These were fivefold: his before-breakfast habits; his after-breakfast habits; his habits of the first watch of the night; his habits of the middle watch of the night; his habits of the last watch of the night.

His before-breakfast habits were as follows :

The Blessed One would rise early in the morning, and when, out of kindness to his body-servant[39] and for the sake of bodily comfort, he had rinsed his mouth and otherwise cared for his person, he would sit retired until it was time to go begging. And when it came time, he would put on his tunic, girdle, and robes, and taking his bowl, he would enter the village or the town for alms. Sometimes he went alone, sometimes surrounded by a congregation of priests; sometimes without anything especial happening, sometimes with the accompaniment of many prodigies.

While, namely, the Lord of the World is entering for alms, gentle winds clear the ground before him; the clouds let fall drops of water to lay the dust in his pathway, and then become a canopy over him; other winds bring flowers and scatter them in his path; elevations of ground depress themselves, and depressions elevate themselves; wherever he places his foot, the ground is even and pleasant to walk upon,[40] or lotus-flowers receive his tread. No sooner has he set his right foot within the city-gate than the rays of six different colors which issue from his body race hither and thither over palaces and pagodas, and deck them, as it were, with the yellow sheen of gold, or with the colors of a painting. The elephants, the horses, the birds, and other animals give forth melodious sounds; likewise the tom-toms, lutes, and other musical instruments, and the ornaments worn by the people.

By these tokens the people would know, "The Blessed One has now entered for alms;" and in their best tunics and best robes, with perfumes, flowers, and other offerings, they issue forth from their houses into the street. Then, having zealously paid homage to The Blessed One with the perfumes, flowers, and other offerings, and done him obeisance, some would implore him, "Reverend Sir, give us ten priests to feed;" some, "Give us twenty;" and some, "Give us a hundred priests." And they would take the bowl of The Blessed One, and prepare a seat for him, and zealously show their reverence for him by placing food in the bowl.

When he had finished his meal, The Blessed One, with due consideration for the different dispositions of their minds, would so teach them the Doctrine that some would become established in the refuges, some in the five precepts, some would become converted, some would attain to the fruit of either once returning, or of never returning, while some would become established in the highest fruit, that of saint-ship, and would retire from the world. Having shown this kindness to the multitude, he would rise from his seat, and return to the monastery.

On his arrival there, he would, take his seat in a pavilion, on the excellent Buddha-mat which had been spread for him, where he would wait for the priests to finish their meal. When the priests had finished their meal, the body-servant would announce the fact to The Blessed One. Then The Blessed One would enter the perfumed chamber.

These, then, were his before-breakfast habits.

Then The Blessed One, having thus finished his before-breakfast duties, would first sit in the perfumed chamber, on a seat that had been spread for him by his body-servant, and would wash his feet. Then, taking up his stand on the landing of the jeweled staircase which led to the perfumed chamber, he would exhort the congregation of the priests, saying—

"O priests, diligently work out your salvation; for not often occur the appearance of a Buddha in the world and existence among men[41] and the propitious moment and retirement from the world and the opportunity to hear the true Doctrine."

At this point some would ask The Blessed One for exercises in meditation, and The Blessed One would assign them exercises suited to their several characters. Then all would do obeisance to The Blessed One, and go to the places where they were in the habit of spending the night or the day— some to the forest, some to the foot of trees, some to the hills, and so on, some to the heaven of the Four Great Kings, . . . and some to Vāsavatti's heaven.

Then The Blessed One, entering the perfumed chamber, would, if he wished, lie down for a while, mindful and conscious, and on his right side after the manner of a lion. And secondly, his body being now refreshed, he would rise, and gaze over the world. And thirdly, the people of the village or town near which he might be dwelling, who had given him breakfast, would assemble after breakfast at the monastery, again in their best tunics and their best robes, and with perfumes, flowers, and other offerings.

Thereupon The Blessed One, when his audience had assembled, would approach in such miraculous manner as was fitting; and taking his seat in the lecture-hall, on the excellent Buddha-mat which had been spread for him, he would teach the Doctrine, as suited the time and occasion. And when he perceived it was time, he would dismiss the audience, and the people would do obeisance to The Blessed One, and depart.

These were his after-breakfast habits.

When he had thus finished his after-breakfast duties, he

would rise from the excellent Buddha-seat, and if he desired to bathe, he would enter the bath-house, and cool his limbs with water made ready by his body-servant. Then the body-servant would fetch the Buddha-seat, and spread it in the perfumed chamber. And The Blessed One, putting on a tunic of double red cloth, and binding on his girdle, and throwing his upper robe over his right shoulder, would go thither and sit down, and for a while remain solitary, and plunged in meditation. After that would come the priests from here and from there to wait on The Blessed One. And some would propound questions, some would ask for exercises in meditation, and some for a sermon; and in granting their desires The Blessed One would complete the first watch of the night.

These were his habits of the first watch of the night.

And now, when The Blessed One had finished his duties of the first watch of the night, and when the priests had done him obeisance and were departing, the deities throughout the entire system of ten thousand worlds would seize the opportunity to draw near to The Blessed One and ask him any questions that might occur to them, even such as were but four syllables long. And The Blessed One in answering their questions would complete the middle watch of the night.

These were his habits of the middle watch of the night.

The last watch of the night he would divide into three parts, and as his body would be tired from so much sitting since the morning, he would spend one part in pacing up and down to free himself from the discomfort. In the second part he would enter the perfumed chamber, and would lie down mindful and conscious, and on his right side after the manner of a lion. In the third part he would rise, and taking his seat, he would gaze over the world with the eye of a Buddha, in order to discover any individual who, under some former Buddha, with alms-giving, or keeping the precepts, or other meritorious deeds, might have made the earnest wish.

These were his habits of the last watch of the night.

NOTES AND REFERENCES

39. In order to give him a chance to acquire merit by waiting on a Buddha.
40. Compare *Isaiah* xl. 4: Every valley shall be exalted, and every mountain and hill shall be made low: . . . and the rough places plain.
41. It is necessary to be a human being in order to attain to saintship, though gods can become converted and animals can keep the precepts.

Chapter XII

THE DEATH OF THE BUDDHA

Translated from the Mahā-Parinibbāna-Sutta (v. and vi.) of the Dīgha-Nikāya.

दीघनिकाये, महापरिनिब्बानसुत्त

परिनित्वानम्वद्यनिपन्नो भगवा

अथ खो भगवा आयस्मन्तं आनन्दं आमन्तेसि–"आयामानन्द, येन हिरञ्ञवतिया नदिया पारिमं तीरं येन कुसिनारा उपवत्तनं मल्लानं सालवनं तेनुपसङ्कमिस्सामा"ति। "एवं, भन्ते"ति खो आयस्मा आनन्दो भगवतो पच्चस्सोसि। अथ खो भगवा महता भिक्खुसङ्घेन सद्धिं येन हिरञ्ञवतिया नदिया पारिमं तीरं येन कुसिनारा उपवत्तनं मल्लानं सालवनं तेनपसङ्कमि तेनुपसङ्कमित्वा आयस्मन्तं आनन्दं आमन्तेसि – "इङ्घ मे त्वं, आनन्द, अन्तरेन यमकसालानं उत्तरसीसकं मञ्चकं पञ्ञपेहि। किलमन्तोस्मि, आनन्द, निपज्जिस्सामी"ति। "एवं, भन्ते"ति खो आयस्मा आनन्दो भगवतो पटिस्सुत्वा अन्तरेन यमकसालानं उत्तरसीसकं मञ्चक पञ्ञपेसि। अथ खो भगवा दक्खिणेन पस्सेन सीहसेय्यं कप्पेसि, पादे पादं अच्चाधाय, सतो सम्पजानो

तेन खो पन समयेन यमकसाला सब्बफालिफुल्ला होन्ति अकालपुप्फेहि। तथागतस्स सरीरं ओकिरन्ति अज्झोकिरन्ति अभिप्पकिरन्ति तथागतस्स पूजाय। दिब्बानि पि मन्दारवपुप्फानि अन्तलिक्खा पपतन्ति। तानि तथागतस्स सरीरं ओकिरन्ति अज्झो

किरन्ति अभिप्पकिरन्ति तथागतस्स पूजाय। दिब्बानि पि चन्दनचुण्णानि अन्तलिक्खा पपतन्ति। तानि तथागतस्स सरीरं ओकिरन्ति अज्झोकिरन्ति अभिप्पकिरन्ति तथागतस्स पूजाय। दिब्बानि पि तूरियानि अन्तलिक्खे वज्जन्ति तथागतस्स पूजाय, दिब्बानि पि सङ्गीतानि अन्तलिक्खे वत्तन्ति तथागतस्स पूजाय।

अथ खो भगवा आयस्मन्तं आनन्दं आमन्तेसि –"सब्बफालिफुल्ला खो, आनन्द, यमकसाला अकालपुप्फेहि। ते तथागतस्स सरीरं ओकिरन्ति अज्झोकिरन्ति अभिप्पकिरन्ति तथागतस्स पूजाय। दिब्बानि पि मन्दारवपुप्फानि अन्तलिक्खा पतन्ति। तानि तथागतस्स सरीरं ओकिरन्ति अज्झोकिरन्ति अभिप्पकिरन्ति तथागतस्स पूजाय। दिब्बानि पि चन्दनचुण्णानि अन्तलिक्खा पपतन्ति। तानि तथागतस्स सरीरं ओकिरन्ति अज्झोकिरन्ति अभिप्पकिरन्ति तथागतस्स पूजाय। दिब्बानि पि तूरियानि अन्तलिक्खे वज्जन्ति तथागतस्स पूजाय, दिब्बानि पि सङ्गीतानि अन्तलिक्खे वत्तन्ति तथागतस्स पूजाय। न खो, आनन्द, एत्तावता तथागतो सक्कतो वा होति गरुकतो वा मानितो वा पूजितो वा अपचितो वा। यो खो, आनन्द, भिक्खु वा भिक्खुनी वा उपासको वा उपासिका वा धम्मानुधम्मप्पटिपन्नो विहरति सामीचिप्पटिपन्नो आनुध म्मचारी, सो तथागतं सक्करोति गरुं करोति मानेति पूजेति अपचियति परमाय पूजाय। तस्मातिहानन्द 'धम्मानुधम्मप्पटिपन्ना विहरिस्साम सामीचिप्पटिपन्ना अनुधम्मचारिनो' ति–एवं हि वो, आनन्द, सिक्खितब्बं"ति।

उपवाणत्थेरं अपसारेसि

तेन खो पन समयेन आयस्मा उपवाणो भगवतो पुरतो ठितो होति भगवन्तं बीजयमानो। अथ खो भगवा आयस्मन्तं उपवाणं अपसारेसि–"अपेहि, भिक्खु, मा मे पुरतो अट्ठासी"ति। अथ खो आयस्मतो आनन्दस्स एतदहोसि–"अयं खो आयस्मा उपवाणो दीघरत्तं भगवतो उपट्ठाको सन्तिकावचरो समीपचारी। अथ च पन भगवा पच्छिमे काले आयस्मन्तं उपवाणं अपसारेति–'अपेहि, भिक्खु मा मे

पुरतो अट्ठासी' ति। को नु खो हेतु, को पच्चयो, यं भगवा आयस्मन्तं उपवाणं अपसारेति–'अपेहि, भिक्खु, मा मे पुरतो अट्ठासी'"ति? अथ खो आयस्मा आनन्दो भगवन्तं एतदवोच–"अयं, भन्ते आयस्मा उपवाणो दीघरत्तं भगवतो उपट्ठाको सन्तिकावचरो समीपचारी। अथ च पन भगवा पच्छिमे काले आयस्मन्तं उपवाणं अपसारेति–'अपेहि, भिक्खु, मा मे पुरतो अट्ठासी' ति। को नु खो, भन्ते, हेतु, को पच्चयो, यं भगवा आयस्मन्तं उपवाणं अपसारेति–'अपेहि, भिक्खु, मा मे पुरतो अट्ठासी'"ति?

"येभुय्येन, आनन्द, दससु लोकधातूसु देवता सन्निपतिता तथागतं दस्सनाय। यावता, आनन्द, कुसिनारा उपवत्तनं मल्लानं सालवनं समन्ततो द्वादस योजनानि, नत्थि सो पदेसो वालग्गकोटिनितुदनमत्ते पि महेसक्खाहि देवताहि अप्फुटो। देवता, आनन्द, उज्झायन्ति–'दूरा च वतम्ह आगता तथागतं दस्सनाय। कदाचि करहचि तथागता लोके उप्पज्जन्ति अरहन्तो सम्मासम्बुद्धा। अज्जेव रत्तिया पच्छिमे यामे तथागतस्स परिनिब्बानं भविस्सति। अयं च महेसक्खो भिक्खु भगवतो पुरतो ठितो ओवारेन्तो। न मयं लभाम पच्छिमे काले तथागतं दस्सनाय"ति।।

"कथम्भूता पन, भन्ते, भगवा देवता मनसिकरोती"ति?

"सन्तानन्द, देवता आकासे पथवीसञ्ञिनियो केसे पकिरिय कन्दन्ति, बाहा पग्गय्ह कन्दन्ति, छिन्नपातं पपतन्ति, आवट्टन्ति–'अतिखिप्पं भगवा परिनिब्बायिस्सति, अतिखिप्पं सुगतो परिनिब्बायिस्सति, अतिखिप्पं चक्खुं लोके अन्तरधायिस्सती"ति।

"सन्तानन्द, देवता पथवियं पथवीसञ्ञिनियो केसे पकिरिय कन्दन्ति, बाहा पग्गय्ह कन्दन्ति, छिन्नपातं पपतन्ति, आवट्टन्ति, विवट्टन्ति–'अतिखिप्पं भगवा परिनिब्बायिस्सति, अतिखिप्पं सुगतो परिनिब्बायिस्सति, अतिखिप्पं चक्खुं लोके अन्तरधायिस्सती"ति।

"या पन ता देवता वीतरागा ता सता सम्पजाना अधिवासेन्ति–'अनिच्चा सङ्खारा, तं कुतेत्थ लब्भा'"ति।

चत्तरि संवेजनीयट्ठानानि

"पुब्बे, भन्ते, दिसासु वस्सं वुत्था भिक्खू आगच्छन्ति तथागतं दस्सनाय। ते मयं लभाम मनोभावनीये भिक्खू दस्सनाय, लभाम पयिरुपासनाय। भगवतो पन मयं, भन्ते, अच्चयेन न लभिस्साम मनोभावनीये भिक्खू दस्सनाय न लभिस्साम पयिरुपासनाया"ति। "चत्तारिमानि, आनन्द, सद्धस्स कुलपुत्तस्स दस्सनीयानि संवेजनीयानि ठानानि। कतमानि चत्तारि? (1) इध तथागतो जातो ति, आनन्द, सद्धस्स कुलपुत्तस्स दस्सनीयं संवेजनीयं ठानं। (2) इध तथागतो अनुत्तरं सम्मासम्बोधिं अभिसम्बुद्धो ति, आनन्द, सद्धस्स कुलपुत्तस्स दस्सनीयं संवेजनीयं ठानं। (3) इध तथागतेन अनुत्तरं धम्मचक्कं पवत्तितं ति, आनन्द, सद्धस्स कुलपुत्तस्स दस्सनीयं संवेजनीयं ठानं।(4) इध तथागतो अनुपादिसेसाय निब्बानधातुया परिनिब्बुतो ति, आनन्द, सद्धस्स कुलपुत्तस्स दस्सनीयं संवेजनीयं ठानं। इमानि खो, आनन्द, चत्तारि सद्धस्स कुलपुत्तस्स दस्सनीयानि संवेजनीयानि ठानानि।"

"आगमिस्सन्ति खो, आन्नद, सद्धा भिक्खू भिक्खुनियो उपासका उपासिकायो–इध तथागतो जातो ति पि, इध तथागतो अनुत्तरं सम्मासम्बोधिं अभिसम्बुद्धो ति पि, इध तथागतेन अनुत्तरं धम्मचक्कं पवत्तितं ति पि, इध तथागतो अनुपादिसेसाय निब्बानधातुया परिनिब्बुतो ति पि। ये हि केचि, आनन्द, चेतियचारिकं आहिण्डन्ता पसन्नचिता कालं करिस्सन्ति, सब्बे ते कायस्स भेदा परं मरणा सुगतिं सग्गं लोकं उपपज्जिस्सन्ती"ति।

आनन्दपुच्छा

"कथं मयं, भन्ते, मातुगामे पटिपज्जामा"ति?

"अदस्सनं, आनन्दा"ति।

"दस्सने, भगवा, सति कथं पटिपज्जितब्बं"ति?

"अनालापो, आनन्दा"ति।

"आलपन्तेन पन, भन्ते, कथं पटिपज्जितब्बं"ति?

"सति, आनन्द, उपट्ठापेतब्बा"ति (1)

"कथं मयं, भन्ते, तथागतस्स सरीरे पटिपज्जामा"ति?

"अब्यावटा तुम्हे, आनन्द, होथ तथागतस्स सरीरपूजाय। इङ्घ तुम्हे, आनन्द, सारत्थे घटथ अनुयुज्जथ; सारत्थे अप्पमत्ता आतापिनो पहितत्ता विहरथ। सन्तानन्द, खत्तियपण्डिता पि ब्राह्मणपण्डिता पि गहपतिपण्डिता पि तथागते अभिप्पसन्ना। ते तथागतस्स सरीरपूजं करिस्सन्ती"ति। (2)

"कथं पन, भन्ते, तथागतस्स सरीरे पटिपज्जितब्बं"ति?

"यथा खो, आनन्द, रञ्ञो चक्कवत्तिस्स सरीरे पटिपज्जन्ति, एवं तथागतस्स सरीरे पटिपज्जितब्बं"ति। (3)

"कथं पन, भन्ते, रञ्ञो चक्कवत्तिस्स सरीरे पटिपज्जन्तो"ति?

"रञ्ञो, आनन्द, चक्कवत्तिस्स सरीरं अहतेन वत्थेन वेठेन्ति, अहतेन वत्थेन वेठेत्वा विहतेन कप्पासेन वेठेन्ति, विहतेन कप्पासेन वेठेत्वा अहतेन वत्थेन वेठेन्ति, एतेनुपायेन पञ्चहि युगसतेहि रञ्ञो चक्कवत्तिस्स सरीरं वेठेत्वा आयसाय तेलदोणिया पक्खिपित्वा अञ्ञिस्सा आयसाय दोणिया पटिकुज्जित्वा सब्बगन्धानं चितकं करित्वा रञ्ञो चक्कवत्तिस्स सरीरं झापेन्ति। चातुमहापथे रञ्ञो चक्कवत्तिस्स थूपे करोन्ति। एवं खो, आनन्द, रञ्ञो चक्कवत्तिस्स सरीरे पटिपज्जन्ति।

यथा खो, आनन्द, रञ्ञो चक्कवत्तिस्स सरीरे पटिपज्जन्ति, एवं तथागतस्स सरीरे पटिपज्जितब्बं। चातुमहापथे तथागतस्स थूपो कातब्बो। तत्थ ये मालं वा गन्धं वा चुण्णकं वा आरोपेस्सन्ति वा अभिवादेस्सन्ति वा चित्तं वा पसादेस्सन्ति तेसं तं भविस्सति दीघरत्तं हिताय सुखाय।"

थूपारहपुग्गला

"चत्तारोमे, आनन्द, थूपारहा। कतमे चत्तारो? (1) तथागतो अरहं सम्मासम्बुद्धो थूपारहो, (2) पच्चेकसम्बुद्धो थूपारहो, (3) तथागतस्स सावको थूपारहो, (4) राजा चक्कवत्ती थूपारहो ति।"

"किं चानन्द, अत्थवसं पटिच्च तथागतो अरहं सम्मासम्बुद्धो थूपारहो? 'अयं तस्स भगवतो अरहतो सम्मासम्बुद्धस्स थूपो'ति, आनन्द, बहुजना चित्तं पसादेन्ति। ते तत्थ चित्तं पसादेत्वा कायस्स भेदा परं मरणा सुगतिं सरगं लोकं उपपज्ञन्ति। इदं खो, आनन्द, अत्थवसं पट्िच्च तथागतो अरहं सम्मासम्बुद्धो थूपारहो। (1)

"किं चानन्द, अत्थवसं पटिच्च पच्चेकसम्बुद्धो थूपारहो? 'अयं तस्स भगवतो पच्चेकसम्बुद्धस्स थूपो'ति, आनन्द, बहुजना चित्तं पसादेन्ति। ते तत्थ चित्तं पसादेत्वा कायस्स भेदा परं मरणा सुगतिं सग्गं लोकं उपपज्ञन्ति। इदं खो, आनन्द, अत्थवसं पटिच्च पच्चेकसम्बुद्धो थूपारहो। (2)

"किं चानन्द, अत्थवसं पटिच्च तथागतस्स सावको थूपारहो? 'अयं तस्स भगवतो अरहतो सम्मासम्बुद्धस्स सावकस्स थूपो'ति, आनन्द, बहुजना चित्तं पसादेन्ति। ते तत्थ चित्तं पसादेत्वा कायस्स भेदा परं मरणा सुगतिं सग्गं लोकं उपपज्ञन्ति। इदं खो, आनन्द, अत्थवसं पटिच्च राजा चक्कवत्ती थूपारहो। (3)

"किं चानन्द, अत्थवसं पटिच्च राजा चक्कवत्ती थूपारहो? 'अयं तस्स धम्मिकस्स धम्मरञ्ञो थूपो'ति, आनन्द, बहुजना चित्तं पसादेन्ति। ते तत्थं चित्तं पसादेत्वा कायस्स भेदा परं मरणा सुगतिं सग्गं लोकं उपपज्ञन्ति। इदं खो, आनन्द अत्थवसं पटिच्च राजा चक्कवती थूपारहो। (4)

इमे खो, आनन्द चत्तारो थूपारहा"ति।

आनन्दे अच्छरियधम्मा

अथ खो आयस्मा आनन्दो विहारं पविसित्वा कपिसीसं आलम्बित्वा रोदमानो अट्ठासि–"अहं च वतम्हि सेखो सकरणीयो, सत्थु च मे परिनिब्बानं भविस्सति यो मम अनुकम्पको"ति। अथ खो भगवा भिक्खू आमन्तेसि–"कहं नु खो, भिक्खवे, आनन्दो"ति?

"एसो, भन्ते, आयस्मा आनन्दो विहारं पविसित्वा कपिसीसं

आलम्बित्व रोदमानो ठितो–'अहं च वतम्हि सेखो सकरणीयो, सत्थु च मे परिनिब्बानं भविस्सति यो मम अनुकम्पको'"ति। अथ खो भगवा अञ्ञतरं भिक्खुं आमन्तेसि–"एहि त्वं, भिक्खु, मम वचनेन आनन्दं आमन्तेहि–'सत्था तं, आवुसो आनन्द, आमन्तेती"ति। "एवं, भन्ते"ति खो सो भिक्खु भगवतो पटिस्सुत्वा येनायस्मा आनन्दो तेनुपसङ्कमि; उपसङ्कमित्वा आयस्मन्तं आनन्दं एतदवोच–"सत्था तं, आवुसो आनन्द, आमन्तेती"ति। "एवमावुसो" ति खो आयस्मा आनन्दो तस्सभिक्खुनो पटिस्सुत्वा येन भगवा तेनुपसङ्कमि; उपसङ्कमित्वा भगवन्तं अभिवादेत्वा एकमन्तं निसीदि। एकमन्तं निसिन्नं खो आयस्मन्तं आनन्दं भगवा एतदवोच–"अलं, आनन्द, सा सोचि, सा परिदेवि। ननु एतं, आन्नद, मया पटिकच्चेव अक्खातं–सब्बेहेव पियेहि मनापेहि नानभावो विनाभावो; तं कुतेत्थ, आनन्द, लब्भा। यं तं जातं भूतं सङ्खतं पलोकधम्मं तं वत तथागतस्सा पि सरीरं मा पलुज्जी ति नेतं ठानं विज्जति। दीघरत्तं खो ते, आनन्द, तथागतो पच्चुपट्ठितो मेत्तेन कायकम्मेन हितेन सुखेन अद्वयेन अप्पमाणेन, मेत्तेन वचीकम्मेन हितेन सुखेन अद्वयेन अप्पमाणेन, मेत्तेन मनोकम्मेन हितेन सुखेन अद्वयेन अप्पमाणेन। कतपुञ्ञोसि त्वं, आनन्द, पधानमनुयुञ्ज, खिप्पं होहिसि अनासवो"ति।

अथ खो भगवा भिक्खू आमन्तेसि–"ये पि ते, भिक्खवे, अहेसुं अतीतमद्धानं अरहन्तो सम्मासम्बुद्धा तेसं पि भगवन्तानं एतप्परमायेव उट्ठाका अहेसुं, सेय्यथापि मय्हं आनन्दो। ये पि ते, भिक्खेन भविस्सन्ति अनागतमद्धानं अरहन्तो सम्मासम्बुद्धा, तेसं पि भगवन्तानं एतप्परमायेव उपट्ठाका भविस्सन्ति, सेय्यथापि मय्हं आनन्दो। पण्डितो, भिक्खवे, आनन्दो; मेधावी, भिक्खवे, आनन्दो। जानाति अयं कालो तथागतं दस्सनाय उपसङ्कमितुं भिक्खूनं, अयं कालो भिक्खुनीनं, अयं कालो उपासकानं, अयं कालो उपासिकानं, अयं कालो रञ्ञो राजमहामत्तानं तित्थियानं तित्थियसावकानं ति।"

"चत्तारोमे, भिक्खवे, अच्छरिया अब्भुता धम्मा आनन्दे। कतमे

चत्तारो? (1) सचे, भिक्खवे, भिक्खुपरिसा आनन्दं दस्सनाय उपसङ्कमति, दस्सनेन सा अत्तमना होति। तत्र चे आनन्दो धम्मं भासति, भासितेन पि सा अत्तमना होति। अतित्ता व, भिक्खवे, भिक्खुपरिसा होति, अथ खो आनन्दो तुण्ही होति। (2) सचे, भिक्खवे, भिक्खुनीपरिसा आनन्दं दस्सनाया उपसङ्कमति, दस्सनेन सा अत्तमना होति। तत्र चे आनन्दो धम्मं भासति, भासितेन पि सा अत्तमना होति। अतित्ता व, भिक्खवे, भिक्खुनीपरिसा होति, अथा खो आनन्दो तुण्ही होति (3) सचे, भिक्खवे, उपासकपरिसा आनन्दं दस्सनाय उपसङ्कमति, दस्सनेन सा अत्तमना होति। तत्र चे आनन्दो धम्मं भासति, भासितेन पि सा अत्तमना होति। अतित्ता व, भिक्खवे, उपासकपरिसा होति, अथ खो आनन्दो तुण्ही होति। (4) सचे, भिक्खवे, उपासिकापरिसा आनन्दं दस्सनाय उपसङ्कमति, दस्सनेन सा अत्तमना होति। तत्र चे, आनन्दो, धम्मं भासति, भासितेन पि सा अत्तमना होति। अतित्ता व, भिक्खवे, उपासिकापरिसा होति, अथ खो आनन्दो तुण्ही होति। इमे खो, भिक्खवे, चत्तारो अच्छरिया अब्भुता धम्मा आनन्दे।

"चत्तारोमे, भिक्खवे, अच्छरिया अब्भुता धम्मा रञ्ञे चक्कवत्तिम्हि। कतमे चत्तारो? (1) सचे, भिक्खवे, खत्तियपरिसा राजानं चक्कवत्तिं दस्सनाय उपसङ्कमति, दस्सनेन सा अत्तमना होति। तत्र चे राजा चक्कवत्ती भासति, भासितेन पि सा अत्तमना होति। अतित्ता व, भिक्खवे, खत्तियपरिसा होति, अथ खो राजा चक्कवत्ती तुण्ही होति। (2) सचे, भिक्खवे, ब्राह्मणपरिसा........पे०.....। (3) गहपतिपरिसा.....पे०.....। (4) समणपरिसा राजानं चक्कवत्तिं दस्सनाय उपसङ्कमति, दस्सनेन सा अत्तमना होति। तत्र चे राज चक्कवत्ती भासति, भासितेन पि सा अत्तमना होति। अति ता व, भिक्खवे, समणपरिसा होति, अथ खो राजा चक्कवत्ती तुण्ही होति। एवमेव खो, भिक्खवे, चत्तारोमे अच्छरिया अब्भुता धम्मा आनन्दे। (1) सचे, भिक्खवे, भिक्खुपरिसा आनन्दं दस्सनाय उपसङ्कमति, दस्सनेन

सा अत्तमना होति। तत्र चे आनन्दो धम्मं भासति, भासितेन पि सा अत्तमना होति। अतित्ता व, भिक्खवे, भिक्खुपरिसा होति, अथ खो आनन्दो तुण्ही होति। (2) सचे भिक्खुनीपरिसा....पे॰....। (3) उपासकपरिसा....पे॰....। (4) उपासिकापरिसा आनन्दं दस्सनाय उपसङ्कमति, दस्सनेन सा अत्तमना होति। तत्र चे आनन्दो धम्मं भासति, भासितेन पि सा अत्तमना होति। अतित्ता व, भिक्खवे, उपासिकापरिसा होति, अथ खो आनन्दो तुण्ही होति। इमे खो, भिक्खवे, चत्तारो अच्छरिया अब्भुता धम्मा आनन्दे"ति।

महासुदस्सनकथा

एवं वुत्ते, आयस्मा आनन्दो भगवन्तं एतदवोच–"मा, भन्ते, भगवा इमस्मिं खुद्दकनगरके उज्जङ्गलनगरके साखानगरके परिनिब्बायि। सन्ति, भन्ते, अञ्ञानि महानगरानि, सेय्यथिदं–चम्पा, राजगहं, सावत्थी, सकेतं, कोसम्बी, बाराणसी, एत्थ भगवा परिनिब्बायतु। एत्थ बहू खत्तियमहासाला ब्राह्मणमहासाला गहपतिमहासाला तथागते अभिप्पसन्ना। ते तथागतस्स सरीरपूजं करिस्सन्ती"ति।

"माहेवं, आनन्द, अवच; माहेवं, आनन्द, अवच–'खुद्दकनगरकं उज्जङ्गलनगरकं साखानगरकं' ति। भूतपुब्बं, आनन्द, राजा महासुदस्सनो नाम अहोसि चक्कवत्ती धम्मिको धम्मराजा चातुरन्तो विजितावी जनप्पदत्थावरियप्पत्तो सत्तरतनसमन्नागतो। रञ्ञो, आनन्द, महासुदस्सनस्स अयं कुसिनारा कुसावती नाम राजधानी अहोस पुरत्थिमेन च पच्छिमेन च द्वादसयोजनानि आयामेन, उत्तरेन च दक्खिणेन च सत्तयोजनानि वित्थारेन। कुसावती, आनन्द, राजधानी इद्धा चेव अहोसि फीता च बहुजना च आकिण्णमनुस्सा च सुभिक्खा च। सेय्यथापि, (रो. 147) आनन्द, देवानं आळकमन्दा नाम राजधानी इद्धा चेव होति फीता च बहुजना च आकिण्णयक्खा च सुभिक्खा च, एवमेव खो, आनन्द, कुसावती राजधानी इद्धा चेव अहोसि फीता च बहुजना च आकिण्णमनुस्सा च सुभिक्खा च। कुसावती,

आनन्द, राजधानी दसहि सद्देहि अविवित्ता अहोसि दिवा चेव रत्तिं च, सेय्यथिदं–(1) हत्थिसद्देन, (2) अस्ससद्देन, (3) रथसद्देन, (4) भेरिसद्देन (5) मुदिङ्गसद्देन, (6) वीणासद्देन, (7) गातसद्देन, (8) सङ्खसद्देन, सम्मसद्देन, (9) पाणिताळसद्देन, (10) अस्नाथ पिवथ खदथा ति दसमेन सद्देन।

"गच्छ त्वं, आनन्द। कुसनारं पविसत्वा कोसिनारकानं मल्लानं आरोचेहि–'अज्ज खो, वासेट्ठा, रत्तिया पच्छिमे यामे तथागतस्स परिनिब्बानं भविस्सति। अभिक्कमथ, वासेट्ठा, अभिक्कमथ, वासेट्ठा। मा पच्छा विप्पटिसारिनो अहुवत्थ–' अम्हाकं च नो गामक्खेत्ते तथागतस्स परिनिब्बानं अहोसि, न मयं लभिम्हा पच्छिमे काले तथागतं दस्सनाया'"ति। "एवं, भन्ते"ति खो आयस्मा आनन्दो भगवतो पटिस्सुत्वा निवासेत्व पत्तचीवरमादाय अत्तदुतियो कुसिनारं पाविसि।

मल्लानं वन्दना

तेन खो पन समयेन कोसिनारका मल्ला सन्थागारे सन्निपतिता होन्ति केनचिदेव करणीयेन। अथ खो आयस्मा आनन्दो येन कोसिनारकानं मल्लानं, सन्थागारं तेनुपसङ्कमि; उपसङ्कमित्वा कोसिनारकानं मल्लानं आरोचेसि–"अज्ज खो, वासेट्ठा, रत्तिया पच्छिमे यामे तथागतस्स परिनिब्बानं भविस्सति। अभिक्कमथ, वासेट्ठा, अभिक्कमथ, वासेट्ठा। मा पच्छा विप्पटिसारिनो अहुवत्थ–'अम्हाकं च नो गामक्खेत्ते तथागतस्स परिनिब्बानं अहोसि, न मयं लभिम्हा पच्छिमे काले तथागतं दस्सनाया'"ति।

इदमायस्मतो आनन्दस्स सुत्वा मल्ला च मल्लपुत्ता च मल्लसुणिसा च मल्लपजापतियों च अघाविनो दुम्मना चेतोदुक्खसमप्पिता अप्पेकच्चे केसे पकिरिय कन्दन्ति, बाहा पगय्ह कन्दन्ति, छिन्नपातं पपतन्ति, आवट्टन्ति विट्ट्न्ति–'अतिखिप्पं भगवा परिनिब्बायिस्सति, अतिखिप्पं सुगतो परिनिब्बायिस्सति, अतिखिप्पं, चक्खुं लोके अन्तरधायिस्सती' त। अथ खो मल्ला च मल्लपुत्ता च मल्लसुणिसा च मल्लपजापतियो

व अघाविनो दुम्मना चेतोदुक्खसमप्पिता येन उपवत्तनं मल्लानं सालवनं येनायस्मा आनन्दो तेनुपसङ्कमिंसु।

अथ खो आयस्मतो आनन्दस्स एतदहोसि–"सचे खो अहं कोसिनारके मल्ले एकमेकं भगवन्तं वन्दापेस्सामि, अवन्दितो भगवा कोसिनारकेहि मल्लेहि भविस्सति अथायं रत्ति विभायिस्सति यन्नूनाहं कोसिनारके मल्ले कुलपरिवत्तसो कुलपरिवत्तसो ठपेत्वा भगवन्तं वन्दापेय्यं–'इत्थन्नामो, भन्ते, मल्लो सपुत्तो सभरियो सपरिसो समच्चो भगवतो पादे सिरसा वन्दती' ति। अथ खो आयस्मा आनन्दो कोसिनारके मल्ले कुलपरिवत्तसो कुलपरिवत्तसो ठपेत्वा भगवन्तं वन्दापेसि–'इत्थन्नामो, भन्ते, मल्लो सपुत्तो सभरियो सपरिसो सामच्चो भगवतो पादे सिरसा वन्दती' ति। अथ खो आयस्मा आनन्दो एतेन उपायेन पठमेनेव यामन कोसि नारके मल्ले भगवन्तं वन्दापेसि।"

सुभद्दपरिब्बाजकवत्थु

तेन खो पन समयेन सुभद्दो नाम परिब्बाजको कुसिनारायं पटिवसति। अस्सोसि खो सुभद्दो परिब्बाजको–"अज्ज किर रत्तिया पच्छिमे यामे समणस्स गोतमस्स परिनिब्बानं भविस्सती"ति। अथ खो सुभद्दस्स परिब्बाजकस्स एतदाहोसि–"सुतं खो पन मेतं परिब्बाजकानं वुड्ढानं महल्लकानं आचरियपाचरियानं भासमानानं–'कदाचि करहचि तथागता लोके उप्पज्जन्ति अरहन्तो सम्मपासम्बुद्धा' ति। अज्जेव रत्तिया पच्छिमे यामे समणस्स गोतमस्स परिनिब्बानं भविस्सति। अत्थि च मे अयं कङ्खाधम्मो उप्पन्नो–'एवं पसन्नो अहं समणे गोतमे। पहोति मे समणो गोतमो तथा धम्मं देसेतुं यथाहं इमं कङ्खाधम्मं पजहेय्यं'"ति। अथ खो सुभद्दो परिब्बाजको येन उपवत्तनं सालवनं येनायस्मा आनन्दो तेनुपसङ्कमि; उपसङ्कमित्वा आयस्मन्तं आनन्दं एतदवोच–"सुतं मेतं, भो आनन्द, परिब्बाजकानं वुड्ढानं महल्लकानं आचरियपाचरियानं भासमानानं–'कदाचि करहचि तथागता लोके उप्पज्जन्ति अरहन्तो सम्मासम्बुद्धा' ति। अज्जेव रत्तिया पच्छिमे यामे समणस्स गोतमस्स

परिनिब्बानं भविस्सति। अत्थि च मे अयं कङ्खाधम्मो उप्पन्नो–'एवं पसन्नो अहं समणे गोतमे, पहोति मे समणो गोतमो तथा धम्म देसेतुं यथहं इमं कङ्खाधम्मं पजहेय्यं' ति। साधाहं, भो आनन्द, लभेय्यं समणं गोतमं दस्सनाया"ति। एवं वुत्ते, आयस्मा आनन्दो सुभद्दं परिब्बाजकं एतदवोच–"अलं, आवुसो सुभद्द, मा तथागतं विहेठेसि। किलन्तो भगवा"ति। दुतयं पि खो सुभद्दो परिब्बाजको....पे0....ततियं पि खो सुभद्दो परिब्बाजको आयस्मन्तं आनन्दं एतदवोच–"सुतं मेतं, भो आनन्द, परिब्बाजकानं वुडढानं महल्लकानं आचरियपाचरियकानं भासमानानं–'कदाचि करहचितथागता लोके उप्पज्जन्ति अरहन्तो सम्मासम्बुद्धा' ति। अज्जेव रत्तिया पच्छिमे यामे समणस्स गोतमस्स परिनिब्बानं भविस्सति। अत्थि च मे अयं कङ्खाधम्मो उप्पन्नो–एवं पसन्नो अहं समणे गोतमे, पहोति मे समणो गोतमो तथा धम्मं देसेतुं यथाहं इमं कङ्खाधम्मं पजहेय्यं' ति। साधाहं, भो आनन्द, लभेय्यं समणं गोतमं दस्सनाया"ति। ततियं पि खो आयस्मा आनन्दो सुभद्दं परिब्बाजकं एतदवोच–"अलं, आवुसो सुभद्द, मा तथागतं विहेठेसि। किलन्तो भगवा"ति।

अस्सोसि खो भगवा आयस्मतो आनन्दस्स सुभद्देन परिब्बाजकेन सद्धिं इमं कथासल्लापं। अथ खो भगवा आयस्मन्तं आनन्दं आमन्तेसि–"अलं, आनन्द, मा सुभद्दं वारेसि। लभतं, आनन्द, सुभद्दो तथागतं दस्सनाय। यं किञ्चि मं सुभद्दो पुच्छिस्सति सब्बं तं अञ्ञापेक्खो व पुच्छिस्सति, नो विहेसापेक्खो। यं चस्साहं पुट्ठो ब्याकरिस्सामि, तं खिप्पमेव आजनिस्सती"ति। अथ खो आयस्मा आनन्दो सुभद्दं परिब्बाजकं एतदवोच–"गच्छावुसो सुभद्द, करोति ते भगवा ओकासं"ति। अथ खो सुभद्दो परिब्बाजको येन भगवा तेनुपसङ्कमि; उपसङ्कमित्वा भगवता सद्धिं सम्मोदि। सम्मोदनीयं कथं सारणीयं वीतिसारेत्वा एकमन्तं निसीदि। एकमन्तं निसिन्नो खो सुभद्दो परिब्बाजको भगवन्तं एतदवोच–"येमे, भो गोतम, समणब्राह्मणा सङ्घिनो गणिनो गणाचरिया ञाता यसस्सिनो तित्थकरा साधुसम्मता बहुजनस्स, सेय्यथिदं–पूरणो

कस्सपो, मक्खलि गोसालो, अजितो केसकम्बलो, पकुधो कच्चायनो, सञ्जयो बेलट्ठपुत्तो, निगण्ठो नाटपुत्तो, सब्बेते सकाय पटिञ्ञाय अब्भञ्ञिंसु? सब्बेव न अब्भञ्ञिंसु? उदाहु एकच्चे अब्भञ्ञिंसु एकच्चे न अब्भञ्ञिंसु"ति?

"अलं, सुभद्द; तिट्ठतेतं–सब्बेते सकाय पटिञ्ञाय अब्भञ्ञिंसु, सब्बेव न अब्भञ्ञिंसु, उदाहु एकच्चे अब्भञ्ञिंसु एकच्चे न अब्भञ्ञिंसु ति। धम्मं ते, सुभद्द, देसेस्सामि, तं सुणाहि, साधुकं मनसिकरोहि, भासिस्सामी"ति।

"एवं, भन्ते"ति खो सुभद्दो परिब्बाजको भगवतो पच्चस्सोसि। भगवा एतदवोच–

"यस्मिं खो, सुभद्द, धम्मविनये अरियो अट्ठङ्गिको मग्गो न उपलब्भति, समणो पि तत्थ न उपलब्भति। दुतियो पि तत्थ समणो न उपलब्भति। ततियो पि तत्थ समणो न उपलब्भति। चतुत्थो पि तत्थ समणो न उपलब्भति। यस्मिं च खो, सुभद्द, धम्मविनये अरियो अट्ठङ्गिको मग्गो उपलब्भति, समणो पि तत्थ उपलब्भति। दुतियो पि तत्थ समणो उपलब्भति। ततियो पि तत्थ समणो उपलब्भति। चतुत्थो पि तत्थ समणो उपलब्भति। इमस्मिं खो, सुभद्द, धम्मविनये आरियो अट्ठङ्गिको मग्गो उपलब्भति। इधेव, सुभद्द, समणो, इध दुतियो समणो, इध ततियो समणो, इथ चतुत्थो समणो। सुञ्ञा परप्पवादा समणेभि अञ्ञेहि। इमे च, सुभद्द, भिक्खू सम्मा विहरेय्युं, असुञ्ञो लोको अरहन्तेहि अस्स"ति।

एकूनतिंसो वयसा सुभद्द, यं पब्बजिं किंकुसलानुएसी।

वस्सानि पञ्ञास समाधिकानि, यतो अहं पब्बजितो, सुभद्द!।

ञायस्स धम्मस्स पदेसवत्ती, इतो बहिद्धा समणो पि नत्थि।।

"दुतियो पि समणो नत्थि। ततियो पि समणो नत्थि। चतुत्थो पि समणो नत्थि। सुञ्ञा परप्पवादा समणेहि अञ्ञेहि। इमे च, सुभद्द, भिक्खू सरमा विहरेय्यूं, असुञ्ञो लोको अरहन्तेहि अस्सा"ति।

एवं वुत्ते, सुभद्दो परिब्बाजको भगवन्तं एतदवोच–"अभिक्कन्तं,

भन्ते, अभिक्कन्तं, भन्ते। सेय्यथापि, भन्ते, निक्कुज्जितं वा उक्कुज्जेय्य, पटिच्छन्नं वा विवरेय्य, मूळहस्स वा मग्गं आचिक्खेय्य, अन्धकारे वा तेलपज्जोतं धारेय्य–चक्खुमन्तो रूपानि दक्खन्तो ति; एवमेवं भगवता अनेकपरियायेन धम्मो पकासितो। एसाहं, भन्ते, भगवन्तं सरणं गच्छामि धम्मं च भिक्खुसङ्घं च। लभेय्याहं, भन्ते भगवतो सन्तिके पब्बज्जं लभेय्यं उपसम्पदं"ति।

"यो खो, सुभद्द, अञ्ञतित्थियपुब्बा इमस्मिं धम्मविनयं आकङ्खति पब्बज्जं आकङ्खति उपसम्पदं, सो चत्तारो मासे परिवसति। चतुन्नं मासानं अच्चयेन आरद्धचित्ता भिक्खू पब्बाजेन्ति उपसम्पादेन्ति भिक्खुभावाय। अपि च मेत्थ पुग्गलवेमत्तता विदिता"ति।

"सचे, भन्ते, अञ्ञतित्थियपुब्बा इमस्मिं धम्मविनये आकङ्खन्ता पब्बज्जं आकङ्खन्ता उपसम्पदं चत्तारो मासे परिवसन्ति, चतुन्नं मासानं अच्चयेन आरद्धचित्ता भिक्खू पब्बाजेन्ति उपसम्पादेन्ति भिक्खुभावाय; अहं चत्तारि वस्सानि परिवसिस्सामि, चतुन्नं वस्सानं अच्चयेन आरद्धचित भिक्खू पब्बाजेन्तु उपसम्पादेन्तु भिक्खुभावाया"ति।

अथ खो भगवा आयस्मन्तं आनन्दं आमन्तेसि–"तेनहानन्द, सुभद्दं पब्बाजेही"ति। "एवं, भन्ते"ति खो आयस्मा आनन्दो भगवतो पच्चस्सोसि। अथ खो सुभद्दो परिब्बाजको आयस्मन्तं आनन्दं एतदवोच–"लाभा वो, आवुसो आनन्द; सुलद्धं वो, आवुसो आनन्द, ये एत्थ सत्थु सम्मुखा अन्तेवासिकाभिसेकेन अभिसित्ता"ति। अलत्थ खो सुभद्दो परिब्बाजको भगवतो सन्तिके पब्बज्जं अलत्थ उपसम्पदं। अचिरूपसम्पन्नो खो पनायस्मा सुभद्दो एको वूपकट्ठो अप्पमत्तो आतापी पहितत्तो विहरन्तो नचिरस्सेव–यस्सत्थाय कुलपुत्ता सम्मदेव अगारस्मा अनगारियं पब्बजन्ति, तदनुत्तरं–ब्रह्मचरियपरियोसनं दिट्ठेव धम्मे सयं अभिञ्ञा सच्छिकत्वा उपसम्पज्ज विहासि। "खीणा जाति, वुसितं ब्रह्मचरियं, कतं करणीयं नापरं इत्थत्तताया"ति अब्भञ्ञासि। अञ्ञतरो खो पनायस्मा सुभद्दो अरहतं अहोसि। सो भगवतो पच्छिमो सक्खिवसावको अहोसी ति।।

पञ्चमो भाणवारो

तथागतस्सपच्छिमावाचा

अथ खो भगवा आयस्मन्तं आनन्दं आमन्तेसि–"सिया खो पनानन्द, तुम्हाकं एवमस्स–'अतीतसत्थुकं पावचनं। नत्थि नो सत्था' ति। न खो पनेतं, आनन्द, एवं दट्ठब्बं। यो वो, मया धम्मो च विनयो च देसितो पञ्ञत्तो, सो वो ममच्चयेन सत्था। यथा खो पनानन्द, एतरहि भिक्खू अञ्ञमञ्ञं आवुसोवादेन समुदाचरन्ति, न खो ममच्चयेन एवं समुदाचरितब्बं। थेरतरेन, आनन्द, भिक्खुना नवकतरो भिक्खु नामेन वा गोत्तेन वा आवुसोवादेन वा समुदाचरितब्बो। नवकतरेन भिक्खुना थेरतरो भिक्खु 'भन्ते' ति वा 'आयस्मा' ति वा समुदाचरितब्बो। आकङ्खमानो, आनन्द, सङ्घो ममच्चयेन खुद्दानुखुद्दकानि सिक्खापदानि समूहनतु। छन्नस्स, आनन्द, भिक्खुनो ममच्चयेन ब्रह्मदण्डो दातब्बो"ति।

"कतमो पन, भन्ते, ब्रह्मदण्डो"ति।

"छन्नो, आनन्द, भिक्खु यं इच्छेय्य तं वदेय्य, सो भिक्खूहि नेव वत्तब्बो न ओवदितब्बो न अनुसासितब्बो"ति।

अथ खो भगवा भिक्खू आमन्तेसि–"सिया खो पन, भिक्खवे, एकभिक्खुस्सा पि कङ्खा वा विमति वा बुद्धे वा धम्मे वा सङ्घे वा मग्गे वा पटिपदाय वा, पुच्छथ, भिक्खवे, मा पच्छा विप्पटिसारिनो अहुवत्थ–'सम्मुखीभूतो नो सत्था अहोसि, न मयं सक्खिम्हा भगवन्तं सम्मुखा पटिपुच्छितुं'"ति। एवं वुत्ते, ते भिक्खू तुण्ही अहेसुं। दुतियं पि खो भगवा....पे०....ततियं पि खो भगवा भिक्खू आमन्तेसि–"सिया खो पन, भिक्खवे, एकभिक्खुस्सा पि कङ्खा वा विमति वा बुद्धे वा धम्मे वा सङ्घे वा मग्गे वा पट्पिदाय वा, पुच्छथ, भिक्खवे, मा पच्छा विप्पटिसारिनो अहुवत्थ–'सम्मुखीभूतो नो सत्था अहोसि, न मयं सक्खिम्हा भगवन्तं सम्मुखा पटिपुच्छितुं'"ति। ततियं पि खो ते भिक्खू तुण्ही अहेसुं। अथ खो भगवा भिक्खू आमन्तेसि–"सिया खो पन, भिक्खवे, सत्थुगारवेन पि न पुच्छेय्याथ। सहायको पि, भिक्खवे, अथ खो आयस्मा आनन्दो भगवन्तं एतदवोच–"अच्छरियं,

भन्ते, अब्भुतं, भन्ते! एवं पसन्नो अहं, भन्ते, इमस्मिं भिक्खुसङ्घे, नत्थि एकभिक्खुस्सा पि कङ्खा वा विमति वा बुद्धे वा धम्मे वा सङ्घे वा मग्गे वा पट्पिदाय वा"ति।

"पसादा खो त्वं, आनन्द, वदेसि। ञाणमेव हेत्थ, आनन्द, तथागतस्स। नत्थि इमस्मिं भिक्खुसङ्घे एकभिक्खुस्सा पि कङ्खा वा विमति वा बुद्धे वा धम्मे वा सङ्घे वा मग्गे वा पटिपदाय वा। इमेसं हि, आनन्द, पञ्चन्नं भिक्खुसतानं यो पच्छिमको भिक्खु सो सोतापन्नो अविनिपातधम्मो नियतो सम्बोधिपरायणो"ति।

अथ खो भगवा भिक्खू आमन्तेसि–"हन्द दानि, भिक्खवे, आमन्तयामि वो–वयधम्मा सङ्खारा, अप्पमादेन सम्पादेथा"ति। अयं तथागतस्स पच्छिमा वाचा।

परिनिब्बुतकथा

अथ खो भगवा पठमं झानं समापज्जि। पठमज्झाना वुट्ठहित्वा दुतियं झानं समापज्जि। दुतियज्झाना वुट्ठहित्वा ततियं झानं समापज्जि। ततियज्झाना वुट्ठहित्वा चतुत्थं झानं समापज्जि। चतुत्थज्झाना वुट्ठहित्वा आकासानञ्चयतनं समापज्जि। आकासानञ्चायतन- समापत्तिया वुट्ठहित्वा विञ्ञाणञ्चायतनं समापज्जि। विञ्ञाणञ्चायतनसमापत्तिया वुट्ठहित्वा आकिञ्चञ्ञायतनं समापज्जि। आकिञ्चञ्ञायतनसमापत्तिया वुट्ठहित्वा नेवसञ्ञानासञ्ञायतनं समापज्जि। नेवसञ्ञानासञ्ञायतन- समापत्तिया वुट्ठहित्वा सञ्ञावेदयितनिराधं समापज्जि। अथ खो आयस्मा आनन्दो आयस्मन्तं अनुरुद्धं एतदवोच–"परिनिब्बुतो, भन्ते अनुरुद्ध, भगवा"ति।

"नावुसो आनन्द, भगवा परिनिब्बुतो, सञ्ञावेदयितनिराधं समापन्नो"ति।

अथ खो भगवा सञ्ञानासञ्ञायतनसमापत्तिया वुट्ठहित्वा सहायकस्स आरोचेतू"ति। एवं वुत्ते, ते भिक्खू तुण्ही अहेसुं।

नेवसञ्ञानासञ्ञायतनं समापज्जि। नेवसञ्ञानासञ्ञायतन-

समापत्तिया वुट्ठहित्वा आकिञ्चञ्ञायतनं समापज्जि। अकिञ्चञ्ञायतन-समापत्तिया वुट्ठहित्वा विञ्ञाणञ्चायतनं समापज्जि। विञ्ञाणञ्चायतन-समापत्तिया वुट्ठहित्वा आकासानञ्चायतनं समापज्जि। आकासानञ्चयन-समापत्तिया वुट्ठहित्वा चतुत्थं झानं समापज्जि। चतुत्थज्झाना वुट्ठहित्वा ततियं झानं समापज्जि। ततियज्झाना वुट्ठहित्वा दुतियं झानं समापज्जि। दुतियज्झाना वुट्ठहित्वा पठमं झानं समापज्जि। पठमज्झाना वुट्ठहित्वा दुतियं झानं समापज्जि। ततियं झानं समापज्जि। ततियज्झाना वुट्ठहित्वा चतुत्थं झानं समापज्जि। चतुत्थज्झाना वुट्ठहित्वा समनन्तरा भगवा परिनिब्बायि।

Thek The Blessed One addressed the venerable Ānanda:

"Let us go hence, Ānanda. To the further bank of the Hiraññavatī river, and to the city of Kusinārā and the sal-tree grove Upavāttana of the Mallas will we draw near."

"Yes, Reverend Sir," said the venerable Ānanda to The Blessed One in assent.

Then The Blessed One, accompanied by a large congregation of priests, drew near to the further bank of the Hiraññavatī river, and to the city of Kusinārā and the sāl-tree grove Upavāttana of the Mallas; and having drawn near, he addressed the venerable Ānanda:

"Be so good, Ānanda, as to spread me a couch with its head to the north between twin sāl-trees. I am weary, Ānanda, and wish to lie down."

"Yes, Reverend Sir," said the venerable Ānanda to The Blessed One in assent, and spread the couch with its head to the north between twin sāl-trees. Then The Blessed One lay down on his right side after the manner of a lion, and placing foot on foot, remained mindful and conscious.

Now at that time the twin sāl-trees—had completely burst forth into bloom, though it was not the flowering season; and the blossoms scattered themselves over the body of The Tathāgata,[42] and strewed and sprinkled themselves in worship of The Tathāgata. Also heavenly Erythrina flowers fell from the sky; and these scattered themselves over the body of The Tathāgata, and strewed and sprinkled themselves in worship of The Tathāgata. Also heavenly sandal-wood powder fell from the sky; and this scattered itself over the body of The Tathāgata, and strewed and sprinkled itself in worship of The Tathāgata. And music sounded in the sky in worship of The Tathāgata, and heavenly choruses were heard to sing in worship of The Tathāgata.

Then The Blessed One addressed the venerable Ānanda:

"The twin sāl-trees, Ānanda, have completely burst forth into bloom, though it is not the flowering season; and the blossoms have scattered themselves over the body of The Tathāgata, and have strewn and sprinkled themselves in worship of The Tathāgata. Also heavenly Erythrina flowers have fallen from the sky; and these have scattered themselves over the body of The Tathāgata, and have strewn and sprinkled themselves in worship of The Tathāgata. Also heavenly sandal-wood powder has fallen from the sky; and this has scattered itself over the body of The Tathāgata, and has strewn and sprinkled itself in worship of The Tathāgata. Also music is sounding in the sky in worship of The Tathāgata, and heavenly choruses are heard to sing in worship of The Tathāgata. But it is not by all this, Ānanda, that The Tathāgata is honored, esteemed, revered, worshiped, or venerated; but the priest, Ānanda, or the priestess, or the lay disciple, or the female lay disciple, who shall fulfil all the greater and lesser duties, conducting himself with propriety and in accordance with the precepts, by him is The Tathāgata honored, esteemed, revered, and worshiped with the best of worship. Accordingly, Ānanda, train yourselves, and fulfil all the greater and lesser duties, and conduct yourselves with propriety and in accordance with the precepts."

Now at that time the venerable Upavāṇa was standing in front of The Blessed One, and fanning him. Then The Blessed One was harsh to the venerable Upavāṇa, saying, –

"Step aside, O priest; stand not in front of me."

Then it occurred to the venerable Ānanda as follows:

"Here, this venerable Upavāṇa has for a long time been the body-servant of The Blessed One, and kept himself at his beck and call; yet, although his last moments are near, The Blessed One is harsh to the venerable Upavāṇa, saying, 'Step aside, O priest; stand not in front of me.' What, pray, was the reason, and what was the cause, that The Blessed One was harsh to the venerable Upavāṇa, saying, 'Step aside, O priest; stand not in front of me'?"

Then the venerable Ānanda spoke to The Blessed One as follows:

"Reverend Sir, here this venerable Upavāṇa has for a long time been the body-servant of The Blessed One, and kept himself at his beck and call; yet, although his last moments are near, The Blessed One is harsh to the venerable Upavāṇa, saying, 'Step aside, O priest; stand not in front of me.' Reverend Sir, what, pray, was the reason, and what was the cause, that The Blessed One was harsh to the venerable Upavāṇa, saying, 'Step aside, O priest; stand not in front of me'?"

"Ānanda, almost all the deities throughout ten worlds have come together to behold The Tathāgata. For an extent, Ānanda, of twelve leagues about the city Kusinārā and the sāl-tree grove Upavattana of the Mallas, there is not a spot of ground large enough to stick the point of a hair into, that is not pervaded by powerful deities. And these deities, Ānanda, are angered, saying, 'From afar have we come to behold The Tathāgata, for but seldom, and on rare occasions, does a Tathāgata, a saint, and Supreme Buddha arise in the world; and now, to-night, in the last watch, will The Tathāgata pass into Nirvāṇa; but this powerful priest stands in front of The Blessed One, concealing him, and we have no chance to see The Tathāgata, although his last moments are near.' Thus, Ānanda, are these deities angered."

"What are the deities doing, Reverend Sir, whom The Blessed One perceives?"

"Some of the deities, Ānanda, are in the air with their minds engrossed by earthly things, and they let fly their hair and cry aloud, and stretch out their arms and cry aloud, and fall headlong to the ground and roll to and fro, saying, 'All too soon will The Blessed One pass into Nirvāṇa; all too soon will The Happy One pass into Nirvāṇa; all too soon will The Light of the World vanish from sight!' Some of the deities, Ānanda, are on the earth with their minds engrossed by earthly things, and they let fly their hair and cry aloud, and stretch out their arms and cry aloud, and fall headlong on the ground and roll to and fro, saying, 'All too soon will The Blessed One pass into Nirvāṇa; all too soon will The Happy One pass into Nirvāṇa; all too soon will The Light of the World vanish from sight.' But those deities which are free from passion, mindful and conscious, bear it patiently, saying, 'Transitory are all things. How is it possible [that whatever has been born, has come into being, and is organized and perishable, should not perish? That condition is not possible.]'"

(Chapter v., page 53)

Then the venerable Ānanda entered the monastery, and, leaning against the bolt of the door, he wept, saying, –

"Behold, I am but a learner and not yet perfect, and my Teacher is on the point of passing into Nirvāṇa, he who was so compassionate to me."

Then The Blessed One addressed the priests:

"Where, O priests, is Ānanda?"

"Reverend Sir, the venerable Ānanda has entered the monastery, and leaning against the bolt of the door, he weeps, saying, 'Behold, I am but a learner, and not yet perfect, and my Teacher is on the point of passing into Nirvāṇa, he who was so compassionate to me.' "

Then The Blessed One addressed a certain priest, saying –

"Go, O priest, and say to the venerable Ānanda from me, 'The Teacher calleth thee, brother Ānanda.'"

"Yes, Reverend Sir," said the priest to The Blessed One in assent, and drew near to where the venerable Ānanda was; and having drawn near, he spoke to the venerable Ānanda as follows:

"The Teacher calleth thee, brother Ānanda."

"Yes, brother," said the venerable Ānanda to the priest in assent, and drew near to where The Blessed One was; and having drawn near and greeted The Blessed One, he sat down respectfully at one side. And the venerable Ānanda being seated respectfully at one side, The Blessed One spoke to him as follows:

"Enough, Ānanda, do not grieve, nor weep. Have I not already told you, Ānanda, that it is in the very nature of all things near and dear unto us that we must divide ourselves from them, leave them, sever ourselves from them? How is it possible, Ānanda, that whatever has been born, has come into being, is organized and perishable, should not perish? That condition is not possible. For a long time, Ānanda, have you waited on The Tathāgata with a kind, devoted, cheerful, single-hearted, unstinted service of body, with a kind, devoted, cheerful, single-hearted, unstinted service of voice, with a kind, devoted, cheerful, single-hearted, unstinted service of mind. You have acquired much merit, Ānanda; exert yourself, and soon will you be free from all depravity."

Then The Blessed One addressed the priests:

"Priests, of all those Blessed Ones who aforetime were saints and Supreme Buddhas, all had their favorite body-servants, just as I have now my Ānanda. And, priests, of all those Blessed Ones who in the future shall be saints and Supreme Buddhas, all will have their favorite body-servants, just as I have now my Ānanda. Wise, O priests, is Ānanda—he knows when it is a fit time to draw near to see The Tathāgata, whether for the priests, for the priestesses, for the lay disciples, for the female lay disciples, for the king, for the king's courtiers, for the leaders of heretical sects, or for their adherents.

"Ānanda, O priests, has four wonderful and marvellous qualities. And what are the four? O priests, if an assembly of priests draw near to behold Ānanda, it is delighted with beholding him; and if then Ānanda hold a discourse on the Doctrine, it is also delighted with the discourse; and when Ānanda, O priests, ceases to speak, the assembly of priests is still unsated. O priests, if an assembly of priestesses . . . an assembly of lay disciples ... an assembly of female lay disciples draw near to behold Ānanda, it is delighted with beholding him; and if then Ānanda hold a discourse on the Doctrine, it is also delighted with the discourse; and when Ānanda, O priests, ceases to speak, the assembly of female lay disciples is still unsated.

"A Universal Monarch, O priests, has four wonderful and marvellous qualities. And what are the four? O priests, if an assembly of men of the warrior caste ... an assembly of men of the Brāhmaṇa caste ... an assembly of householders ... an assembly of monks draw near to behold the Universal Monarch, it is delighted with beholding him; and if then the Universal Monarch hold a discourse, it is also delighted with the discourse; and when the Universal Monarch, O priests, ceases to speak, the assembly of monks is still unsated.

"In exactly the same way, O priests, Ānanda has four wonderful and marvellous qualities. O priests, if an assembly of priests ... an assembly of priestesses ... an assembly of lay disciples ... an assembly of female lay disciples draw near to behold Ānanda, it is delighted with beholding him; and if then Ānanda hold a discourse on the Doctrine, it is also delighted with the discourse; and when Ānanda, O priests, ceases to speak, the assembly of female lay disciples is still unsated. These, O priests, are the four wonderful and marvellous qualities possessed by Ānanda."

When The Blessed One had thus spoken, the venerable Ānanda spoke to him as follows:

"Reverend Sir, let not The Blessed One pass into Nirvāṇa in this wattel-and-daub town, this town of the jungle, this branch village. For there are other great cities, Reverend Sir, to wit, Campā, Rājagaha, Sāvatthi, Sāketa, Kosāmbī, and Benares. Let The Blessed One pass into Nirvāṇa in one of them. In them are many wealthy men of the warrior caste, many wealthy men of the Brāhmaṇa caste, and many wealthy householders who are firm believers in The Tathāgata, and they will perform the funeral rites for The Tathāgata."

"O Ānanda, say not so! O Ānanda, say not so, that this is a wattel-and-daub town, a town of the jungle, a branch village. There was once, Ānanda, a king called Sudassana the Great, who was a Universal Monarch, a virtuous king of justice, a victorious ruler of the four quarters of the earth, possessing a secure dominion over his territory and owning the seven precious gems.[43] This city Kusinārā, Ānanda, was the capital of king Sudassana the Great, and had then the name of Kusāvatī. From the east to the west it was twelve leagues in length, and from the north to the south it was seven leagues in breadth. Kusāvatī, the capital, Ānanda, was prosperous and nourishing, populous and thronging with people, and well provided with food. As Āḷakamandā, the capital of the gods, Ānanda, is prosperous and flourishing, populous and thronging with gods, and is well provided with food, in exactly the same way, Ānanda, Kusāvatī, the capital, was prosperous and flourishing, populous and thronging with people, and well provided with food. Kusāvatī, the capital, Ānanda, was neither by day nor night without the ten noises, – to wit, the noise of elephants, the noise of horses, the noise of chariots, the noise of drums, the noise of tabors, the noise of lutes, the noise of song, the noise of cymbals, the noise of gongs, and the tenth noise of people crying, 'Eat ye, and drink !'

"Go thou, Ānanda, and enter the city Kusinārā, and announce to the Kusinārā-Mallas :

"'To-night, O ye Vāseṭṭhas, in the last watch, The Tathāgata will pass into Nirvāṇa. Be favorable, be favorable, O ye Vāseṭhas, and suffer not that afterwards ye feel remorse, saying, "The Tathāgata passed into Nirvāṇa while in our borders, but we did not avail ourselves of the opportunity of being present at the last moments of The Tathāgata."

"Yes, Reverend Sir," said the venerable Ānanda to The Blessed One in assent; and putting on his tunic, and taking his bowl and his robes, he went to Kusinārā with another member of the Order.

Now at that time the Kusinārā-Mallas were assembled together in the town-hall on some matter of business. And the venerable Ānanda drew near to the town-hall of the Kusinārā-Mallas; and having drawn near, he made announcement to the Kusinārā-Mallas, as follows :

"To-night, O ye Vāseṭṭhas, in the last watch, The Tathāgata will pass into Nirvāṇa. Be favorable, be favorable, O ye Vāseṭhas, and suffer not that afterwards ye feel remorse, saying, 'The Tathāgata passed into Nirvāṇa while in our borders, but we did not avail ourselves of the opportunity of being present at the last moments of The Tathāgata.'"

The Mallas, on hearing this speech of the venerable Ānanda, and their children and their daughters-in-law and their wives were grieved and sorrowful and overwhelmed with anguish of mind, and some let fly their hair and cried aloud, and stretched out their arms and cried aloud, and fell headlong to the ground and rolled to and fro, saying, "All too soon will The Blessed One pass into Nirvāṇa; all too soon will The Happy One pass into Nirvāṇa; all too soon will The Light of the World vanish from sight." Then the Mallas and their children and their daughters-in-law and their wives, being grieved and sorrowful and overwhelmed with anguish of mind, drew near to the sāl-tree grove Upavāttana of the Mallas, and to where the venerable Ānanda was.

Then it occurred to the venerable Ānanda as follows:

"If I shall cause the Kusinārā-Mallas one by one to do reverence to The Blessed One, the day will dawn ere they have finished. What if now I marshal the Mallas by families, and cause them by families to do reverence to The Blessed One, and say, 'Reverend Sir, a Malla named so-and-so, with his children, his wife, his following, and his friends, bows low in reverence at the feet of The Blessed One.'"

And the venerable Ānanda marshalled the Mallas by families, and caused them by families to do reverence to The Blessed One, saying, "Reverend Sir, a Malla named so-and-so, with his children, his wife, his following, and his friends, bows low in reverence at the feet of The Blessed One." And the venerable Ānanda by this device succeeded in causing all the Kusinārā-Mallas to do reverence to The Blessed One before the end of the first watch of the night.

Now at that time Subhadda, a wandering ascetic, was dwelling at Kusinārā. And Subhadda, the wandering ascetic, heard the report:

"To-night, in the last watch, the monk Gotama will pass into Nirvāṇa."

Then it occurred to Subhadda, the wandering ascetic, as follows:

"I have heard wandering ascetics, that were old men, advanced in years, teachers, and teachers' teachers, declare, 'But seldom, and on rare occasions, does a Tathāgata; saint, and Supreme Buddha arise in the world.' And to-night, in the last watch, the monk Gotama will pass into Nirvāṇa. And a certain question has arisen in my mind, and I am persuaded of the monk Gotama that he can so teach me the Doctrine that I shall be relieved of this my doubt."

Then Subhadda, the wandering ascetic, drew near to the sāl-tree grove Upavāttana of the Mallas, and to where the venerable Ānanda was, and having drawn near, he spoke to the venerable Ānanda as follows:

"Ānanda, I have heard wandering ascetics, that were old men, advanced in years, teachers, and teachers' teachers, declare, 'But seldom, and on rare occasions, does a Tathāgata, a saint, and Supreme Buddha arise in the world.' And to-night, in the last watch, the monk Gotama will pass into Nirvāṇa. And a certain doubt has arisen in my mind, and I am persuaded of the monk Gotama that he can so teach me the Doctrine that I shall be relieved of this my doubt. Let me, then, Ānanda, have an opportunity of seeing the monk Gotama."

When Subhadda, the wandering ascetic, had so spoken, the venerable Ānanda spoke to him as follows:

"Enough of that, brother Subhadda; trouble not The Tathāgata. The Blessed One is weary."

And a second time Subhadda, the wandering ascetic, . . .

And a third time Subhadda, the wandering ascetic, spoke to the venerable Ānanda as follows:

"Ānanda, I have heard wandering ascetics, old men, advanced in years, teachers, and teachers' teachers, when they said, 'But seldom, and on rare occasions, does a Tathāgata, a saint, and Supreme Buddha arise in the world.' And to-night, in the last watch, the monk Gotama will pass into Nirvāṇa. And a certain doubt has arisen in my mind, and I am persuaded of the monk Gotama that he can so teach me the Doctrine that I shall be relieved of this my doubt. Let me, then, Ānanda, have an opportunity of seeing the monk Gotama."

And a third time the venerable Ānanda spoke to Subhadda, the wandering ascetic, as follows:

"Enough of that, brother Subhadda; trouble not The Tathāgata. The Blessed One is weary."

Now The Blessed One chanced to hear the conversation between the venerable Ānanda and the wandering ascetic Subhadda. And The Blessed One called to the venerable Ānanda:

"Enough, Ānanda; hinder not Subhadda. Let Subhadda,

Ānanda, have an opportunity of beholding The Tathāgata. Whatever Subhadda shall ask of me, he will ask for the sake of information, and not for the sake of troubling me, and he will quickly understand my answers to his questions."

Then the venerable Ānanda spoke to Subhadda, the wandering ascetic, as follows :

"You may come, brother Subhadda; The Blessed One grants you an audience."

Then Subhadda, the wandering ascetic, drew near to where The Blessed One was; and having drawn near, he exchanged greetings with The Blessed One; and having passed with him the greetings of friendship and civility, he sat down respectfully at one side. And seated respectfully at one side, Subhadda, the wandering ascetic, spoke to The Blessed One as follows :

"Gotama, all those monks and Brāhmaṇas who possess a large following and crowds of hearers and disciples, and who are distinguished, renowned leaders of sects, and highly esteemed by the multitudes, – to wit, Pūraṇa Kassapa, Makkhali Gosāla, Ajita Kesakambali, Pakudha Kaccāyana, Sañjaya Belaṭṭhiputta, Nigaṇṭha Nāthaputta, – have they all done as they maintain, discovered the truth, or have they not? or have some of them done so, and others not?"

"Enough, O Subhadda; let us leave the question, 'Have they all done as they maintain, discovered the truth, or have they not? or have some of them done so, and others not?' The Doctrine will I teach you, Subhadda. Listen to me, and pay strict attention, and I will speak."

"Yes, Reverend Sir," said Subhadda, the wandering ascetic, to The Blessed One in assent. And The Blessed One spoke as follows :

"Subhadda, in whatever doctrine and discipline the noble eightfold path is hot found, therein also is not found the monk of the first degree, nor the monk of the second degree, nor the monk of the third degree, nor the monk of the fourth degree;

and in whatever doctrine and discipline, O Subhadda, the noble eightfold path is found, therein also are found the monk of the first degree, and the monk of the second degree, and the monk of the third degree, and the monk of the fourth degree. Now in this Doctrine and Discipline, O Subhadda, the noble eightfold path is found: and therein alone, O Subhadda, are found the monk of the first degree, and the monk of the second degree, and the monk of the third degree, and the monk of the fourth degree. Destitute of true monks are all other creeds. But let these my priests, O Subhadda, live rightly, and the world will not be destitute of saints."

"What time my age was twenty-nine,
Subhadda, I left the world to seek the summum bonum.
Now fifty years and more have passed, Subhadda,
Since I renounced the world and lived ascetic
Within the Doctrine's pale, that rule of conduct
Outside of which no genuine monk existeth,

nor the monk of the second degree, nor the monk of the third degree, nor the monk of the fourth degree. Destitute of monks are all other creeds. But let these my priests, O Subhadda, live rightly, and the world will not be destitute of saints."

When The Blessed One had thus spoken, Subhadda, the wandering ascetic, spoke to him as follows:

"O wonderful is it, Reverend Sir! O wonderful is it, Reverend Sir! It is as if, Reverend Sir, one were to set up that which was overturned, or were to disclose that which was hidden, or were to point out the way to a lost traveller, or were to carry a lamp into a dark place that they who had eyes might see forms. Even so has The Blessed One expounded the Doctrine in many different ways. Reverend Sir, I betake myself to The Blessed One for refuge, to the Doctrine, and to the Congregation of the priests. Suffer me to retire from the world under The Blessed One; suffer me to receive ordination."

"Subhadda, any one who aforetime has been an adherent of another sect and afterwards desires to retire from the world and receive ordination under this Doctrine and Discipline, must first spend four months on probation; and after the lapse of four months, strenuous-minded priests receive him into the Order and confer on him the priestly ordination. Nevertheless, in this matter of probation I recognize a difference in persons."

"Reverend Sir, if all they who aforetime have been adherents of other sects and afterwards desire to retire from the world and receive ordination under this Doctrine and Discipline, must first spend four months on probation, and after the lapse of four months strenuous-minded priests receive them into the Order, and confer on them the priestly ordination, then am I ready to spend four years on probation, and after the lapse of four years, let strenuous-minded priests receive me into the Order and confer on me the priestly ordination." Then The Blessed One said to the venerable Ānanda, "Well, then, Ānanda, receive Subhadda into the Order." "Yes, Reverend Sir," said the venerable Ānanda to The Blessed One in assent.

Then Subhadda, the wandering ascetic, spoke to the venerable Ānanda as follows:

"How fortunate you priests are, brother Ānanda! How supremely fortunate, brother Ānanda, that you all have been sprinkled with the sprinkling of discipleship at the hands of The Teacher himself."

And Subhadda, the wandering ascetic, retired from the world under The Blessed One, and received ordination. And without delay, after he had received ordination, the venerable Subhadda began to live solitary and retired, vigilant, strenuous, and zealous; and in no long time, and while yet alive, he came to learn for himself, and to realize, and to live in the possession of that highest good to which the holy life conducts, and for the sake of which youths of good family so nobly retire from the household life to the houseless one. And he knew that for him rebirth was exhausted, that he had lived the holy life, that he had done what it behooved him to do, and that he was no more for this world. So the venerable Subhadda became of the number of the saints, and he was the last disciple made by The Blessed One himself.

End of the Hiraññavatī Recitation, which is the Fifth.

Then The Blessed One addressed the venerable Ānanda :

"It may be, Ānanda, that some of you will think, 'The word of The Teacher is a thing of the past; we have now no Teacher.' But that, Ānanda, is not the correct view. The Doctrine and Discipline, Ānanda, which I have taught and enjoined upon you is to be your teacher when I am gone. But whereas now, Ānanda, all the priests address each other with the title of 'brother,' not so must they address each other after I am gone. A senior priest, Ānanda, is to address a junior priest either by his given name, or by his family name, or by the title of 'brother;' a junior priest is to address a senior priest with the title 'reverend sir,' or 'venerable.' If the Order, Ānanda, wish to do so, after I am gone they may abrogate all the lesser and minor precepts. On Channa,[44] Ānanda, after I am gone, the higher penalty is to be inflicted."

"Reverend Sir, what is this higher penalty?"

"Let Channa, Ānanda, say what he likes, he is not to be spoken to nor admonished nor instructed by the priests."

Then The Blessed One addressed the priests:

"It may be, O priests, that some priest has a doubt or perplexity respecting either The Buddha or the Doctrine or the Order or the Path or the course of conduct. Ask any questions, O priests, and suffer not that afterwards ye feel remorse, saying, 'Our Teacher was present with us, but we failed to ask him all our questions.'"

When he had so spoken, the priests remained silent.

And a second time The Blessed One, and a third time The Blessed One addressed the priests:

"It may be, O priests, that some priest has a doubt or perplexity respecting either The Buddha or the Doctrine or the

Order or the Path or the course of conduct. Ask any question, O priests, and suffer not that afterwards ye feel remorse, saying, 'Our Teacher was present with us, but we failed to ask him all our questions.'"

And a third time the priests remained silent.

Then The Blessed One addressed the priests:

"It may be, O priests, that it is out of respect to The Teacher that ye ask no questions. Then let each one speak to his friend."

And when he had thus spoken, the priests remained silent.

Then the venerable Ānanda spoke to The Blessed One as follows:

"It is wonderful, Reverend Sir! It is marvellous, Reverend Sir! Reverend Sir, I have faith to believe that in this congregation of priests not a single priest has a doubt or perplexity respecting either The Buddha or the Doctrine or the Order or the Path or the course of conduct."

"With you, Ānanda, it is a matter of faith, when you say that; but with The Tathāgata, Ānanda, it is a matter of knowledge that in this congregation of priests not a single priest has a doubt or perplexity respecting either The Buddha or the Doctrine or the Order or the Path or the course of conduct. For of all these five hundred priests, Ānanda, the most backward one has become converted, and is not liable to pass into a lower state of existence, but is destined necessarily to attain supreme wisdom."

Then The Blessed One addressed the priests :

"And now, O priests, I take my leave of you; all the constituents of being are transitory; work out your salvation with diligence."

And this was the last word of The Tathāgata.

Thereupon The Blessed One entered the first trance; and rising from the first trance, he entered the second trance; and rising from the second trance, he entered the third trance; and rising from the third trance, he entered the fourth trance; and rising from the fourth trance, he entered the realm of the infinity of space; and rising from the realm of the infinity of space, he entered the realm of the infinity of consciousness; and rising from the realm of the infinity of consciousness, he entered the realm of nothingness; and rising from the realm of nothingness, he entered the realm of neither perception nor yet non-perception; and rising from the realm of neither perception nor yet non-perception, he arrived at the cessation of perception and sensation.

Thereupon the venerable Ānanda spoke to the venerable Anuruddha as follows:

"Reverend Anuruddha, The Blessed One has passed into Nirvāṇa."

"Nay, brother Ānanda, The Blessed One has not passed into Nirvāṇa; he has arrived at the cessation of perception and sensation."

Thereupon The Blessed One rising from the cessation of his perception and sensation, entered the realm of neither perception nor yet non-perception; and rising from the realm of neither perception nor yet non-perception, he entered the realm of nothingness; and rising from the realm of nothingness, he entered the realm of the infinity of consciousness; and rising from the realm of the infinity of consciousness, he entered the realm of the infinity of space; and rising from the realm of the infinity of space, he entered the fourth trance; and rising from the fourth trance, he entered the third trance; and rising from the third trance, he entered the second trance; and rising from the second trance, he entered the first trance; and rising from the first trance, he entered the second trance; and rising from the second trance, he entered the third trance; and rising from the third trance, he entered the fourth trance; and rising from the fourth trance, immediately The Blessed One passed into Nirvāṇa.

NOTES AND REFERENCES

42. *Tathāgata* is a term most commonly used by the Buddha in referring to himself. Its meaning, like that of its Jaina equivalent *Tatthagaya,* possibly is, "He who has arrived there *(tatra* or *tattha), i.e.* to emancipation or Nirvāṇa." See "Sacred Books of the East," vol. xiii, p. 82. [Chalmers, "Journal of the Royal Asiatic Society," 1898, p. 113, takes it as "One who has come at the real truth."]
43. The wheel of empire, the elephant, the horse, the gem, the empress, the treasurer, and the crown-prince.
44. Not the Channa who had been the Future Buddha's charioteer.

GLOSSARY

Abhidharma **:** Philosophical exposition of the *dharma*. The Philosophy of *Abhidharma* was compiled in Sanskrit by Vasubandhu in a book of eight chapters, known as Abhidharmakośa. *Abhidharma* is one of the branches of Buddhist Tripiṭaka. It is the higher doctrine of the Buddha, expounds the quintessence of his profound teachings. The Abhidharma Piṭaka is composed of the following seven works: (1) Dhammasaṅgaṇi (classification of Dharma), (2) Vibhaṅga (divisions), (3) Dhātukathā (discourse on elements), (4) Puggala Paññati (the book on individuals), (5) Kathāvatthu (points of controversy), (6) Yamaka (the book of pairs), (7) Paṭṭhāna (the book of causal relations). To the wise truth-seekers, Abhidharma is an indispensable guide and an intellectual treat.

Ahiṁsā **:** Lit. means non-vilolence, harmlessness, absence of cruelty. Both Buddhist and Jainas lay great stress on virtue of *ahiṁsā*. The thought of non-violence is one of the three constituents of Right Thought.

Aṇu* or *paramāṇu **:** Both the terms are synonymous and denote an atom, i.e. an indivisible particle of matter.

Arhat **:** A Buddhist monk or Bodhisattva, who has attained the forth and final path (*magga*) and for whom existences have come to an end, i.e. he is freed from further rebirth (*punarjanma*).

***Ariya* :** The noble one; one who has entered the path, i.e. one who has realized at least one of the four *maggas* (*mārgas*).

***Asura* :** Lit. means an evil spirit, demon, a general name for the enemies of gods, known as *daityas* and *dānavas*.

This term also appears in the Pāli scriptures. Whenever there is a discussion about *devaputras* (sons of gods), there is a reference to the *asuras* in the same context. The gods are famous for their pious deeds and the *asuras* for their evil deeds (Saṁyutta Nikāya, Vol. I, 228). The *asuras* are considered and classed with inferior deities, such as *yakṣas, gandharvas,* etc. It is evident from the Asura Vagga that the *asuras* are generally considered to be wicked, who indulge impious deeds (Aṅguttara Nikāya, Vol. I, p. 96). According to the Mahāsamaya Sutta, the *asuras* lived in the Ocean (Dīgha Nikāya, Vol. II, p. 192). The *asuras* whose names are mentioned in the Buddhist scriptures are: Rāhu, Pahārada, Baicitrāsura, etc.

***Bhikṣu* or *Bhikkhu* (Pāli) :** A Buddhist monk, who follow the rules of Saṅgha.

***Bhūmisparśa-mudrā* :** The earth touching posture of Buddha images. The right hand (of Buddha) exhibits this *mudrā*; the palm turned inward and the fingers outstretched with the tips touching the earth. This *mudrā* indicates that Buddha has defeated Māra and obtained *Nirvāṇa*. It is a symbol of victory over Māra. The earth has witnessed this great victory.

***Bimba* :** It means the disc of the sun or moon or any round or disc-like surface. In the commentary of Amarakośa, Kṣīrasvāmin explains the term as: '*bimbati bhāti bimbam ābhogaḥ*.' *Bimba* is derived from the root *bimba-*, 'to shine' and *ābhoga* here means circuit, circumference, etc. Hence, *bimba* denotes a solar or lonar orb, shape and any round surface (*maṇḍala*), face, mark, shadow or reflected form, etc.. The Buddhacarita of Aśvaghoṣa mentions that Buddha sees the whole world reflected within himself just like a reflection in mirror.

Bodhisattva **:** In the Buddhist thought it generally means all the previous existences of Gautama Buddha. The Pāli term Bodhisatta is composed of *bodhi* which means 'wisdom' or enlightenment and *satta* means 'devoted to' or 'intent- on'. A Bodhisatta, therefore, means one who is devoted to, or intent on, wisdom or enlightenment. The popular term is Bodhisattva which means 'wisdom being' or a being aspiring to become a Buddha. The methods of becoming a Bodhisattva and the stages or *bhūmis* of his mental, moral and intellectual attainments to the extent of realising *dharmaśūnyatā* were carefully outlined The Bodhisattvas take keen interest in all forms of homage. The image of Buddha is a great inspiration to them. It should be understood that Buddhists do not worship an image. They pay homage to what it represents and reflects on the virtues of the Buddha. A Bodhisattva always intends the good and welfare of the world. He loves all beings as a mother, who loves her only child. Therefore, it is known that he is like a mother, a father, a friend, a teacher, to all beings in this universe.

Bodhivṛkṣa **or Bodhi tree** (*Fiscus religious*) **:** The most religious tree at Bodhgaya under which Lord Buddha meditated and finally got *Nirvāṇa*. This tree is also known as the symbol of the enlightened Buddha.

Dharma **:** Lit. means religion, sect, law, usage, practice, custom, ordinance, etc. The term is derived from the root *dhṛ-* 'to hold' with the suffix *man*, denoting 'one that holds or sustains'. Various meanings of *dharma* like religious merit (*puṇya*), *yama*, fitness, nature, uses and drinker of a Soma, etc. are recorded in the Amarakośa (*dharmāḥ puṇyaya-manyāyasvabhāvācārasomapāḥ*— III.3. 138). According to the Gautama Dharmasūtra, *dharma* is that which is enjoined by the Vedas and Smṛtis. Etymologically the term *dharma* conveys the concept of eternal custom of disciplined people. According to Mīmāṁsakas *dharma* is identical with Vedic laws which enjoins the performance of a variety of actions in different walks of life. *Codanālakṣaṇo'rtho dharmaḥ*—Mīmāṁsā Sūtra, I.1.2). This interpretation was followed in the Brāhmaṇical tradition which equated *dharma* with law and behaviour. According to Buddhism, *dharma* is one of the three jewels (*triratna*) with Buddha and Saṁgha and one of the ten Recollections (*anussati*). The Buddha used the term *dharma* to denote the moral laws prescribed by him. Consequently, the term came to be used in the sense of nature, duty, and phenomenon or elements, truth, doctrine, justice, virtue, laws, quality, etc. in Buddhism. The *dhamma* or *dharma* as the liberating law discovered and proclaimed by the Buddha, is summed up in the four Noble Truths. *Dharma*, as an object of mind (*dhammāyatana*) may be anything past, present or future, corporeal or mental, conditioned or not, real or imaginary.

Dharmacakra : Wheel of the Law and also the symbol of Buddha's first sermon (*upadeśa*) at Sarnath (Varanasi), coupled with the symbol of *triratna*.

Dhātu : The word *dhātu* is derived from the root *dhā-*, 'to place, to put', with the suffix *tu*. In the Nirukta (I.20), Yāska defines *dhātu* as '*dhāturdadhāteḥ*'-

dhātu is so called, because it puts words in a proper form. The word can also be traced back to the root *dhṛ*- 'to hold or to bear'. The basic idea of supporting or holding has developed into different technical nuances in different systems which offer different etymologies of *dhātu*. Āyur-vedācārya Suśruta gives the etymology of *dhātu* from the root *dhṛ*-, which holds true for all body elements as: '*ta ete śarīradhāraṇāddhātava etyucyante*' (Suśruta Saṁhitā, Sūtra-sthāna, XIV.20). In the Buddhist text Abhidharmakośa (III.3cd), *dhātu* is derived from the root *dhṛ*- with a different meaning like: '*svalakṣ aṇadhāraṇād dhātuḥ'*—physical and material elements are called *dhātus*, because of holding their own characteristics. Here, *dhātu* is used in the sense of element (*bhūta*). The four physical elements (*dhātu* or *mahābhūta*), popularly called earth, water, fire and wind are to be understood as the primary qualities of matter. They are named in Pāli as: *paṭhavī dhātu, āpo dhātu, tejo dhātu* and *vāyo dhātu*. The Buddhists speak of eighteen *dhātus* which include the six sense organs, their objects, as well as their perceptions, like: *cakkhudhātu, rūpadhātu, cakkhuvijñāṇadhātu, sotadhātu, saddhadhātu*, etc. (Vibhaṅga Pāli, 401- 402, P.T.S.). The Pāli texts speak of three states of existence, viz. *kāmadhātu* 'element of desire', *rūpadhātu* 'element of form' and *ārūpyadhātu* 'element of formlessness'. However, in the Buddhist literature both in Pāli as well as in Sanskrit, the term *dhātu* conveys psycho-physical states (*viññāṇa*) of human personality in respect of all elements. It also denotes mortal remains of Lord Buddha which are worshipped as the relics.

Dukkha : Lit. means suffering, sorrow, misery, pain, etc. The first of the four Noble Truths preached by Lord

Buddha. As a feeling *dukkha (duḥkha)* means that which is difficult to be endured As an abstract truth *dukkha* is used in the sense of contemptible ('*du*') and emptiness ('*kha*'). The world rests on suffering, hence it is contemptible. It is devoid of any reality, hence it is empty or void. Hence, *dukkha* is meant 'existence in the world with concomitant pain and pleasure' which are without any real substance (*anattā*) and are impermanent (*anicca*). The Visuddhimagga (498.99) refers to seven kinds of *dukkha*, viz. *dukkha, vipariṇāma, saṅkhārā, paticchanna, appaṭicchanna, pariyāya* and *nippriyāya*. There is a way leading to this cessation of suffering. There is an ethical and spiritual path (eight fold path) by following which misery may be removed and *Nirvāṇa* or liberation can be attained All the systems of Indian Philosophy basically deal with *dukkha* and the permanent means to remove it.

Karma : Lit. means work, action, deed, etc. In the early Vedic ideas *karma* denotes sacrifice, a religious rite. Our Vedas, *śāstras*, seers, teachers, etc. have advised us to perform good, auspicious, and religious acts for obtaining desirable things. Different systems of Indian philosophy, i.e. Bauddha, Jaina, Nyāya, Sāṁkhya, Yoga, Mīmāṁsā, Vedānta, etc. have explained the term according to their own principles.

Karuṇā : Lit. means compassion, pity, tenderness, etc. *Karuṇā*, a strong emotion of deep compassion, is a dynamic force, a source of human inspiration, which compels one to live and die for the suffering mankind.

In Buddhism, *karuṇā* is one of the four qualities of character significant of a human being who has attained enfranchisement of heart (*cetovimutti*) in the four sentiments.

Loka : The term *loka* is derived from the root *lok-* or *loc-* (*bhvādi*) 'to see, to behold, to perceive' or *lok-* or *loc-* (*curādi*) 'to recognize, to know', etc. The second deriving root of *loka* is *ruc-* (*bhvādi*), which means 'to shine, to bright or radiant or resplendant'. An important synonym of *loka* is *bhuvana*. The Amarakośa (III.3.2) defines *loka* as: '*lokastu bhuvane jane*'. Here *loka* means world and people. *Loka* is generally defined as : '*lokyate iti loka*' or '*lokyate asau loka*' (*loka* + *ghañ*). Generally speaking there are three *lokas*, viz. *svarga, pṛthivī* and *pātāla*. According to the Lakṣmī Tantra (XIV.50) *lokas* are fourteen (*lokāścaiva caturdaśa*), seven higher regions rising from the earth one above the other, viz. *bhūloka, bhuvarloka, svarloka, maharloka, janaloka, tapaloka,* and *satyaloka* (cf. Viṣṇu Purāṇa, I.22.80), and the seven successively lower regions, descending from the earth one below the other, viz. *atala, vitala, sutala, rasātala, talātala, mahātala* and *pātāla*.

In the Brahmasūtra Bhāṣya (IV.3.4), *loka* is used to denote 'places of enjoyment of living beings.' In the Caraka Saṁhitā (Śārīrasthāna, V.4) *loka* is conceived as an aggregate of six *dhātus* (5 elements and Brahman). In the Sarasvatīkaṇṭhābharaṇa (I.146), *loka* is accepted as one of the *pramāṇas* and also described as the behaviour of the mobile and immobile beings. According to the Kāvyālaṅkāra Sūtra (I.3.1), *loka* is known as one of the three limbs of *kāvya*.

The Buddhist text Abhidharmakośa Bhāṣya (I.8cd) explains *loka* as: '*lujyata iti loka*'—*loka* is so called because it is in the process of dissolution and discomposition. It is also identified with the body or *yoni*, i.e. form of existence (station) fixed by birth (IV.1). In Jaina philosophy, *loka* is conceived as the conglomeration of five *astikāyas*, viz. *dharma, adharma, ākāśa, jīva* and *pudgala* (Tattvārthasūtra Bhāṣya, III.6).

Maṇḍala : Lit. means round, circular. The Amarakośa defines the term *maṇḍala* as: '*cakravalaṁ tu maṇḍalam* (I.3.6), *bimbo'strī maṇḍalaṁ triṣu* (I.3.15) and *pariveṣastu paridhirūpasūryaka, maṇḍale* (I.3.32).'

Maṇḍala worship is very popular and even important in Tāntric rituals. In Śaivite tradition various *maṇḍalas* are worshipped in different months. Several *maṇḍalas* are described in the Śāradā Tilaka, Pauṣkara Saṁhitā and other Tāntric texts. The Buddhist Tantras also describe *maṇḍalas*, e.g. Sarvatobhadra etc. Now a days *maṇḍala* worship is a common feature in any *pūjā* rituals.

Mudrā : Lit. means a seal, an instrument for sealing or stamping; a stamp, print, mark, impression; an image, a sign; name of certain positions of fingers practised in devotion or religious worship. Generally it is known as posture of the body, especially of hands needed for *yogic* exercise and spiritual attainment. It is called *mudrā* (root *mud*- 'to rejoice', 'to please', with the suffix *rak* and *tāp*), because it gives the bliss of spiritual consciousness. The derivative meaning of the term *mudrā* is: '*mudaṁ harṣaṁ rāti dadāti iti mudrā*'—it gives delight in the heart. *Mudrās* like Abhaya, Varada, Dharmacakra, Bhūmisparśa, Namaskāra, etc. are commonly found in iconic representation symbolising the quality associated with the deity. The Haṭhayoga Pradīpikā devotes a complete chapter on *mudrās*. Some of which are: Mahāmudrā, Mahāvedha, Khecarī, Mahābandha, Uḍḍīyyānabandha, Mūlabandha, Jālandhara-bandha, etc.

However, the scholars explain *mudrā* in different ways denoting 'mystic pose of the hand', 'manual signs indicative of various ideas', finger signs, hand poses adopted during meditation or exposition.

Nāstika-darśana **:** The heterodox schools of Indian Philosophy denying the authority of the Veda. As said '*nāstiko vedanindakaḥ.*' These *Nāstika-darśanas* are: Cārvāka, Jaina and Bauddha.

Nirodha **:** Lit. means confinemet, restraint, check, suppression, control, etc. In Buddhism, it denotes extinction of all sufferings and is regarded as one of the four noble truths, *dukkha-nirodha*.

Perception **:** *Pratyakṣa* or *pratyakṣa-pramāṇa*. It is the first kind of means of knowledge based on sense.

Pratītya-samutpāda **:** The Buddhist causal theory is called Dependent Origination, i.e. there being one thing, the other follows. It explains how the three successive births, viz. past, present & future of a man is related to one another. It is based on a twelve-point law of causation. *Avidyā* (ignorance) in a past- life creates *saṁskāras* (impressions), which lead an individual to *vijñāna*, i.e. birth consciousness of the present life. From this originates the *nāma-rūpa* or mental and physical faculties developing *ṣ aḍāyatana*, or internal organs of sense and mind leading to *sparśa* or contact with the corresponding objects. Contact further leads to *Vedanā* (sensation), which results in *taṇhā* or desire to reborn. From the latter arises *upādāna* (grasping) leading to *bhava*, i.e. becoming, the basis of *jāti* or birth in the next birth. Finally, when the birth takes place it is sure to lead to old age and death (*jarāmaraṇa*). This is the theory of causation in Buddhism.

Rakṣasa **or *Rākṣasa*** **:** Lit. means a demon, an evil spirit, an imp, a goblin, etc. In the Pāli texts the word *rākṣasa* is also occurred several times. It is often mentioned along with the words like: *yakṣa, gandharva, asura, nāga*, etc. (Jātaka, Vol. I, p. 127; Vol. VI, p. 464). Because of their association with inferior gods, *rākṣasas* are treated as minor supernatural beings. Due to their evilmindedness they are considered as demons in the *śāstras*.

The term *rākṣasa* is explained in the sense of a harmful non-human being. They are supposed to possess supernatural powers, excellent valour and energy. It is also said that they can assume any form (*ākāra*) they like. (Jātaka, Vol. I, pp. 556-57).

***Śakti*:** Lit. means energy, power, especially the creative energy that generates and continues to activate the universe. The term *śakti* is derived from the root *śak-* 'to be able', 'to be powerful', with the suffix *ktin*. Kṣīrasvāmin, the commentator of the Amarakośa comments on the term as: *śakyate anayā jetuṁ śakti*. The derivative sense of *śakti* is 'that through which it is possible to conquer or through which something can be conquered (*śakyate jetum ābhiḥ śaktyaḥ*). The Aṣṭādhyāyī of Pāṇini (III.2.129) uses the term *śakti* in the sense of capability. The primordial female principle or the power of the Supreme Being is treated *śakti* through the manifestation of the universe is affected *Parāśakti* is conceived as female principle. It is the energy of Lord Śiva and regarded as the instrumental cause of creation. Besides, Śakti is symbolically represented as the spouse of Śiva and hence She is the immanent principle of Śiva. Devoid of Śakti, Śiva would be insentient (*jaḍa*) and consequently, as good as 'dead' (*śava*). Śiva knows Himself only through His Great Śakti. She is also the power of freedom of the Lord. Śakti has been addressed as *janani, mātri* and *ambā*. Generally, Śakti or Devī is identified with Vidyāmāyā. With the help of Vidyāmāyā, *jīva* proceeds towards spiritual sublimity. Śakti or Devī helps *jīva* in moving towards Paramaśiva. Without the help of Śakti it is not possible for the *jīva* to attain the Supreme Oneness with Paramaśiva.

Samādhi : Collectness of mind in which there is cessation of the fluctuations of the mind; mental absorption. The experience of higher consciousness is known as *samādhi*. It is an advanced state of contemplation, and implies a thought-free mind. In the beginning the strain of the mind is felt in a subtle form, and is, therefore, called *savikalpa samādhi*. It is attained with effort in order to curb mental disturbances. Then there is the higher state known as *nirvikalpa samādhi*, in which the mind is totally quiescent and the experience effortless. The mind gets dissolved in the bliss of higher consciosness.

Sambodhi : Enlightenment that came to Lord Buddha after heroic struggle. The seven qualities or attributes of *sambodhi* are: self-control, understanding of the *dharma*, zeal, tranquility of mind, joy, concentration and compassion.

Saṁsāra : Lit. means passage, course, i.e. the course or circuit of worldly life, mundane existence, the world. '*Saṁsarati iti saṁsāraḥ*', i.e. that which is always on the move. Etymologically the word '*saṁsāra*' also means 'wandering through' (a succession of states) of the *jīva* or individual soul.

Saṅgha : The word *saṅgha* means 'a community' or group, collection, multitude; as *maharshi-saṅgha, manuṣya-saṅgha*, etc. In Buddhist context it means an assembly of Buddhist priests. The community or society of Buddhist monks or mendicants, both (male) *bhikṣu* and (female) *bhikṣuṇī*. The *saṅgha* in widest sense is meant, a community of all those who are walking the Buddhist path. As the third of the three gems (*triratna*) and three refuges (*trisaraṇa*), i.e. *Buddha, Dharma* and *Saṅgha*, it applies to the *ariya-saṅgha*, the real community of the saints. It is the oldest monastic order in the world.

Sarvāstivāda **:** one of the oldest schools of Hīnayāna sect of Buddhism.

Siddhis**:** Super-natural powers attained through the practice of *yoga*. These *siddhis* are eight in number, viz. *aṇimā, laghimā, mahimā, garimā, prāpti, prākāmya, vaśitva*, and *īśitva*.

Śrī**:** Goddess Lakṣmī, the deity and consort of Lord Viṣṇu, who embodies the qualities of prosperity and beauty. She is worshipped especially by the Vaiṣṇavas as inseparable from Viṣṇu.

Śūnya**:** Lit. means empty, void. According to Buddhism it is a state in which there is no distinct consciousness of knower, knowledge and known; an indefinable state of Reality. But according to Kashmir Śaivism it is a state in which no object is experienced.

Śūnya-pramātā **:** The experiment who is identified with the void, *pralayākala* (Kashmir Śaivism).

Sūtra **:** Lit. thread. It means that which like a thread runs through or holds together certain ideas, a rule, a formula, a direction. A *sūtra* must contain the fewest possible words, must be free from ambiguity, must be meaningful and comprehensive, must not contain useless words and pauses and must be faultless.

Svastika **:** It is an auspicious symbol accepted by Bauddhas, Jainas and Hindus.

Taṇhā : Lit. thirst. 'Craving' is the chief root of suffering, and of the ever continuing cycle of rebirths. According to the Dependent Origination, craving is conditioned by feeling. The most frequent synonyms of *taṇhā* are *rāga* and *lobha*.

Tathāgata : A title of Buddha, used by his followers, and also by himself when speaking of himself. It is now usually derived from *tathā-āgata* (thus come) and *tathāgata* (thus gone) and has given the meaning as: he who has come and gone as former Buddhas. The Mahāyāna school says that one who has attained full realization of thatness (*tathātā*), i.e. become one with the Absolute.

Tripiṭaka : Lit. means 'the three baskets'. It is the name for the three main divisions of the Pāli canon, viz. Vinaya Piṭaka (the basket of Discipline), Sutta Piṭaka (the basket of Discourses), and Abhidhamma Piṭaka (the basket of Philosophy).

Triratna : Lit. means 'three Jewels or three Gems, which by all Buddhists are revered as the most venerable things, are the Buddha, the Dhamma and the Holy Saṅgha.

Trisaraṇa : 'Threefold refuge', in which every faithful adherent of the Buddha puts his whole trust, consists in the Buddha, the Dhamma and the Saṅgha. Lord Buddha, the Enlightened One, is the teacher who by himself has discovered, realized and proclaimed to the world of deliverance. The Dhamma is the law of deliverance. The Saṅgha is the community of the holy monks, who have truly realized or are striving to realize the law of deliverance. In Pāli this is known as: *Buddhaṁ śaraṇaṁ gacchāmi, Dharmaṁ śaraṇaṁ gacchāmi* and *Saṅghaṁ śaraṇaṁ gacchāmi*.

Tuṣita Heaven : The heaven of the thirty three gods, the last of the paradises in the sky from where Lord Buddha descended to this earth.

Vihāra : A living place of the Buddhist monks. It is also known as a Buddhist monastery.

Vijñānavāda : One of the four Buddhist school of philosophy, also called Yogācāra which holds the theory of subjective idealism.

Vṛkṣa : Lit. means tree. The term is derived from the root *vraśc-* 'to cut down' with the suffix *sa*. In Nirukta, the etymologies of *vṛkṣa* are given as: (1) *vṛkṣa vraścanāt* (Nir II.6; XII.29), here the term is derived from the root *vraśc*—'to cut down'; (2) *vṛtvā kṣāṁ tiṣṭhatīti vā* (Nir II.6)—here the term stands for having covered (√*vṛ-*) the earth (*kṣā*), i.e. *vṛkṣa* = √*vṛ-* 'to cover' + *kṣā* 'earth'; (3) *vṛtakṣaye vā* (Nir XII.29)—it means the chosen dwelling place (root *vṛ-* 'to choose' + *kṣaya* 'to dwell' = *vṛkṣa*).

Vṛkṣa is a symbol of stability, as it is clear from the above explanations. Lord Viṣṇu is called *Vṛkṣa* on account of His stability, as He is known as the sheltering tree of the wise persons (Viṣṇusahasranāma Bhāṣya 72). In the Saṁhitās, the Brahman is treated as the Primordial tree from which the entire creation is manifested *Vṛkṣa* is explained by the scholars as the body or the orb or region of the Sun or the sacrificial post or the world or the mythical world-tree. In the Śvetāsvatara Upaniṣad the cosmic person is treated as an eternal tree rooted in heaven and the entire world is filled by that Supreme Being (*vṛkṣa iva stabdho divi tiṣṭhatyekastenedaṁ pūrṇaṁ puruṣeṇa sarvam*—III.9).

Vṛkṣa has a great importance in Buddhist Literature as different *vṛkṣas* are related with Buddhas or Bodhisattvas. Aśvattha is the tree of enlightenment of Gautama Buddha.

Wheel of Law : The *dhamma* as an ever-rolling chariot Wheel, the symbol of conquering efficacy; the Buddha, being the *dhammacakka-vattin* or Universal Monarch in the domain of Righteousness. The preaching of the first *upadeśa* in Varanasi is called Dharmacakra pravartana Sutta or the discourse of sitting in motion the chariot of Wheel of the holy law.

Yantra : The term *yantra* is derived from the root *yam-*, 'to control'. It has various meanings like: restraint, curb, check, bind, fasten, force, etc. Besides, it also denotes a fetter, band, tie and rain. In the Ṛgveda (X.149.1) it is used in the sense of bend or fetter. In the Aṣṭāṅgahṛdaya (Sūtrasthāna, XXV.3-28), *yantra* is described as different types of instruments. According to the Sūryasiddhānta (XIII.19-24), various *yantras* were used for measuring time, like: *chāyā-yantra, kapāla-yantra, toya-yantra*, etc. The Mayamata, as an archaeological text, used *yantra* in the sense of a device and machine as: *jala-yantra*. In the Tāntric point of view, *yantra* means an amulet, i.e. a mystical or astronomical diagram used as an amulet. This diagram is engraved or drawn on metal, paper, stone, wood or other materials which are worshiped in the same manner as an image. The *yantra* worship is an essential feature of Tantra *sādhanā* and it is also a mystic process of awakening the Divine Power.

BIBLIOGRAPHY

(Original Texts)

Abhidhammatha Saṅgaho: edited by Bhadanta Revatadharma Shastri, Varanasi: Secretary, Buddha Swadhyaya Satra, 1965 A.D.

Aṅguttara Nikāya: edited with Hindi translation by Swami Dwarikadas Shastri, Buddha Bharati Series-45, Varanasi: Bauddha Bharati, I-IV Vols, 1st edition, 2002.

_____ Dhammagiri-Pāli-Ganthamālā, Dhammagiri, Igatpuri: Vipassana Research Institute.

Cullavagga (under Saŏkhitta Piṭakam): edited by Nathmal Tatia, Nalanda (Bihar):

Navanālandā Mahāvihāra, 2 Vols, 1975.

____ Dhammagiri-Pāli-Ganthamālā, Dhammagiri, Igatpuri: Vipassana Research Institute.

Dhammapada Aṭṭhakathā: edited by C.S. Upasak, Nalanda (Bihar): Navanālandā Mahāvihāra, 1973.

____ Dhammagiri-Pāli-Ganthamālā, Dhammagiri, Igatpuri: Vipassana Research Institute.

Dīgha Nikāya: edited with Hindi translation by Swami Dwarikadas Shastri, Bauddha Bharati Series 34, Varanasi : Bauddha Bharati, I-III Vols, 1996.

____ Dhammagiri-Pāli-Ganthamālā, Dhammagiri, Igatpuri: Vipassana Research Institute, 1993.

Jataka Aṭṭhakathā: Dhammagiri-Pāli-Ganthamālā, Dhammagiri, Igatpuri: Vipassana Research Institute.

Mahāvagga: edited by Bhikkhu J. Kashyap, Nālandā (Bihar): 2 Vols, Navanālandā Mahāvihāra, reprint, 1980.

_____ Dhammagiri-Pāli-Ganthamālā, Dhammagiri, Igatpuri: Vipassana Research Institute.

Majjhima Nikāya: edited with Hindi translation by Swami Dwarikadas Shastri, Bauddha Bharati Series 22, Varanasi: Bauddha Bharati, I-V Vols, 1989.

_____ Dhammagiri-Pāli-Ganthamālā, Dhammagiri, Igatpuri: Vipassana Research Institute.

Milinda Pañha: edited with Hindi translation by Swami Dwarikadas Shastri, Bauddha Bharati Series 13, Varanasi: Bauddha Bharati, 1990.

____ Dhammagiri-Pāli-Ganthamālā, Dhammagiri, Igatpuri: Vipassana Research Institute.

Udāna: Dhammagiri-Pāli-Ganthamālā, Dhammagiri, Igatpuri: Vipassana Research Institute.

Saṁyutta Nikāya: edited with Hindi Translation by Swami Dwarikadass Shastri, Bauddha Bharati Series 40, Varanasi: Bauddha Bharati, 4 Vols., 2000.

_____ Dhammagiri-Pāli-Ganthamālā, Dhammagiri, Igatpuri: Vipassana Research Institute.

Sumaṅgala Vilāsinī (Comm. of Dīgha Nikāya): edited by Mahesh Tiwary , Nālandā Mahāvihāra, 2 Vols., 1974-75.

Visuddhi Magga: edited by D. Kosambi, Bombay: Bharatiya Vidya Bhawan, 1940.

_____ Dhammagiri-Pāli-Ganthamālā, Dhammagiri, Igatpuri: Vipassana Research Institute.

INDEX

N

O

P

R

S

T

U

+++++